HIGH-TECH ESPIONAGE

HIGH-TECH ESPIONAGE

JAY TUCK

St. Martin's Press
New York

327.1
Tu

Library of Congress Cataloging in Publication Data

Tuck, Jay.
  High-tech espionage.

  1. Espionage—Soviet Union.   2. Espionage—Europe.
3. Espionage—United States.   4. Trade
secrets—Europe.   5. Trade secrets—United States.
I. Title.
UB271.R9T83   1986   327.1′2′0947   86-13756
ISBN 0-312-37237-X

First Published in Great Britain by Sidgwick & Jackson Limited.

First U.S. Edition

10 9 8 7 6 5 4 3 2 1

Contents

Preface

A French spy penetrates the innermost circles of a top Soviet espionage ring – and is found dead in the snow on a deserted road in the Alps; an eccentric California inventor launches a successful high-tech enterprise from his garage – and ends up selling one of America's best-kept secrets to Moscow; a chubby Chinese financier travels from Hong Kong to Silicon Valley – on a clandestine shopping spree to purchase California banks for the KGB; a jetsetting German is hunted around the world by intelligence agents from the German BND, the British MI5 and the American CIA – and the computers he is smuggling become a matter of priority for the President of the United States.

These and other episodes in this book may read like the inventions of a novelist. But they are authentic accounts of events in the lives of real people – researched in hundreds of interviews, court records, government hearings and unpublished Eastern bloc literature. Great care has been taken in tracing the accuracy of details. If a phone call is quoted, as in Chapter Eight, then I am in possession of a transcript of the original conversation. If weather conditions or the personal impressions of participants are mentioned, they are based on my interviews with eye-witnesses.

Since embargo-runners pursue their dark trade in all corners of the world, original source material has often been supplemented by the research of my journalistic colleagues. The bulk of the information presented here, however, is based on first-hand investigation by myself. On occasion, press articles are cited – even though they do not include all details described in this book – in order to provide independent verification of an event. The notes on sources listed at the end of each chapter should be sufficient to allow the reader to form his own judgement as to the credibility of the text.

Legally, 'spies' are agents of the KGB, GRU and other intelligence services who knowingly participate in espionage operations. Western businessmen smuggling strategic equipment to the East are not always aware of the involvement of Eastern spies. In such cases, I have avoided judgements as to the legality of the activities of the men and women involved. The laws governing embargo-running differ enormously from country to country.

The research for this book was sometimes quite exciting. In the Elmont case, in fact, I decided to devote an entire chapter to an account of my own investigation. Other cases were more routine. The chapter on Marc André DeGeyter, for example, is based almost entirely on evidence published in United States Senate hearings. Television journalist John Penycate, producer of the excellent BBC documentary 'The High-Tech Trail to Moscow', contributed valuable material on Amos Dawe, and a superb article researched by Ehud Yonay and printed in *New West Magazine* was a major source of information for the chapter on Walter Spawr.

This book has been compiled and written on a word processor, which helped me understand why the Soviets are so hungry for computers. The machine was an invaluable tool for correlating the large quantities of research material and writing the manuscript. Computers also assisted in Washington, where my television colleague Jay Gourley of the Cable News Network quizzed an electronic data bank and produced a large collection of newspaper clippings related to the subject of computer-smuggling.

I gratefully acknowledge the expertise on Warsaw Pact weaponry offered by Bundeswehr test pilot Wolf Dietrich Havenstein, whom I would like to thank here, as I would Klaus Krakat from the federally funded Research Institute for East-West German Economic and Social Affairs (Forschungsstelle für Gesamtdeutsche Wirtschaftliche und Soziale Fragen) in West Berlin, who enhanced the chapter on Eastern electronics with ideas and editing, and Professor Rolf Hasse, who offered valuable tips on CoCom. My family – Marion, Sarah Lee and Jody – allowed this book to disrupt their private lives, yet continued to offer their love and support.

Finally I want to thank Dr Erich Vogt, who handed me a UPI wire service report on 14 July 1982, putting me on the high-tech trail to Moscow.

Jay Tuck
Hamburg in West Germany
4 March 1986

Part I

STARTING POINT

Introduction

On the High-Tech Trail to Moscow: The First Four Days

News of the incident hit the wires at 3:10 pm on 14 July 1982. According to a United Press International file from Washington, forty-one crates of computers valued at $450,000 had been seized at Frankfurt and Munich airports. Agents of a US customs task force called 'Operation Exodus' had intercepted the electronic contraband en route to the Soviet Union. It was the first I had heard of Soviet computer-smuggling, and it sounded like a good story.

I was working on the foreign desk at the ARD German Television News Network in Hamburg on what had begun as a routine shift. The four days that were to follow turned into the most exciting investigative research of my reporting career. The trail led me onto a journalistic odyssey through five European cities, dozens of interviews and, finally, to the door of the smugglers in a small Swiss border town.

Later, I would learn that there was more to the story than the shady dealings of a few fly-by-night electronics bootleggers. They are marginal figures in a global plan – plotted by the Central Committee of the USSR, and judged by most Western counter-intelligence authorities to be 'the central security issue of the coming decade'.

The stunning successes of this Eastern bloc espionage operation are already visible in the arsenals of the Warsaw Pact. Over 160 Eastern weapons systems rely on technology imported from the West. Western main-frame computers co-ordinate troop movements in East Germany; Western microchips guide air-to-air missiles in the Near East. The Red Army rolled into Afghanistan on trucks built with NATO know-how; the Red Fleet repairs Kiev aircraft-carriers in Vladivostok in dry docks purchased in Japan; and the Red Air Force practises shooting down cruise missiles at a flight range in Vladimirovka using radar systems stolen from the United States.

Mobile SS-20 Soviet atomic missiles are trucked from site to site on launch vehicles designed on computer hardware from New York and operated by computer software from Massachusetts. The nose cones are tipped with a carbon-fibre heat shield developed in New Jersey and – should they ever be fired in anger – their three nuclear warheads will be guided into Western targets by a gyroscope system constructed with the help of machine tools from Vermont. In everything from spy satellites and supersonic fighters to artillery and atomic submarines, the Communists are using technology begged, borrowed or stolen from the West.

At the height of détente, Soviet purchasing agents could meet their military needs with relative ease on the open markets of the West. When the US Administration tightened export controls in the wake of the Afghanistan invasion, however, the Kremlin was forced to resort to covert methods of acquisition. Illegal electronics traffic – funnelled through an international maze of phoney companies, post office box addresses and mysterious middlemen – has since become a billion-dollar business threatening the very foundations of Western security. Ever since the end of the Second World War, Western nations have relied on the technological prowess of their industry to counterbalance the enormous number of men and machines deployed in Warsaw Pact forces. In recent years, however, the East has been equipping its armies with know-how from NATO – smuggled to the East by black-market bootleggers – and shifting the balance of power in its favour.

While reading that wire service report on 14 July 1982, I was quite unaware of all this. All I knew was that American and German customs agents had confiscated forty-one crates of illegal freight at two German airports. And I wanted to produce a television report on the incident.

The raid had taken place nine days earlier. The wire service report did not contain details of the airport seizures: no names, no freight companies, not even a description of the electronics equipment involved. A good television report thrives on such details. My problem was how to get them.

German authorities are generally pretty tight-lipped when a criminal investigation is active. In this case, where a foreign government was running the show, they would probably say nothing at all. I decided to start my research elsewhere. An operation this size, involving computers valued at nearly half a million dollars, could hardly be kept secret. Dozens of customs agents – American and German – must have participated in the raid. People talk about things like that.

I reached for the phone and began calling low-level customs and police officials, airline employees, freight agents, switchboard operators and anyone else in Munich or Frankfurt who might be able to reveal a detail. After an hour of working the phones, I was ready for my first political query.

Ministerialdirektor Hans Hutter is director of German customs. I reached him at about 4 pm in his Bonn office: 'Herr Hutter, you have two telexes on the upper left-hand corner of your desk – one from Frankfurt and one from Munich. They contain the names of eleven West German companies involved in this operation. Could you tell me the names?'

The customs chief on the other end of the line took a long, deep breath.

'This is an active investigation,' he replied after a while. 'The legal briefs have yet to be filed. It's an extremely delicate matter.' Hutter was apparently irritated by my question. 'Besides, how do you know what papers I have on my desk?'

The answer was simple enough. Customs officials in Frankfurt and Munich, while refusing to reveal any names, had mentioned their telexes to Hutter in Bonn. When I called his office in Bonn to inquire about them, Hutter's secretary mentioned they were on the upper left-hand corner of his desk. She hardly thought, however, that Herr Ministerialdirektor would answer any questions about them for the press. She knew her boss. Hutter hung up.

I would call back later, I thought, as I returned to my other calls. Each company name, flight time or waybill number, each tip from a secretary, ticket agent or freight handler contributed a piece to the puzzle. Some clues were vague, such as a nameless freight company in the Black Forest area. Others were more fruitful. Using patience, politeness and the Yellow Pages, I made slow but steady progress. After an hour, I had Hutter back on the line:

'I have three of the names: Apollo Air Cargo, HAT-Express and Transsped.'

'I will neither confirm nor deny,' came the icy response.

Back to the puzzle. Each lead revealed new potential sources, or gave cause to return to former ones. I called some freight agents three, four and five times. One trail led from the Frankfurt airport to a computer company in the town of Laichingen, yet another across the frontier into Switzerland. I reported my progress to Hutter at regular intervals and pressed for further details. To little avail.

When our evening news conference convened at 7:30 pm, I took a seat in the front row and presented the results of my research to my colleagues at ARD-News. After a brief discussion, the editor-in-chief assigned me to prepare a report for broadcast on the following day. It was to cover the Frankfurt and Munich raids and include background information on Soviet computer-smuggling practices and the enforcement efforts of 'Operation Exodus'.

The following day, 15 July, began with a slow drizzle, and any Germans watching would not have thought much of the sunrise. Seen from above the clouds through the window of flight 993 to Munich, however, it was a magnificent sight. I felt the exhilaration of any reporter freed from the bonds of desk paperwork and out to cover a story. Chewing sleepily on a Lufthansa breakfast roll, I tried to organize my thoughts. The hectic turmoil of the previous day had left little time to arrange for a camera crew or make interview appointments.

When the plane landed at Riem Airport in the Bavarian capital, I headed for the first available phone booth and called cameraman Axel Reuter at his home. Axel is one of the best in the business – fast, reliable, professional. I could hear in his voice that I had caught him in bed. He promised to appear at the airport with equipment and a crew as soon as possible. We agreed to meet at the customs offices.

Munich airport customs agents work out of a run-down wing at the rear of the terminal building. Posters, calendars and a few dried flowers on the office walls testified to the futile efforts of someone on the staff to give the bare rooms a little warmth. The duty officer sat behind a worn desk, a sandwich and coffee spread out on wax paper in front of him. My arrival coincided with his Brotzeit, a traditional German breakfast break that is sacred in Bavaria. When he saw me standing in the doorway, the man dragged himself to his feet and donned his cap. We shook hands.

'Good morning. I have an appointment to shoot footage of your confiscated computers for network television.'

'So I've heard,' the duty officer mumbled. He was obviously not pleased about the visit, or about the impending disruption of his work-day.

'Bonn granted permission,' I added hopefully. 'My camera crew will be arriving shortly.'

'I have to check this with my superiors.' He glared at me. I waited.

'Can you please wait outside.' I obeyed.

Axel had arrived with two technicians and a welcome smile. I briefed them on the story and our shooting schedule. Time was tight, since I wanted to catch a 2:40 pm flight to Frankfurt for another appointment.

Customs called us in. Yes, we could film the thirteen crates. Before shooting, however, all names and addresses were to be covered from view. A sleepy employee was dispatched to hunt down brown paper and tape. We were in a hurry, so I offered our assistance.

'We'd be glad to help with the taping.'

'I'm sure you would,' the customs man answered, enjoying his brief moment of authority. 'But my instructions are not to reveal any of the names on the crates to anyone. That includes television cameras and nosy reporters.'

I flipped through my notes and began rattling off the data I had gathered on the shipment. By now, it was a pretty complete list of the freight companies, flight times and waybill numbers involved, and it helped convince him that we knew all the details anyway. So why shouldn't we help with the unpleasant task of taping brown paper over the names?

As the customs agent made his way through the dusty corridors to an outdoor freight yard just off the airstrip, I felt my curiosity rising. What would the contraband look like? The brown boxes and styrofoam packages we found looked innocuous enough. It was hard to believe they could be of any military significance to a super-power.

We scrambled across the rows of boxes, carefully covering any name that might be visible to our television camera. Many of the names on the countless stickers and printed labels were new to me, and – hidden between the crates – I entered them in my notebook. Most obvious were the large printed letters 'DEC': abbreviation for the American computer manufacturer Digital Equipment Corporation.

The customs officer, who had kept his distance while we were taping, moved in for a closer look when the shooting began. Axel, who had borrowed a fork-lift truck to use as a camera dolly, was riding around the crates, barking orders to his technicians and making quite a scene.

Knowing he could handle the visuals alone, I had withdrawn to a nearby phone booth, where I was talking to public affairs person Claudia Röhricke at DEC. News of the seizure had not yet hit the

Munich office, but she said she would inquire at the head office in Massachusetts. Shortly before air time that evening she relayed valuable information on the Stateside leg of the transaction. But now it was time to move on. We headed for our first interview appointment.

A Munich electronics company called Micrologic had been listed in the freight documents as receiver for the shipment. On the phone, Ferenc Gall, general manager of the company, had insisted his company was not involved in the smuggling operation and knew nothing of the shipment. Up to that point, Gall was the only person prepared to talk about the computer affair in front of a camera. I wanted him for the report.

When the tape started to roll, this is what the lean and polite Hungarian had to say:

'Back in 1979, we were importing computers from America. They were small machines worth between $1,000 and $2,000. Apparently we left a trail in the United States as an electronics import company. My guess is, someone got our names from trade papers or catalogues and decided to use it for this illegal action.'

'You didn't order anything?'

'No.'

I had no reason to doubt his claim. Later, one of the smugglers confirmed Gall's story. A notorious embargo-runner named Gerald Gessner admitted using the Micrologic address – without their knowledge – to conceal the true recipients of the contraband from the authorities. Gessner had instructed a Munich freight company to notify him directly when the shipment arrived. If all had gone well, he would have reshipped the strategic electronics, paid the bill and no one at Micrologic would have been any the wiser.

We shot some visuals of Gall's workshop and drove back to Riem. Before my flight at 2:30 pm there was time for a brief visit to the airport offices of HAT-Express, where the DEC computers had been seized. I was hoping for an eye-witness account of the raid. But company officials refused to make a statement.

On the flight to Frankfurt I thought about the day's work: there were enough visuals in the can for a four-minute news report. I had plenty of colourful details. But who were the smugglers? How had they concocted their plan and why? At Hansa Allee 141, the offices of the Frankfurt customs authorities, I hoped to find answers to these questions. Another camera crew was waiting when I arrived. We recorded the following statement from German customs officer Ernst Eckstein:

'We're still in the midst of our investigation. At this point, we cannot tell which freight offices were actively participating in criminal activities, and which were the innocent victims of a clever ploy. We believe that businessmen in Switzerland were running the illegal part of the operation. But our enforcement activities there are limited. Switzerland is a neutral country.'

When TV lights go down, many interviewees warm up. Not Ernst Eckstein. His tip on the Swiss connection – in the midst of an active investigation – was risky enough, and we both knew it. I didn't press him. The camera crew headed to the Frankfurt TV station, where the report was edited and fed by cable to ARD headquarters in Hamburg. It was aired that night at 10:30 pm on the German network news show *Tagesthemen*.

For a journalist, sources are vital. They must be carefully cultivated. Many people who are cautious during their first encounter with a reporter can become invaluable informants later, when they see that their information has been handled responsibly in the published product. It was 10:10 am on 16 July when I began a round of telephone calls to the sources of the previous day.

Two customs investigators were willing to meet me briefly before my return flight to Hamburg. We rendezvoused at a streetside café in downtown Frankfurt, and were soon huddled together over coffee at a back table. My pretext for the meeting was some sensitive information which I had allegedly run across in my research and which might be crucial to their investigation. Their faces were expectant. When I concluded my remarks, however, they were frowning.

'That's not new,' one of the men objected. 'We saw that on television yesterday. I thought you had some new information for us.'

'That was it,' I responded.

'I don't understand then,' the man continued, his consternation growing. 'What's the purpose of this meeting supposed to be then?'

The other investigator understood, and was nudging his colleague's shoulder. 'I have to see a man about a horse,' he said, rising from his chair.

His colleague didn't react. 'You do too,' he added, pulling his colleague gently to his feet.

As I watched the two men walk to the gents' room, I couldn't help thinking of schoolgirls I had seen in similar situations, disappearing to powder their noses when things got critical.

The men behind the computer caper were a Swiss businessman named Freddie Schiavo and a German physicist named Dieter

Enderlein. They had run the operation through companies called Trans Travel and Elmont AG. A few telephone calls from the café confirmed the tip from the two customs officers and at 1:40 pm I boarded a Swiss Air flight to Zürich.

At Frankfurt airport before leaving I rang up a freight company in Zürich called Fracht AG , which was listed in freight documents as the next forwarding address for the contraband. An employee there confirmed that Elmont was a regular customer of his company and had sent hundreds of foreign shipments through Zürich – many destined for Warsaw Pact countries. I was getting closer. With some difficulty, I managed to persuade the employee to meet me at the Zürich airport bar. Two hours later we were chatting over a drink.

'One false word can ruin a freight company these days,' the man announced slowly in Swiss-German. His calloused hands, which were obviously accustomed to lifting heavy crates, wrestled with each other on the table as he spoke. Someone had obviously warned him not to talk to reporters.

'In my field, discretion is everything,' he said.

'In my field too,' I responded. 'A journalist who exposes a confidential source is finished.'

'I don't know what's in the crates that I shove around every day. Maybe guns, maybe heroin, maybe even a dead horse. I don't know and I don't care. It isn't healthy to ask too many questions in this business.'

Dead horse? The guy had a sense of humour. I ordered another round of drinks and pressed on: 'This time we know what was in the crates: four complete PDP-11 computers from the Digital Equipment Corporation. That is strategically relevant equipment. We also know where they originated – Phoenix, Arizona – and where they were headed – for the Eastern bloc. If you've been working on shipments for Elmont for several years, you're bound to know some details about their transactions with the East?'

He shrugged his shoulders.

'At least you're familiar with the management at Elmont?'

Another shrug.

'What can you tell me about the men behind this operation?'

'Nothing.'

'I don't believe you.'

'Not a damn thing. The only thing that I can tell you. . .' he hesitated, then continued, '. . . is the name of the guy at Elmont who runs their freight department. We dealt with him regularly. But he's small fry.'

I jotted down the name. Not a particularly productive interview, I thought, as my taxi jostled through the winding cobblestone streets of the old city. It was after eleven. Normally, this Swiss banking town was dead by this time of night. But it was 16 July and Zürich was celebrating a *Volksfest*. Local tavern-owners had pitched colourfully lighted beer tents in the market-places. Makeshift wine bars were nailed to telephone poles, and a large, not-too-sober crowd was pushing its indiscriminate way through the streets. At the hotel I donned a clean shirt and stepped back into the warm Swiss summer air.

There were few natives out that night. The cheerful crowds consisted mostly of Italians and French, English and Americans, Germans and Austrians, and the conversations at their tables were lively and dull at the same time. Most people seemed interested in dancing, drinking, and generally enjoying the cross-cultural opportunities offered by such occasions. My thoughts, however, were occupied with cross-cultural exchanges of a more serious nature.

Who were Schiavo and Enderlein? Apparently they had been pursuing their dark trade for several years. Now they had been caught, their computers seized. What were they doing and thinking now? Who were their business partners? What if Eastern espionage services were involved? I had dropped my name and even my business card at dozens of the freight agencies and companies. Did Schiavo and Enderlein already know that I was on their trail?

Tomorrow I would know more. Tomorrow I would look them up in the small Swiss border town of Kreuzlingen. Today I needed sleep. On my way back to the hotel through the narrow medieval streets of the city I looked behind me several times. No one was following. You're starting to see ghosts, I thought.

It was midday on 17 July when I parked my rented Ford Fiesta on the main street of Kreuzlingen. The sixty-eight kilometres from Zürich had taken about fifty minutes. Boutiques, cafés and souvenir shops lined the street where I was parked. Down the road, Swiss border guards were checking passports at the German frontier.

The city of Kreuzlingen skirts picturesque Lake Constance and draws bustling crowds of families from both Germany and Switzerland on sunny summer weekends. It was Saturday, and tourists were flocking round the postcard racks and cake buffets. Beer-bellied men with cameras hanging like trophies from their necks, and women in flowered dresses, trying their best to tame the kids hanging from their arms, streamed across the sidewalks into the traffic, where cars waited patiently to pass the border checkpoint.

For a while I remained seated and watched the jovial crowds filing past my car. From my vantage point I enjoyed an unobstructed view of the offices of the Trans Travel tourist agency across the street. According to my information, this was where the computer caper had begun. I took a couple of snapshots through the windshield before getting out and approaching the travel bureau. But the offices of Trans Travel at Hauptstrasse 40 were closed, as was the other branch of the company at Konstanzer Strasse 6. I quizzed a few neighbours, jotted down a few notes and set my hopes on my third and final address.

Elmont AG occupied a small suite in a nearby office building. I found the main entrance open when I arrived. The reception area was deserted and no one challenged me. A plaque on the wall indicated that Elmont resided on the sixth floor, so I took the elevator up. When the electric doors opened, I was confronted with total darkness. I had to feel for the switch. The neon lights buzzed on, revealing three office doors, one with the bronze inscription: Elmont AG. I took out my camera and photographed the door. Then I asked myself, 'What now?'

No one would be working in an office at the weekend, certainly not in Switzerland. My expense account had expired, and all I had to show was a photograph of a door. Without additional information, I would never be able to use the picture.

The door. Before returning to the elevator I decided to try the door. I pushed against it gently, and it opened.

The offices of Elmont AG sprawled out brightly in front of me. About six rooms branched off from the carpeted hall, some with a pleasant view of the lake. The furniture was modern. I felt my heart thumping. Where does investigative reporting end and burglary begin, I asked myself, rapping loudly on the open door. A male voice on the phone could be heard from one of the back rooms. But no one responded. The man apparently had not noticed my arrival. For a moment I just stood there. Then, taking a deep breath, I marched inside.

On the way to the back room I passed a sign on one of the office doors: 'Fred Schiavo, President'.

The man on the phone sat with his back to the door, immersed in what appeared to be a routine conversation. When I knocked on his office door, he shot up:

'How did you get in here? And who are you?'

'My name is Tuck. I'm a journalist. The door was open.'

'You found us pretty quick.' He had seen the broadcast.

'I see you watch German television here in Switzerland. How did you like my report?'

'I didn't.' The man glared angrily. I could sense him sizing me up, slowly recovering from the shock of my sudden intrusion.

'And what's your name?' I asked.

'I can tell you my name. It won't mean a thing to you.' It was the name I had been given in the Zürich airport bar. I took to the offensive.

'Of course your name means something to me. You run the freight department here at Elmont. You've arranged over 300 shipments through Trans Travel in Kreuzlingen and Fracht AG in Zürich. Most of them were destined for the East.'

The man paled. I was asked to take a seat out in the hallway and offered a glass of orange juice while he returned to his telephone. This time, the voice from the back room had lost its routine ring. It sounded thin and nervous. Twenty minutes later the two men I had been tracking for four days walked through the door. Schiavo came in first, a muscular man with a strong step and a powerful voice. He was obviously the boss: manager and motor of whatever happened here. Following him – tall, thin and stooped – came German physicist Dieter Enderlein, the man for detail. An odd couple, I thought. Their respective talents are probably a good mix for the job.

It may seem quite irrational that two men involved in a shady deal should consent voluntarily to a conversation with a journalist. But their decision was completely logical. Computer gear belonging to them and valued at over $400,000 had been impounded at Munich and Frankfurt airports. Their lawyer in Frankfurt was doing his best to retrieve it. Thus, it was important for Enderlein and Schiavo to find out how much the press knew. There was a lot at stake for them. Enderlein sank into an armchair and limited his role to an occasional nod. His eyes remained riveted on Schiavo, who began drilling me with questions.

Schiavo and Enderlein may have been excellent electronics traders. After all, that was their business. Questioning people, however, is mine. It took about ten minutes to reverse the interview situation and start getting answers. More about the Elmont case will be revealed in Chapter Five. Suffice it here to say that they admitted masterminding the smuggling operation, as well as a number of previous West-East electronics deals. After forty minutes of note-taking, I interrupted the conversation.

'That's enough for the interview. Now all we need are a couple of pictures.'

'Pictures?'

'Yes, photographs for the story.'

'You must be out of your mind,' Schiavo objected, louder than necessary. 'We've given you an extensive interview, sacrificed our free time at the weekend and probably said much more than we should have. That's enough.'

'Let me show you something.' I opened the small black travelling-case at my feet. Schiavo moved closer.

'I just want to show you some lenses.' I smiled and passed my Canon FTb to Enderlein, who was watching my movements with curiosity.

'This is a Tokina 500mm mirrored-lens telephoto. Normally a lens with this magnifying power would be half a yard long and much heavier.' Enderlein fiddled helplessly with the camera. 'You have to go to the window. You won't see anything in here.'

Enderlein strode to the window and pointed the lens down towards Lake Constance.

'With this lens, one can take professional pictures from the roof of the building across from your company parking lot or from the bushes near your home. When you come out of your house with a bag of garbage. . . .'

'You don't know where we live,' Schiavo interrupted.

'Home addresses are listed in public records of the company.' I thumbed my notes.

'Kreuzstrasse 1C in Engelburg. Herr Enderlein lives at Am See 28 in Constance. Photo editors love pictures like that: man with briefcase steps from Mercedes, foreground out of focus. They have an authentic air to them. I prefer to take normal pictures of people who co-operate. The long-lens stuff makes them look so guilty.'

It was 3 pm when I pulled my Ford Fiesta out of the parking lot and headed back to Zürich airport and my flight home. In my suit-case I carried forty-three exposed negatives showing Schiavo and Enderlein – posing as a pair and individually, standing in front of their computers and sitting behind their desks. They had been co-operative.

The story was published in *Stern* magazine three weeks later.

The research that began with a UPI wire service report on 14 July 1982 continued over a period of three years. I interviewed experts on computer security and East-West trade, on Kremlin-watchers and the KGB, strategic systems and sophisticated software. I tracked several smuggling rings across Germany, France, Switzer-land, England, Holland, Scandinavia, and several cities in the

United States. Their trail leads from the labs and drawing boards of Silicon Valley in California across a wide network of European embargo-runners and mysterious middlemen to Zeleenograd, a secretive city twenty-five kilometres north of Moscow, where the Soviets construct the components for their nuclear missiles on machines 'made in USA'.

Computer piracy is now the number one priority of Eastern espionage services. Stereotype trenchcoat spies who send their coded messages to Moscow from secret hideaways, or mild-mannered moles like Günther Guillaume who spend years penetrating the upper echelons of Western politics, are no longer regarded as the prime danger. Today, it's the white-collar wizards of the illicit electronics trade – living in a weird world of waybill numbers and wads of cash, calculating in microseconds and megabucks – who pose the most serious threat to Western security.

Directorate 'T', a special branch of the Soviet intelligence service KGB, has been staffed with experts specializing exclusively in the theft of Western technology. A total of some 20,000 highly qualified agents are now in their service around the world. Their directives come from the highest policy-making levels within the Kremlin. The illegal acquisition of defence know-how is co-ordinated with the legal purchases of the State Committee for Science and Technology, the foreign outposts of Soviet trade missions and other official government offices working in the West. They are targeted at the central nervous system of NATO.

To meet this challenge, the Atlantic Alliance maintains an office for embargo policies in Paris called the Committee for East-West Trade (CoCom). But the West has assigned a total of only fourteen employees to control strategically sensitive technology and co-ordinate the international enforcement activities of its member states. They are trade diplomats – most of them without either military or electronics training – and they spend their working days translating documents, copying correspondence and distributing protocols. CoCom is a toothless watchdog, and a lot of Europeans would like to keep it that way.

This book describes eight cases of embargo-smuggling, examines the consequences of such dealings for the strategic balance of power, and describes what price we can and should pay to stop the computer spies. But will we? ·

Part II

CASES

ONE

Secrets From the Garage:
The Spawr Case

'My wife Fran and I love our country.' The small man in the rumpled suit had tears in his eyes as he glanced over to his wife from the defence stand. With his thick horn-rimmed spectacle-frames, short hair and short trousers, he looked like a relic from the 1950s. Walter Spawr was an inventor. 'We would never do anything to harm it. I was brought up to love our country, our flag and our heritage.'

Mr Spawr didn't seem like a spy, or even a smuggler. Friends knew him as a quiet businessman, a patriotic citizen and a Reaganite Republican. In his spare time he coached neighbourhood kids on a local Little League baseball team. His wife Frances taught Bible lessons in Sunday school.

But in September 1980 they were both indicted by a Los Angeles federal court on charges of embargo-running, accused of selling one of America's hottest military secrets to the Soviets. Neighbours and friends, relatives and acquaintances just couldn't get over it. Even US district judge Matthew Byrne admitted, 'You can't help but wish they weren't here. . . They are good community people.'

Like scores of other Western businessmen and women the Spawrs had been out to earn an easy dollar – perhaps overly ambitious, they admitted, but not unpatriotic. Unwittingly, they became entangled in an international scheme orchestrated by the KGB to pry strategic technology from the West and implement it in the armaments of the Warsaw Pact.

The married couple operated a small family business on the West Coast about forty-five miles east of Los Angeles, and their customer list read like a who's who of the American defence establishment: they were selling to the Redstone Arsenal, to the weapons laboratories of the air force and navy, to the nuclear weapons facilities of Lawrence Livermore and Los Alamos, to cruise missile makers at Rocketdyne and to spy-satellite producers at the TRW Corporation. Their product was a key to one of the most strategically important developments of the coming decade. The Spawrs made mirrors.

In the mid-1970s, almost nothing was known publicly about the military use of lasers. Death-rays were widely regarded as a fantasy product of science fiction authors. In secret, however, the superpowers in East and West were quietly keying up to a strategic struggle for supremacy in space. Low-flying spy satellites had already become the eyes and ears of modern military power, peering deep into installations and communications on the territory of foreign powers. Armaments experts envisioned killer satellites – armed with laser cannons – which could knock out an opponent's entire satellite fleet within twenty-four hours. Think-tank theoreticians were investigating gargantuan orbiting battle stations which could intercept attacking atomic missiles in mid-flight.

According to some estimates, laser weapons would soon be able to destroy intercontinental ballistic missiles within 300 to 500 seconds of their launch from enemy silos. The implications of the highly secret research were later revealed to the general public by President Ronald Reagan in his now famous 'Star Wars' speech of 28 March 1983:

'What if free people could live secure in the knowledge that their security did not rest upon the threat of instant US retaliation to deter a Soviet attack; that we could intercept and destroy strategic ballistic missiles before they reached our own soil or that of our allies?'

At the time, such plans were far from ripe. Mathematicians and physicists were still scribbling theoretical models on blackboards; chemists and engineers were caught up in the trials and errors of small-scale laboratory testing. Among the technical hurdles to be overcome was the unwieldy size and weight of the laser generator. Plans called for space platforms measuring over four metres in diameter and weighing nearly 100 tons. Since the cumbersome devices would be impossible to move quickly and aim precisely, specialists hoped to guide their deadly beams with mobile, lightweight laser mirrors. The best mirrors were being built by a small company in Corona, California, owned by Frances and Walter Spawr.

The Spawrs first set up shop in the garage of their home. The story that led from their backyard beginnings to major defence contracts – and success – could have come straight from Horatio Alger.

Walter Spawr had always loved to work with his hands. As a child he had built model aeroplanes. One of them set a world record for speed. He learned to grind and polish glass at the age of fourteen, when he designed and built his own reflecting telescope. Spawr was never particularly successful at school. He dropped out of college after his second term, and his father got him a job at North American Aviation, a military corporation nearby where he stayed for two years.

On 1 April 1963 Walter Spawr joined the US Air Force. Although he was promoted to sergeant, he quit after four years and returned to his job as lab technician. In the service he had developed a deep resentment towards large organizations. 'There was just too much politics involved,' he says today. 'People were getting promotions because they were so bad nobody wanted to keep them or because they were friends of certain other people.'

Back in the electro-optical lab of his former company, Spawr submerged himself in the exotic world of aerospace technology. He soon became an expert in the confusing tangle of government regulations and, together with his wife Frances, he decided to set up on his own. In 1973 they founded Spawr Optical Research Incorporated (SORI), one of thousands of small high-tech businesses popping out of the fertile California soil during that period.

The first years were no rousing success. Most visitors at SORI were turned off by the makeshift equipment scattered around the garage workshop. A high-tech talent hunter from the US Air Force Weapons Laboratory changed that. Captain Dale Holmes stopped by at SORI on one of his countless trips up and down the California coastline. Holmes knew that some of the most revolutionary high-tech developments came from small innovative companies with initiative, and he left a small piece of molybdenum with the Spawrs for a polishing test. Molybdenum was the metal chosen by air-force scientists for laser mirrors to withstand the bombardment of the death-rays. It was also extremely difficult to work.

When his labs had completed their analysis of the polishing, Holmes rang up the Spawrs to report that it was the best job he had ever seen. It was a breakthrough for SORI and the small California company was soon granted a security clearance by Washington.

At the labs of the TRW Corporation, America's leading producer of espionage satellites, events were unfolding that would eventually lead new purchasing agents to the garage in Corona. Top-secret tests on a project called 'Alpha-2' had revealed that light beams created in an explosive mixture of hydrogen and fluorine gas could be magnified in a long mirrored chamber, producing a laser with weapons-scale energy.

The effectiveness of the chemical laser, which could bore through tanks, aeroplanes and rockets like a hot knife through butter, was directly dependent on the quality of the mirrored surfaces reflecting it. TRW needed mirrors that could reflect 100 per cent of the light beamed onto them. Even the tiniest defect on the finely polished surface could diffuse the bundled light rays, rendering them ineffective. When managers of TRW heard of the quality of SORI mirrors, they were quick to order dozens. Many special surfaces were later developed in co-operation between the highly trained experts at TRW and the home-baked inventor from Corona.

At the atomic test sites of the Lawrence Livermore National Laboratory in Oakland, nuclear physicists were tinkering with other tests, which required even more demanding specifications from metal mirrors. They were trying to tame the neutron bomb. Instead of allowing the pulse of X-rays generated by an atomic detonation to be blown in all directions, their plans called for splitting and funnelling them into dozens of thin, intense and deadly X-rays. A small nuclear device, they figured, could be triggered in New Mexico, blasting the beams into space. From there, a worldwide network of computer-aimed space mirrors would bounce them to dozens of targets around the globe. The rays generated by a single detonation could be slammed simultaneously into fighters in the Far East, rockets in the USSR and even atomic submarines in the Arctic.

It was a weapons development with enormous strategic implications, theoretically capable of countering an all-out nuclear attack. The technical prerequisite was a metal mirror strong enough to withstand the explosive bombardment of the murderous X-ray pulses. The Lawrence Livermore National Lab turned to SORI.

Within just a few years, Walter Spawr had moved from being a backwater inventor to being a major defence contractor in one of America's key strategic technologies. The man who had always worked best when left alone was an overnight success: 'Ever since I was a little boy, I have had two goals – to contribute to my country and to contribute to science. Now I could do both.'

But with success came problems. The self-made inventor didn't blend well into the social scene of the high-tech defence élite of southern California. At cocktail parties, his outdated suits and clumsy comments tended to raise eyebrows. Spawr, who had developed his product inexpensively and quickly, complained constantly about wasteful defence-spending policies, remarks not well received by those earning their livelihoods from them. In Washington, the fact that a crucial new weapons development was becoming increasingly dependent on a shoestring operation in the suburbs was making the Pentagon uneasy.

When the US Air Force proposed a million-dollar research effort to develop its own mirror-polishing procedure, Spawr started to get nervous. If the Pentagon succeeded, SORI would soon lose its biggest account. His business was threatened, and Walter Spawr decided it was time to diversify. When he was approached by a European sales representative offering to sell SORI mirrors abroad, Spawr grasped the opportunity.

Wolfgang Weber was a German entrepreneur with extensive trade contacts in the East. He had read in trade papers of Spawr's success and approached him – as he had a number of other US high-tech companies – by mail. Within months Weber's company, Oriel GmbH in Darmstadt, was selling SORI products to car companies in Italy, hospitals in Israel and a good dozen universities and research institutions across Europe. After two and a half years of close and profitable co-operation, Weber suggested they take a look at Eastern markets.

Walter Spawr's small but strategic business had also attracted Moscow's attention. An organization called 'Welt East European Exhibit Management' had sent him an invitation to the Soviet trade exhibition 'Physics 75', promising that the exhibition would 'affect planning/purchasing attitudes in Eastern Europe for the remainder of the decade'.

The Eastern bloc overtures were no accident. 'Physics 75' was being sponsored by the Soviet Chamber of Commerce. Its president was a KGB general named Yevgeny Pitrovranov, identified by KGB expert John Barron as a key espionage figure who had masterminded kidnappings and assassinations in Western Europe at an earlier stage in his career. Pitrovranov had been transferred to the Chamber of Commerce to concentrate on the illegal acquisition of Western strategic high technology, which had already become a high-priority goal of Eastern intelligence operations. The illicit sales of Spawr's strategic metal mirrors were later organized through the Lebedyev Institute for Physics and the Mashpriborintorg Machine Import Company of Moscow, both of which play major roles in a number of the embargo cases described later in this book.

Walter Spawr had been raised as a patriotic American and he didn't think much of trading with the Soviets. Perhaps more important, he didn't expect they paid well. But he was wrong. The money they later offered – through Weber – was more than enough to bail him out of current difficulties. In fact, it was more than he had ever seen.

On 27 March 1975 Weber started selling the exhibition to Spawr, at first on the phone, finally flying to Los Angeles for personal talks. After some initial hesitation, Spawr was persuaded to participate. They worked out the details over a sandwich at the local diner. There was only one problem: the sale of high-energy laser mirrors to Moscow was illegal.

In 1975 détente was at its peak. Former Cold Warrior Richard Nixon had popped champagne corks with Soviet leader Leonid Brezhnev, US farmers were earning millions on enormous grain sales to the Soviet Union, and high-tech corporations like Sperry Rand and Control Data were opening offices in Moscow with the blessing of the White House. Soviet delegations had been repeatedly invited to tour Western defence facilities and Walter Spawr commented:

'I attended conferences on how to make better mirrors. The Russians were there. The latest, state-of-the-art military advancements on how to make mirrors that will take the most tremendous amounts of energy you'd ever heard of were all presented. So what's the big deal about exporting laser mirrors?'

It was obviously a big deal to high-level Soviets, who had expressed keen interest in SORI mirrors to Mr Weber. They met the German businessman at Moscow airport in November when he arrived with the first twenty SORI specimens and insisted on driving the tired traveller straight to the 'Physics 75' exhibition hall, immediately opening the crates and eagerly examining their contents. Mashpriborintorg bought half of the metal mirrors on sight. Twenty-five more were ordered later, ostensibly for the Lebedyev Institute.

Weber telephoned Spawr several times from Moscow to relay to him the continuing enthusiasm for his mirrors. Soviet interest was understandable. At that time the USSR was heavily involved in its own laser weapons programme at top-secret testing sites in Semipalatinsk and Saryshagen.

The dimensions and design of the large copper mirrors being

ordered by the Soviets should have made it clear that they were intended for military purposes. They measured 25–40 cm in diameter and included a water-cooling system designed to prevent bending when subjected to the extreme temperatures of high-energy lasers. Intelligence sources later revealed that the Soviets, who were having great difficulty with overheating, quickly implemented the SORI metal mirrors in their weapons programme. The US cooling technique, which had been revealed to Spawr on the basis of his security clearance, was then unknown in the Soviet Union.

Colonel Bob L. Francis, Commander of the Air Force Weapons Laboratory at Kirtland Air Force Base, believes that the mirrors exported by Spawr not only advanced the USSR's 'pointing technology', an area where the Soviets were believed to be seriously deficient, but also saved them millions of dollars and nearly 100 man-years in research and development.

By April 1976, the SORI shop was buzzing. Employees spoke openly of the 'Russian order'. And while they ground and polished the precision reflecting surfaces for the Lebedyev Institute, the phone rang. Weber was on the line again from Moscow. His eager customers at Mashpriborintorg wanted another twenty-nine water-cooled mirrors valued this time at $44,000. This was the third order, and the German salesman announced that others would soon follow. For Walter Spawr, who had been sceptical at the outset, East-West trade was growing more interesting by the hour. At the same time, his conservative political conscience was growing uneasy. Wouldn't it be better, he asked his wife Frances, if SORI applied for an export licence, at least for the larger mirrors in the new order? Frances thought it would.

On 4 May 1976 they formally submitted an export application to the US Department of Commerce. On the forms, however, they 'forgot' to mention fifteen of the twenty-nine mirrors ordered by Mashpriborintorg. The twenty-five mirrors for Lebedyev, which weren't mentioned in the export application at all, were secretly smuggled out of the country three months later. Wolfgang Weber stuffed eight of the smaller ones into his luggage and boarded a Lufthansa flight to Frankfurt. No one questioned him. The rest were packed in crates, deceptively labelled, and air-freighted over to Germany. No one examined them. At Frankfurt's Rhein-Main Airport Weber simply removed the fake freight papers and reshipped the crates – that same day – to the Lebedyev Institute in Moscow.

It was that easy to smuggle strategic high technology to the East in the year 1976. The United States export control system was in a state of complete shambles. 'Nothing was being done in that field,' William von Raab, who became US Customs Commissioner in 1981, would later complain. 'We had as many cases on parrot-smuggling as we had involving illegal export of technology to the Soviets. Apparently these crimes had equal priority.'

In October the US government replied to Spawr's export application. It was turned down. In its rejection, the Department of Commerce wrote that the laser mirrors 'have significant predominant use with CO_2 lasers which have important applications in the military arena.'

It was bad news at the wrong time. Two orders had already been sent off secretly without permission. The third one, which was in progress, was now blocked. Spawr was in trouble and he knew it. But instead of finally realizing that he was in serious violation of the law, he decided to blame the government. He sent off a fiery letter of protest to his Congressman.

Things started to converge. Congressman George E. Brown, concerned that a small company in his election district was suffering unjustly at the hands of Washington bureaucracy, quickly forwarded Spawr's letter to the Commerce department with a request for review. Commerce officials, however, were already aware of Spawr's intentions – and their significance for the nation's security. The complaints of two disgruntled former SORI employees, claiming that the California company was involved with mysterious 'Russian orders', had reached Commerce from the FBI. An investigation was started.

Totally unaware of the noose closing round their necks, Frances and Walter Spawr continued their preparations for the third order. This time, however, they intended to disguise the shipments even better: instead of shipping the strategic equipment directly to Weber's company in Germany, they routed it through a Zürich freight company called Fracht AG. From Switzerland Wolfgang Weber arranged for the onward shipment of the mirrors to Mashpriborintorg in Moscow.

In the summer of 1977, Walter Spawr was dining with Wolfgang Weber in the Imperial Terminal at LA airport, chatting about the success of their ventures, when things suddenly took an entirely new direction. The German pulled a contract from his attaché case and presented Spawr with a Soviet proposal to buy the entire production process from SORI. The Soviets wanted him to fly to Moscow to sign the contract, where he was to supply polishing equipment and train Soviet technicians in the art of making high-quality laser mirrors. They were offering $1.5 million for Spawr's secret. For the small-town American inventor, it was a lot of money. For the Soviets, it was a steal.

But the deal never came off.

On 9 March 1978, law enforcement agents appeared at the offices of SORI in Corona, California, and confiscated the files. It was all over. Walter J. Spawr, 39, and his wife Frances, 38, were indicted on charges of conspiracy and of knowingly selling strategic US high technology that would 'be used for the benefit of a Communist-controlled nation'.

On 12 December 1980 the Spawrs were convicted in a Los Angeles federal court on six counts of falsifying export documents and four counts of selling high-power laser mirrors to the Soviet Union. Walter Spawr was sentenced to ten years in prison. All but six months of his sentence was suspended. His wife received a five-year suspended sentence. Both were ordered to perform 500 hours of community service and the company was fined $100,000. Considering the strategic significance of the case, the sentence was mild. At the time, however, it was the hardest punishment ever handed down in a high-tech trading case.

'The Spawrs are not spies,' their defence attorney William Dougherty argued. 'These are very patriotic people.' Perhaps they genuinely thought they were. But their role in the international designs of the black-marketeers at Mashpriborintorg, the Lebedyev Institute and the KGB demonstrates the vulnerability of the Western defence industry. Even the products and processes of small businesses can be of enormous importance to the security of NATO. The strategic SORI secret was invented in a garage. Walter Spawr discovered it by trial and error. 'Anyone could have done it,' he reported in *New West Magazine*.

When news of the Spawr arrest reached the plush offices of Oriel GmbH in Darmstadt, Wolfgang Weber was not unduly alarmed. Since the German constitution protected him from extradition, the California case threatened neither his person nor his business. When the prosecutor in the Spawr case, who had flown to Germany from Los Angeles, rang him up, Mr Weber did however agree to cooperate in the investigation. After an interview at the US Embassy in Bonn – and a promise of a safe-conduct – Wolfgang Weber flew to Los Angeles to testify against Walter Spawr at his trial. It was a major success for the American Federal Prosecutor, a young Chinese lawyer named Dr Theodore Wu.

In the course of his investigation, Dr Wu had discovered that the Spawrs were only small fish in a very large pond. He had developed an acute appetite for a bigger catch. While Theodore Wu travelled through Europe, interviewing witnesses and local officials for his case against Spawr, his hooks had already been baited.

This time, it was no small-time American inventor. The man Theodore Wu wanted had masterminded a huge international ring of professional smugglers, shipping enough electronics equipment to the Soviet Union to equip entire factories.

His name was Werner Jürgen Bruchhausen.

Source Notes

Quotes from Spawr, as well as biographical background, come from an excellent article by Ehud Yonay, 'Mirrors for Moscow', *New West Magazine*, September 1981.

The deal: Dr Theodore Wu, 'Transfer of United States High Technology to the Soviet Union and Soviet-Bloc Nations', US Senate Subcommittee on Investigations, Washington DC 1982, p. 521.

Details of the law enforcement operation were supplied by Dr Theodore Wu (prosecutor) and Robert Rice (special agent) in personal interviews with the author.

Other information on the Spawr case: Michael Mallowe and David Friend, 'Russia's High-Tech Heist', *Life Magazine*, April 1983; *International Herald Tribune*, 6/9/1980; Reuters, 4/9/1980; AP, 4/9/1980; *Washington Post*, 4/4/1981; UPI, 12/3/1981; AP, 4/2/1981; UPI, 19/1/1981; AP, 13/12/1980.

Pitrovranov's KGB past: John Barron, *KGB*, Sherz Verlag, Munich 1974, p. 17.

Laser weapons: Clarence A. Robinson, 'Developing Beam Weapons', *Aviation Week*, 7/11/1983; Clarence A. Robinson, 'Beam Weapon Advances Emerge', *Aviation Week*, 18/7/1983; Ronald Reagan, as quoted in *Wireless Bulletin from Washington*, USIS, Washington DC, 24/3/1983; *New York Times*, 10/2/1980; *New York Times*, 3/3/1980; 'Wechsel in der Grundstrategie', *Der Spiegel*, 30/3/1981; 'Rethinking the Unthinkable', *Newsweek*, 4/4/1983; *Die Welt*, 9/4/1984; Eugene Kozicharow, 'Soviet Union Continues Military Buildup', *Aviation Week*, 23/4/1984.

TWO

Sandtraps:
The Bruchhausen Case

At the Los Angeles prosecutor's office, high-tech cases were regarded as sticky, tedious and unrewarding. Dr Theodore Wu got most of them because he was uniquely qualified to deal with the complex technical issues involved. As a graduate of the US Naval Academy in Annapolis he had an excellent scientific and military background. Perhaps more important was his motivation.

Ted Wu fled China with his family at the age of nine. The Japanese had confiscated their home and belongings in the Second World War and they emigrated to America hoping for a new start. It had been a rough uphill battle for the Chinese youngster. Language problems, prejudice, and plenty of street fights had paved his way. But Wu had fought himself out of the Chinese ghetto with willpower and hard work. Now an accomplished young prosecutor, he believed in the American Dream. And he didn't think much of those who wanted to sell the security of his new homeland to the Soviets.

As Wu leafed through the new file, he felt anger rising inside him. High-level strategic smugglers were at work and the case was inactive, despite extensive incriminating evidence. He read two anonymous letters giving names, addresses and details that had been mailed to the US Consulate in Düsseldorf, Germany. It had taken six months before they were translated into English and relayed to the enforcement branch of the Commerce Department in Washington. When they finally arrived, they had been ignored. No one had initiated even a preliminary investigation.

In addition, a number of high-tech companies had sent written inquiries to the government, expressing concern about the possible smuggling activities of the Bruchhausen group. Perkin-Elmer in

Connecticut reported that embargoed Microlign test equipment valued at $150,000 was on order, probably intended for the USSR. According to the management, the Soviets were known to be offering million-dollar rewards to anyone who could secure the Perkin-Elmer equipment for them. Officials at Watkins-Johnson in California were worried about two extremely sensitive microwave eavesdropping systems (WJ 2140 and WJ 940) which they feared could be diverted to the Eastern bloc. At Fairchild Camera and Instruments in San Jose the same group had aroused suspicion by ordering two Xincom 5581 test machines that were on strategic export lists. The purchasers had alleged that the equipment was destined for West German air-force bases. But they were paying cash and wanted the goods shipped to a post office box in Vienna.

Wu read on.

The suspects had been approached by a Commerce Department investigator. But when the manager of the suspicious company denied any illdoing – and offered to cancel the order in question – the agent had simply dropped the investigation. He should have grown more suspicious than ever, thought Wu, closing the file in disgust.

In his opinion, the evidence was overwhelming. It was certainly more than enough to warrant a serious investigation. Wu didn't understand how a case of this importance could get lost in the bureaucratic shuffle. Here was strategic equipment worth millions of dollars disappearing into uncertain channels. Some of it could be on its way to Moscow within days.

Special agent Robert Rice, who had flown in from Washington with the file, sat across the room from him. The two had developed a close working relationship on the Spawr case and Rice shared the prosecutor's outrage. Together they tried to figure out how they could throw some sand into the gears of the Bruchhausen operation.

Sand?

They had an idea. Why not sand?

Their plan wasn't easy. It would require the co-ordinated efforts of law enforcement agencies in California, Texas, New York and several European countries. Agents from Commerce, Justice and Internal Revenue would have to co-operate, as well as American and German customs authorities. Above all, it would cost money. But the chances of success were good. They both agreed on that.

Their superiors weren't exactly enthusiastic about the scheme. Commerce Department officials felt it was too risky and the price, which they estimated at $10,000, too high. After several delays, Wu was able to persuade the customs department to bear the costs.

When federal prosecutor Theodore Wu and special agent Robert Rice boarded a plane in July 1980 to trace Spawr's laser mirrors on the last leg of their journey through Germany and Switzerland to the USSR, the trap had already been set. They didn't know, however, that their target – German jetsetter Werner Bruchhausen – had just left the United States. For good.

Werner Bruchhausen was born on 5 November 1939 in Dortmund, Germany – the same dreary industrial city in which Wolfgang Weber later operated his Oriel GmbH. Bruchhausen started off earning a modest living in the electronics trade. With Soviet help, he later rose to become a multimillionaire with domiciles in Los Angeles, Germany, Vienna and Monte Carlo.

Bruchhausen first connected with his Soviet partners at an international trade fair in Munich, when USSR representatives approached him at his electronics booth. They spoke of good earnings; Bruchhausen showed interest and soon they were in business together. As it happened, his major trade contact was none less than Viktor Kedrov, Vice-President of the Moscow company Elorg (Electronorg-Technika) and number two man in the Soviet electronics industry.

Before assuming his post in Moscow, Viktor Kedrov had served many years abroad. He was a spy. In England, Kedrov had been assigned to the Soviet Embassy, until British authorities identified him as an officer of the Soviet military intelligence service GRU – and he was extradited. From there he travelled to Copenhagen to continue his espionage activities. He was exposed there also. When Moscow called him home, Kedrov was promoted to the Elorg job. It was an assignment far more important than routine intelligence collection in the field. The experienced spy was given major responsibility for the illegal acquisition of Western high technology, by then a top priority of the Kremlin intelligence services. Werner Bruchhausen fitted nicely into his plans.

After his first contacts with the Soviets, Bruchhausen headed for Los Angeles, where he founded four companies on 23 October 1974. Later, his empire grew to over a dozen companies plus a wide assortment of phoney addresses, shady freight agencies and middlemen – each with its own role to play in the unobtrusive movement of Bruchhausen's illegal shipments around the world.

Outwardly, Bruchhausen blended well with the business land-scape on the Pacific coast. The agile young German businessman was quick to learn the ropes. He was often sighted chatting up sales personnel and engineers at high-tech offices and exhibitions. But Bruchhausen preferred to leave official business to his American partner, Anatoli Maluta, whom he recruited through a classified ad in the *Los Angeles Times*.

Mr Maluta (alias 'Tony Metz') was born in Kharkov in the USSR. At first glance he seems an unlikely choice for the ominous Eastern business deals that the smuggling ring was soon pulling off. But in American security circles, Maluta had impeccable credentials. He had served with US Air Force intelligence and held a 'top secret' security clearance.

Maluta's assistant – and lover – was a German lady named Sabine Tittel from Gumbsheim. Together they formed the first link in a complex international chain of genuine companies and paper cor-porations, shipping companies and phoney post office box addres-ses, smuggling more than 300 illegal freight shipments from the USA into the USSR. Almost without exception these contained state-of-the-art technology that fell under the embargo restrictions of NATO. Among their customers were Mashpriborintorg and Elorg in Moscow, VEB Carl Zeiss Jena and Dr Günther Forgber in East Germany, Metronex and Unitra in Poland, Tungsram in Budapest and Isotimpex in Bulgaria. Their total sales topped $12 million.

The Bruchhausen Network

California

CTC California Technology Corp., 4676 Admiralty Way, Marina Del Ray, CA

Interorga International Components and Equipment Sales, 4676 Admi-ralty Way, Marina Del Ray, CA

Interedbo Edbo International Inc., 4676 Admiralty Way, Marina Del Ray, CA

Electronic Continental Industries Inc., 4676 Admiralty Way, Marina Del Ray, CA

Interorga Europe Inc., 4676 Admiralty Way, Marina Del Ray, CA

Atlantic Universal Supply Inc., 4804 Macafee Road, Torrance, CA

Universal Digital Corp., 4804 Macafee Road, Torrance, CA

Consolidated Protection Development Corp., 21515 Hawthorne Boulevard, Torrance, CA

Continental Technology Corp., 21515 Hawthorne Boulevard, Torrance, CA

American Data Technology Corp., 231 Calle Mayor, Redondo Beach, CA
Digital Security Corporation, 231 Calle Mayor, Redondo Beach, CA

Europe
Elubat Vertriebsgesellschaft für Elektronik und Batterien mbH, Göthes-
trasse 11, D-4000 Düsseldorf
ADT Analog und Digital Technik, D-8019 Niederseeon 21
Ing. Ulrichshofer, Ulrich Vertrieb Elektronischer Bauelemente und Elek-
tronischer Geraete, Baderstrasse 5, D-823 Bad Reichenhall
Electronik Elektrotechnische Bauelemente Handelsgesellschaft mbH,
4951 Ameisasse, A-1140 Wien
Techma Technische Maschinenhandelsgesellschaft mbH, Königstrasse 10,
D-4000 Düsseldorf
Elmasch Vertriebsgesellschaft für Produkte der Elektrotechnik und des
Maschinenbaus mbH, Bergstrasse 185, D-5300 Bonn

(Source: US Senate Subcommittee on Investigations, Washington DC, 4
May 1982.)

This is the way it worked: the Soviets would place their orders
with Bruchhausen in Europe. Bruchhausen passed them on to
Maluta in California, who then made the purchase through one of
the Los Angeles companies. On the surface, it looked legitimate.
One American company was buying from another. The strategic
electronics would then be shipped and reshipped – with changing
waybill numbers and falsified freight documents – along a tangled
international route within NATO, until they finally dropped out of
sight of the Western authorities. Some of the typical stations
included California, Düsseldorf, Munich, Bad Reichenhall, Bonn,
Vienna, Zürich and Amsterdam. On paper, the ownership changed
several times within the company network. It was the typical shell
game used by all strategic smugglers to conceal the illegal recipients
of their shipments.

At the purchasing end, Mr Maluta had drawers full of let-
terheads, business cards and addresses to choose from: 'Continental Technology', 'California Technology', 'Consolidated Protection', 'Interorga', 'Atlantic Universal', 'Universal Digital', and so
on. Sometimes Maluta would use his real name; on other occasions
he would call himself 'Tony Metz'. He described his position as
'President', or as 'Vice-President' or – modestly – 'Sales Manager'.
Several of the companies had overlapping directorships; often they
worked from the same office; some existed solely on paper; one was
run from a desk in the German-American Club of Los Angeles.

On the other side of the Atlantic, things weren't much different.
Werner Bruchhausen's European outfits were often little more than

transition points on the roundabout route to the USSR. The highly sophisticated electronics – occasionally so sensitive that the US did not allow even NATO countries to import them – were declared in freight documents to be 'ovens' or 'machine equipment'. When customs papers required the listing of a 'final' destination, the smugglers simply listed the next country on the route. It wasn't until the shipments reached the penultimate destination that the true recipients appeared on paper.

The group was well aware of the sensitivity of its doings. For fear their lines could be tapped by the authorities, they avoided using the names of their true customers on the phone. Instead, they referred to secret passwords they had agreed upon in advance. Any mention of a purchase order using the number 7200, for example, meant the speaker was referring to a Bulgarian deal.

Bruchhausen described his view of the legal situation in a television interview with the BBC several years later:

Bruchhausen: 'It was not against the law to ship that material from the States to Germany and it was not against the law to ship it from Germany to Switzerland, and it is not against the law to ship it from Switzerland to the Soviet Union. It might be an infringement of rules, but it's no crime.'

BBC: 'But it is against the law to ship it from America to the Soviet Union.'

Bruchhausen: 'Yes.'

BBC: 'You're saying whether this equipment was on the restricted list or not. . .'

Bruchhausen: '. . . was not checked by me.'

BBC: 'You didn't mind, whether it was on the restricted list or not? You were still making the money?'

Bruchhausen: 'Yes. It was a good trade and we made some extra money on that. That's why I took the chance.'

At the beginning of 1980, the risks started to increase. Customs agents stormed aboard a Soviet freighter anchored off the California coast and found an illegal electronics shipment valued at several thousand dollars. In the United States, where embargo-violators were now facing the stiffest penalties, things started getting too hot for Mr Bruchhausen. In March he decided to return to his home in West Germany.

About that time, Bruchhausen's company in Düsseldorf received a new order from Elorg in Moscow. Viktor Kedrov wanted two

HiPox (high-pressure oxidation) ovens (model no. 5025). The state-of-the-art equipment, made by Gasonics in Mountain View, California, was a decisive link in the production of electronic microchips and was listed in the export restrictions of the US government. There was real money to be made.

Bruchhausen had no idea that a Chinese prosecutor named Wu was on his trail. He confirmed the Soviet order by telex ('Attn. Mr V. Kedrov') and asked Maluta in Los Angeles to purchase the equipment from Gasonics. 'Get plenty for this,' Maluta cabled back. Company officials had been asking him very direct questions about the destination of the goods.

When purchasing sensitive electronics in the United States, Maluta had discovered that one technique was particularly useful in achieving maximum success. He paid cash. 'You show up with money and they're going to sell you anything, no questions asked.'

Well, some companies did ask questions. Maluta assured them, however, that the equipment was bound for a top-secret US army facility in Arizona, and any inquiries sent to the FBI were answered with reassuring references to Maluta's background as a former US intelligence agent. The Bruchhausen ring was having no trouble buying what it wanted.

Gasonics sold the two HiPox systems to Maluta. After all, the 'final' destination listed in the sales documents was the United States. As soon as the Gasonics equipment was in Maluta's possession it was resold to another American company in the group. And on 5 May 1980 Maluta brought the equipment to Los Angeles airport and booked it on a Lufthansa flight to Munich. The supermodern microchip-production equipment was labelled simply 'ovens'. Maluta declared the value to be $3,500. 'Final' destination was now listed as the Federal Republic of Germany.

In Munich, the shipment was received by Bruchhausen's European partner, Dietmar Ulrichshofer, who paid for it upon delivery. The two ovens, which had cost $250,000 in California, were now priced at $400,000. Yet Ulrichshofer was happy to pay. In his pocket he had a contract with the Soviets – written in both German and Russian. Viktor Kedrov and his friends at Elorg had agreed to pay a final price of $764,525 for the embargoed American electronics equipment. The mark-up on the original US purchase price was to be divided between Maluta (who had run the purchasing end in California), Bruchhausen (who organized the deal from Germany) and Ulrichshofer (who was about to make the final shipment to Moscow).

As he drove to Vienna airport on the evening of 3 June Dietmar Ulrichshofer reckoned he'd made a handsome profit for a single transaction. His freight agents had already forwarded the HiPox equipment from Munich to Vienna. On paper, it had been sold from Ulrichshofer's German company in Bad Reichenhall to his Austrian firm. The shipment was now in Vienna – out of NATO territory and home free for the final run. Connecting flights on the KLM 940 to Amsterdam, and from there on the Aeroflot 702 to Moscow, had already been booked. On Austria's neutral soil, Ulrichshofer felt safe. At the airport he was going to insert the original HiPox data sheets into the shipping crates. The Soviets would need them, when the shipment arrived.

It was shortly before midnight when Ulrichshofer pulled his car into the airport parking lot. He headed straight for the freight hall at the back of the terminal building, where the shipment was waiting. But when Ulrichshofer opened the crates, the data sheets in his hand, he discovered something horrible. The HiPox equipment was gone. In its place he found sand. Just sand.

The Austrian businessman was beside himself. He paced back and forth through the empty terminal halls, asking himself what had gone wrong. Ulrichshofer was far too upset to notice an unobstrusive American watching him from a distance. The American was smiling. US customs agent Roger Urbanski had been sent to Vienna from the American Embassy in Bonn, and Urbanski understood the Austrian's confusion. He knew that the electronics equipment was missing from the crates. The HiPox ovens had never left Los Angeles.

At 1:10 in the morning, a worn and weary Ulrichshofer appeared at the freight agents' window and cancelled the flights to Amsterdam and Moscow. The American agent reported the success back to Los Angeles. Theodore Wu's plan had worked.

The District Attorney's office had been tipped off on the illegal shipment. They wanted to let the shipment continue on its way, tracking its movements and the men it met on the way. But they didn't want to risk losing the original equipment. It was too sensitive. Wu: 'That was so state-of-the-art that even if one were to export it to West Germany an export licence was required and there was the question whether Commerce would have granted one.'

Customs agents had thus been instructed to remove the original equipment at Los Angeles airport and replace it with sand. The crates had been resealed in original Gasonics boxes by professional packers.

'Naturally, I was very surprised,' recalls Ulrichshofer today. 'I thought it was Bruchhausen, or one of his companies, because I had made a down payment for those machines of $400,000. I never got it back.'

Retracing the shipment's movements, the authorities got their first inside look at the internal workings of the Bruchhausen operation. And what they saw was sufficient. American lawmen raided its offices in California, while German officials swooped on European accomplices in Bad Reichenhall, Düsseldorf, Bonn and Munich. They netted over 400 freight documents, purchase orders and other papers which Dr Wu and his associates had to sort through. Slowly, they began to grasp the dimensions of the operation – and the damage done to Western security interests.

In former days, the Soviets had concentrated on the theft of prototypes of new NATO weapons systems – carefully dismantling and painstakingly reverse-engineering them for their own production. The Bruchhausen case, however, revealed a new strategy. They were now pursuing manufacturing equipment, apparently finding it easier to reproduce Western technology on the West's own equipment. They were stealing computer-aided design systems for planning integrated circuits, and printers for plotting them; photo-lithographic masks, copiers and etchers for transferring them onto silicon; saws for cutting the crystals and scribers for separating the circuits on the wafers; ion-implantation devices and diffusion ovens for circuit production; bonding equipment for connecting leads; solderers for mounting them and test equipment for quality control – all 'made in USA'.

The Soviets knew exactly what they wanted – right down to ten-digit spare-parts numbers – and they had been able to obtain it, more or less with impunity. US control efforts had proved almost useless. 'What we have here,' complained one of the investigators on the case, 'is a sieve.'

'Using Bruchhausen and the CTC connection,' computer expert Dr Lara Baker concluded, 'the Soviets were able to acquire all the hardware to build a complete modern integrated-circuit plant with 100 per cent spares. They got the best they could get – all state-of-the-art equipment. And they showed very good taste in getting it.'

In 1983 the products of the new Soviet microchip factories – already fielded in Warsaw Pact weapons – were washed up on the Pacific beaches of the United States, finally prompting Washington to take decisive action. But more about that later.

Anatoli Maluta and Sabine Tittel were apprehended in their car by FBI agents on 19 August 1980. Two pistols were found on the back seat at the time of their arrest. That very day, the Los Angeles prosecutor's office filed a sixty-count indictment against them – and against the two European co-conspirators Bruchhausen and Ulrichshofer – in federal court. They were accused of violating American export laws, as well as of a number of tax offences. The indictment was signed by Dr Theodore Wu.

Anatali Maluta was convicted and sentenced to five years in prison. Sabine Tittel received a two-year sentence and a fine of $25,000. Werner Bruchhausen and Dietmar Ulrichshofer didn't show up at the trial. They were protected in the same way that Wolfgang Weber had been protected in the Spawr case: export violations were not regarded by their governments as extraditable offences. US law enforcement agencies registered the names Bruchhausen and Ulrichshofer – somewhat helplessly – as 'fugitive'.

Bruchhausen, who was able to continue his dealings with impunity from West German soil, did not suffer financially. He lived in a magnificent villa, drove expensive cars and purchased lavish jewellery. One of his wildest wishes was a million-dollar wristwatch. He commissioned Spanish painter Salvador Dali to do the watch face. The price for the hand-painted work of art was to be $1 million. But Bruchhausen's luck was changing. The old master collected a $160,000 down payment – and was never heard from again. Soon afterwards, Bruchhausen was arrested by German police on charges of illegal high-tech trading with the Soviets.

In spite of his extravagant tastes, the dealer from Düsseldorf does not regard himself as a big fish. In a telephone interview with the Associated Press, he later commented, 'Volume-wise, what I've done is Mickey Mouse.'

Disneyland was not far from Bruchhausen's main base of operations in Los Angeles. Neither was Fantasyland. And further north, in a valley on the Bay of San Francisco, the big fish were biting.

Source Notes

The deal, including times, dates, model types and quantities of smuggled equipment, names of participating companies, etc.: US Senate Subcommittee on Investigations, Washington DC 1982, pp. 54, 350-65, 384-425, 524-32.
Investigation: Theodore Wu and Robert Rice in personal interviews with the author.
Interview with Bruchhausen, as well as quotes from Ulrichshofer: 'High-

Tech Trail to Moscow', *Panorama*, BBC Television, 21/2/1983 (referred to hereafter as BBC *Panorama*).

Victor Kerov: Danisa counter-intelligence and KGB-convicted spy Bent Weibel in personal interviews with the author.

Bruchhausen quote: ('Mickey Mouse'), AP, 1/6/1983.

Trial in Germany and watch from Dali: *Süddeutsche Zeitung*, 17/1/1981; *Tagesspiegel*, 15/6/1983; *Express*, 15/6/1983; *Neue Rhein Zeitung*, 15/6/1983; *Westdeutsche Zeitung*, 15/6/1983; *Rheinische Post*, 15/6/1983; AP, 1/6/1983; *Weltwoche*, 17/11/1982 and 12/8/1983.

Bruchhausen's arrest: Munich *Abendzeitung*, 11/5/1985.

Other details of the Bruchhausen case: Christopher Simpson, 'Electronics Underworld', *Computer World*, 31/8/1981; *New York Times*, 20/8/1981; Christopher Simpson, 'Faule Ware', *Stern*, no. 40/1981; *Die Zeit*, 10/9/1982; *Newsweek*, 23/11/1981.

THREE

From Hong Kong to Silicon Valley: The Dawe Case

They came from all corners of the country and settled in thousands in a wide fertile valley on the southern tip of San Francisco Bay. They spoke in strange tongues like COBOL, OLTEP, ALGOL and FORTRAN. They dressed like students and worked out in corporate swimming pools. They were easy-going and hard-working, and everyone was expected to call them by their first names. Their settlement was soon named after a common substance that composes a quarter of the earth's crust. But the achievements of the computer freaks of California were anything but common. They changed the world. The nickname of their new home soon became an international symbol of the electronic age they had created: Silicon Valley.

The first computer chips – microscopic electronic circuits – were developed here. They were packed into small black boxes with wire centipede legs and built into toasters and telephones, traffic lights and televisions, quartz watches and quadrophony. They run mighty power-plants and tiny toys, automobile assembly-lines and aeroplane flight-paths. Schoolchildren use them for their homework, multinational corporations to calculate billion-dollar transactions. They catapulted the Western world irreversibly into a new age. Almost overnight, entire sectors of the economy were out of date; dozens of professions had lost their meaning.

Today, the stars of San Jose, Santa Clara and Sunnyvale are as celebrated as the Western heroes of yesteryear. Like Jesse James, Wyatt Earp and Billy the Kid before them, many became legends in their own time.

There was the eccentric engineer at Sperry Univac back in the 1950s, who dreamed of computers able to calculate 200 million transactions per second. He was met with mild amusement when he quit his lucrative job one day to pursue that dream. The man was Seymour Cray, and he had soon designed a machine that more than doubled that goal. His Cray-1 now sits at the strategic nodes of defence and intelligence establishments, where the most rigorous demands are placed on high-speed computers: at the nuclear testing facilities in Los Alamos and Lawrence Livermore, at NASA control rooms in the Houston space centre and at cryptographers' puzzle parlours in the supersecret basement complex of the National Security Agency. His Cray-2 computer, which hit the market in 1984, reaches a speed of two billion transactions per second. Seymour Cray, a lover of breakneck skiing and Boolean algebra, is now a multimillionaire.

Condescending smiles also greeted Steven Jobs when he gathered with his friends Sandy Kurtzig, Jerry Sanders and Stephan Wozniak in the family garage. Jobs was concerned with two problems: the first was his weight, which he combated as best he could with an apple diet. The second was a 'people's computer' the group was developing. They named their product after Steven Jobs' diet. Today, the Apple Computer is a legacy, and the corporation that builds it has sales topping $600 million a year.

The family garage was also the starting point for two other neighbourhood youngsters named Bill and David. Their last names tell the rest of the story: Hewlett and Packard. Nearby, Nolan Bushnell (Atari), Bob Noyce (Intel), Ken Oshman (Rolm), Jimmy Treybig (Tandem) and scores of others were soon on their way to fame and fortune.

In Silicon Valley the American Dream was turning into reality. Time after time tangle-haired kids with nothing but bits and bytes in their heads were skyrocketing out of neighbourhood back yards into plush executive suites atop their own multinational corporations. In an age of elephant mergers, when the United States economy seemed stuck in an irreversible process of corporate concentration, the computer cowboys from California were offering living proof of the vitality of the free-enterprise system.

If California seemed a little confused in those days, Wall Street was insanity. Backwater electronics shops could suddenly be worth millions. Venture capital was in high demand and the prospect of overnight earnings was attracting investors from around the world. There was money to be made, big money, and the conservative financial markets of the West were abuzz with ecstasy – and confusion. West Coast brokers were unfamiliar with the mysterious mechanics of RAM and ROM, where millionths of a millimetre or billionths of a second could mean life or death to an up-and-coming young company.

No one took particular note when Amos Dawe, a chubby banker from Hong Kong, checked into this bizarre world one foggy afternoon in February 1973. He arrived at the Hyatt Regency Hotel in San Francisco with three associates and a lot of money.

The wealthy Asian businessman was accustomed to unpredictable financial situations. He had earned his reputation – and his millions – on the wild and woolly stock exchanges of the Far East. He had come to buy American banks, about twenty of them. But Amos Dawe was not seeking sound investments for himself.

He had been sent by the Soviets.

The Kremlin leadership was well aware of the potential of the electronics revolution in California. They knew that its products were not going solely into consumer goods, that a good portion of the money spent there came from the Pentagon, and that computer innovations would have a decisive influence on the strategic struggle for military supremacy in the coming decades. California computers were guiding the missiles and planes, tanks and ships, helicopters and howitzers of NATO. The Kremlin had admired the finely tuned electronic engineering they found in captured weapons systems during the Vietnam War. They envied America's spy satellites, which could peer deeply into their own territory. They envied them, and they feared them. The Soviets were watching Silicon Valley.

Their own rudimentary electronics industry was unable to design comparable weapons systems, their own roughshod factories unable to produce them. So they decided to steal. Three years before Amos Dawe checked into the Hyatt Hotel in San Francisco, Kremlin spy chief Yuri Andropov had set up a new branch of the KGB called Directorate 'T'. Its sole function was the theft of modern Western technology. Scientists and students, engineers and academics had been recruited for the new centre from the best Soviet institutes and universities across the country. Housed in a modern concrete and glass office building in the suburbs of Moscow, they were soon operating a top-priority programme to rob strategic secrets quickly, quietly and efficiently.

Western law enforcement agencies dealing with high-tech smuggling cases had often been amazed at Soviet luck in finding companies and individuals that were susceptible to their designs. It was not luck. Directorate T's experts ran a thorough intelligence operation to locate vulnerable targets. They were devoted to the dirty details: a company's financial squeeze (that could make 'overseas business' seem attractive), heavy indebtedness (that could make an individual susceptible to bribery), or personal weaknesses, like homosexuality or drugs (that invite blackmail).

Obviously, an ideal source of confidential information of this nature would be a bank in northern California. Along with the accounts of hundreds of Silicon Valley scientists, engineers and businessmen, Andropov's outfit could hope to find intimate details on debts, alimony payments, liquor-store bills and other soft spots – any of which could lead to a potential smuggler.

When looking for an undercover agent who could scout the Silicon Valley scene for Moscow, the KGB did not do the obvious and turn to a loyal leftist. Instead they approached an Oriental financier who had earned millions through the capitalist system. Amos Dawe was perfect.

First of all, Hong Kong was good cover for the operation. It is absolutely paranoid about suggestions of Soviet influence. Neither Soviets nor Communist nationals from East European countries are allowed even to enter the territory without a visa – and visas are nearly always refused to them. Even sailors from Soviet ships are not permitted to set foot on land. The setting was ideal.

And then there was Dawe's personal history. He was no spoiled son of a wealthy family, susceptible to romantic ideological notions. He had started from humble beginnings and worked his way up the hard way – a rugged self-made man.

Until 1964 he had worked as a clerk at a Singapore post office. Together with his schoolteacher wife he saved enough money to buy some land on a small island in the harbour. Shortly afterwards a bridge was built and real-estate prices hit the ceiling. Dawe, then twenty-nine, suddenly had money. He quit his job and went into the investment business with an Indonesian friend.

Although neither educated nor experienced in investment matters, Dawe showed a skilled hand. His new company bought some plantation land across the causeway from Singapore, dividing it into forty housing sites and selling at a quick profit. From there, he moved into rubber and palm-oil plantations. Before too long he was all over the stock markets of Hong Kong, Singapore, Malaysia and Kuala Lumpur. Within ten years his Mosbert Holdings Limited owned a number of international corporations with names like

Allstate Enterprises, South Jahore Amalgamated Holdings and Raja Enterprises.

In the shady and often corrupt financial world of the Orient, Dawe advanced rapidly from being whiz-kid to the major leagues. He soon moved from Singapore to Hong Kong, where tax laws were more merciful towards wealthy men. At the height of his career the former postal clerk controlled over 200 companies in six Asian countries, valued at an estimated total of some $100 million. Amos Dawe looked like a very successful businessman. On the surface.

Those who had access to his book-keeping, or were plugged in to the Far Eastern financial grapevine, had a quite different picture. Dawe was having liquidity problems. In fact, bankruptcy was knocking at his door. One year he approached five auditors before he could find one willing to sign his corporate records. And the one who signed insisted on a disclaimer stating that the balance sheet 'is not properly drawn up and does not exhibit a true and correct view of the state of the company's affairs'.

As far as serious accounting goes, he might just as well have written 'pack of lies' all over it in thick red ink.

'Operation Amos Dawe' was initiated by the Moscow Narodny Bank (MNB) in Singapore. MNB is a poker-faced financial arm of the Soviet Union, established by Lenin in 1919 as a small concession to Western capitalist ways. Over the years, the London headquarters had won recognition as a reputable, conservative – almost British – financial institution. By comparison, its Singapore sister was absolutely wild.

The ebullient Soviet branch manager Vachislav Rykhov and his windy Indonesian sidekick Teo Kong had a reputation for throwing caution to the wind – and with it millions of Singapore dollars. By 1974 – only three short years after opening its doors – MNB accounted for over 13 per cent of all bank lending in Singapore. A year later it had distributed some $833 million in loans and advances to its customers, so that the total exposure of the 'restricted' Soviet bank was far greater than that of many of the oldest established 'full' banks in the area. In some cases, the Narodny Bank was even observed borrowing money at 11 per cent and re-lending it at 9 per cent. Professionals began to question whether the Soviets were in it for the money at all.

Mr Rykhov and Mr Teo first approached Amos Dawe in 1972. They offered to underwrite his Mosbert Holdings, including a considerable international expansion, and Dawe eagerly agreed. A year later they told him the rest of the story. Their plan was to send

Dawe to the United States to acquire banks for MNB, something the Moscow bank could hardly do alone. They made it clear to Dawe that his current loans, already running at several million dollars, would be extended only if he consented. Dawe felt the gentle squeeze of an iron hand at his throat – and consented.

The self-made millionaire, long accustomed to working only for himself, found himself checking into the Hyatt Regency Hotel in San Francisco as an errand boy for the Soviets. They had instructed him to scout the local banking scene for appropriate targets. When he returned to Singapore to report his findings, he discovered his Soviet friends had used him only to cross-check intelligence they already possessed. In an interview with the BBC, Dawe said:

Dawe: 'To my surprise, they already had all the information under the table. They had maps and everything – which banks were to be acquired, all the information on the banks. They had more details than I could imagine. They had done their homework.'

BBC: 'Why do you think the Moscow Narodny Bank had all the details of the banks in San Francisco?'

Dawe: 'They were trying to get someone within the group, within the Moscow bank, that would be suitable for the job, you know, to take over the banks in San Francisco.'

That role was reserved for the banker from Hong Kong, and soon Amos Dawe found himself back in the United States, continuing down the strange path he had somehow stumbled onto. He didn't want to be there. But there he was.

At least Dawe understood the trade. One US banker described his entourage as 'three lightweights and a shark to do the nibbling. He made a pass at every bank worth under $100 million.'

To his American business partners, the Chinaman was a complete unknown. Although he had announced his intention to purchase some twenty American financial institutions in the most vital strategic industrial area of the nation, no one showed particular concern. Why should they? United States banking regulations were known to be among the stiffest in the world. The Americans, if they had any reservations at all, could be sure the authorities would take a close look at the foreigner. Regulations required that.

But Dawe knew the regulations better. Strict controls were required only of foreign companies buying in America. Amos Dawe was buying as a private individual. So no one checked him.

Until later.

His first acquisition was the Peninsula National Bank in the sleepy San Francisco suburb of Burlington, across the street from the bowling alley. Dawe paid $3 million for it, twice the market value, and the deal was closed in December 1974. Peninsula National was no big financial corporation. Neither did it control any significant industrial portfolios. It was just a regular drive-in-and-cash-your-cheque bank, earning a mere $165,000 a year. For the price, it was a questionable investment at best. Dawe could have earned more if he had put his money in an ordinary savings account.

But Dawe was not out for earnings.

Within six months, he had brought two more West Coast banks under Soviet control: the Tahoe National Bank and the Fresno 1st National. (All three banks are now back in American hands.) The package price this time was $7.9 million, nearly three times the market value.

The source of the money was to be kept carefully concealed. The million-dollar transactions were not transferred directly from the Moscow Narodny Bank to Dawe, but rather channelled through a complicated web of international accounts. Another Chinese banker named Eddy Wong, also a major recipient of MNB money, proved a willing conduit. His Pacific Atlantic Bank in Panama received a $2.7 million letter of credit from the Soviets out of Singapore and transferred the money to the Commerce Union Bank in Nashville, Tennessee. From there, it was re-transferred to Dawe.

In spite of all the precautions taken to disguise the source, the doings of Dawe and his Eastern masters had not escaped the watchful eyes of American intelligence. Undercover agents at the CIA station in Singapore were closely monitoring his movements and radioing their intelligence back to headquarters.

'The plot,' according to CIA consultant Harry Martin, 'was to learn the entire financial structure of Silicon Valley, which is a very high-defence, high-technology area. They wanted to get access to the boardrooms, to get access to individuals' finances and thereby assess who was the most vulnerable and which pressures to apply.'

At Langely headquarters, disturbed CIA officials debated as to the best course of action. They decided publicly to expose the ominous Soviet ploy, and leaked the results of their investigation to an influential Hong Kong-based journalist named Raymond M. Sacklyn. In his computerized financial newsletter *Target*, Sacklyn published the story of the Soviet-Singapore sting in all its intriguing detail. Sacklyn's revelations sent out shock waves that reached all the way to California.

Under normal circumstances, Amos Dawe was a low-key, poker-faced man of notorious Oriental reserve. But when he stormed into the offices of the Narodny Bank at eleven in the morning on 20 October 1975 his pudgy face was glowing red. In his trembling hand he held a telex from Peninsula National asking lots of embarrassing questions about the *Target* revelations. The American banking world was in uproar, and Dawe was hoping for advice and comfort from his masters. He found neither.

In fact, he didn't even get past Teo's secretary. When Dawe, after incessant dialling, finally reached Teo on the phone, it was 4:30 in the afternoon. Dawe couldn't believe what he then heard.

'There's been too much publicity,' Teo was screaming. 'Under the circumstances, I'm afraid we will not be able to extend your credit for the Peninsula Bank. You will have to pay the $2.7 million yourself.' Dawe felt his stomach and his financial empire slip.

Teo Kong and his Soviet boss were having problems of their own. In Moscow, all hell had broken loose. For years the Kremlin had worked quietly and discreetly at establishing a financial foothold in the Far Eastern capital. MNB had succeeded in spreading its silent influence through insurance companies, shipping agencies, hotel chains and travel offices on the entire continent. No one had become suspicious. The only critical voice heard thus far had been from Peking. 'The ruse used by the bank,' Hsinhua had complained, 'is to extend credit to various businesses on very severe terms and then press them for repayment.' The official Chinese news agency had gone on to detail a number of Moscow takeovers instigated by the Narodny Bank.

The Soviets could live with the ravings of the Peking press. No one had taken them seriously. A public scandal in the West, however, was a different matter entirely. Now in Fresno, headlines were screaming 'Soviet Money in California'. In Hong Kong, *Target* continued to fire off its accusations of 'Commercial Warfare'. Illicit dealings at the Moscow Narodny Bank had become the talk of the town, and Moscow had to find a scapegoat. They went looking in Singapore and found Mr Teo, who was removed from his post, and Mr Rykhov, who was called home. Both were blamed for the enormous losses incurred by the operation.

Amos Dawe, who was in the midst of preparing his fourth bank takeover, in Santa Ana, had become worthless. His cover was blown. A few days after the demise of Teo and Rykhov, it was official: the Narodny Bank withdrew all loans from Dawe's enterprises. To make things worse, authorities in Australia and Hong Kong were starting investigations. His empire collapsed like a house of cards. Dawe knew he was finished. He could even land behind bars. There was only one alternative: flight.

The Hong Kong financier disappeared into the underground – first hiding in Bangkok, later commuting between Thailand, the Philippines and Taiwan. Occasionally, he risked a side-trip to Europe. But in spite of the wealth of money he had squirreled away for this eventuality, Dawe was hardly amusing himself. He knew too much, and feared that KGB agents were on his heels. On one occasion, Dawe returned to his London hotel room to find it ransacked. Important documents were missing – and whoever had taken them had left a $1 Singapore note as a warning.

A few days later, on 12 December 1975, a stranger approached him in a London subway: 'If you value your life, go home.' The man repeated the sentence twice – and vanished in the crowd.

Dawe took the warning seriously and returned to Asia. But he found no peace. He continued to live on the run. Although travelling on a Canadian passport and using unlisted telephone numbers and anonymous hotel rooms, his hunters found him again and again. The postman brought hate mail and anonymous callers hurled death threats at him in the night. In a plush hotel in Bangkok he was savagely assaulted and beaten almost to death by Thai hoodlums. Amos Dawe was convinced they had been hired by the KGB. Whatever the case, he no longer felt safe where he was. The resourceful Oriental millionaire had come a long way since the heyday of Hong Kong. After two and a half years in hiding, Amos Dawe decided to surface.

He figured the safest place to go was to the United States. In August 1978 he flew to San Francisco International Airport and surrendered to FBI agents. A US federal court later dismissed embezzlement charges against him. But an endless chain of civil suits followed: the Bank of America sued Mosbert Holdings, Mosbert sued Dawe, who in turn sued the Narodny Bank, and so on and so forth. The seemingly endless litigation went on for years in courtrooms in various parts of the world. The sums involved were enormous.

While Dawe's lawyers battled the countless civilian suits on one front, criminal charges were brought against him on another. Several countries asked US authorities to release him to face charges in their own courts. Dawe fought them with a vengeance, claiming he would be killed by the KGB if he ever left America. An extradition request from Singapore was denied. But another – from Hong Kong – was then granted. And Dawe had to leave.

In Hong Kong he was acquitted of fraud charges. Then, in a reversal of the decision made by the appeals courts on 1 December 1982, he was convicted and sentenced to five years in prison. But the Far Eastern financier was nowhere to be found. Amos Dawe had slipped from sight again.

This time, perhaps, for ever.

Source Notes

Silicon Valley (background): 'Storm Clouds over Silicon Valley', *INC*, 9/ 1982; *International Herald Tribune*, 28/5/1983; 'Amerika liegt in Kalifornien', *Der Spiegel* no. 48/1983; 'The Race to Build a Supercomputer', *Newsweek*, 14/7/1983; 'Chipmaking Machines Come Roaring Back', *Fortune*, 3/10/1983.

Quotes from Amos Dawe and CIA adviser Harry Martin: BBC *Panorama*.

Quote from Teo: Dawe describes this meeting with Teo in an article in *Asian Banking*, June 1981.

Quote from Hsinhua: 'Charting the Asian Trail', *Far Eastern Economic Review*, 28/7/1978.

Other sources for the Dawe case: *International Herald Tribune*, 28/5/1983; Robert S. Dudney, 'How Russia Steals US Defense Secrets', *US News and World Report*, 25/5/1981; Anthony Cook, 'The Singapore Sting', *New West*, 21/6/1976; 'CIA Documents Shed Light on Soviet Banks', *Asian Wall Street Journal*, 8/1/1979; 'Long-Running Saga of Amos Dawe Moves to San Francisco', *Asian Wall Street Journal*, 9/1/1979; Peter Weintraub, 'Amos Dawe switches to the offensive', *Far Eastern Economic Review*, 17/11/1978; *Wall Street Journal*, 11/5/1981; 'The Russian Connection', *Target*, 28/8/1975; *Daily Telegraph*, 18/5/1981; 'Lifting the Veil of Secrecy', *Far Eastern Economic Review*, 11/4/1980.

FOUR

Roubles For Ryad:
The IBM Case

The adroit young Germans in white overalls made their way quietly through the darkened corridors of Neckermann's department store in Frankfurt. It was Sunday, 22 December 1974, and Christmas decorations hung eerily over the sales displays in the empty rooms they passed. Outside, the streets of downtown Frankfurt were deserted.

There had been no difficulties at the door. They had told the guard they were IBM maintenance men on an urgent repair mission. But the equipment at Neckermann's was not in need of repair. And no one had called them. Once inside the air-conditioned computer room of the department store, the intruders pulled microfilm cameras from their briefcases and systematically began photographing the 2,000-page IBM manuals they found there.

The two men were so engrossed in their work they didn't notice the other Sunday visitors lurking in an adjoining room. Detectives from the Wiesbaden state police, tipped off by a company employee, were waiting for them. For two hours the lawmen let the men in their white overalls go about their work. Then, with guns drawn, they moved in to arrest them.

Under police interrogation the burglars confessed quickly. But the startled Wiesbaden detectives were soon hearing more than they had bargained for. The story of the Neckermann break-in was just a small part of the fascinating international intrigue that unfolded as the suspects' statements slowly filled over 150 pages of police transcripts. Chatting easily, the two explained they were only low-level members of a larger group that was smuggling high-tech equipment to the East. Their tale told of secret Soviet shopping lists, million-dollar deals and couriers travelling with contraband on mysterious missions to Moscow and East Berlin. The events at the Hanauer Landstrasse in Frankfurt that cold December afternoon were taking on dramatic East-West dimensions.

Phones started ringing at the Attorney General's office in Karlsruhe, at the headquarters of the federal police in Weisbaden and at West German counter-intelligence in Cologne. Over 100 law enforcement officers were ordered to cancel their plans for the Christmas holidays and join the mounting investigation. Search warrants were issued and hastily-formed detective squads, fanned out in the German cities of Frankfurt, Solingent, Stuttgart, Düsseldorf and Krefeld. In private apartments and obscure business offices across the country police confiscated large quantities of telltale evidence, including Eastern bloc acquisition lists, exposed films, a Soviet 35mm camera and nearly $100,000 in cash.

By 13 January authorities had rounded up a total of twelve suspects – all of them German electronics experts aged between 30 and 35. One was carrying $30,000 in notes rolled in a rubber band in his trouser pocket at the time of his arrest. Another had almost as much cash neatly stacked in a bank safe deposit box. The results of the police sweep were announced two days later at a press conference by German Attorney General Siegfried Buback.

The twelve men, Buback charged, had 'operated a high-level espionage ring for the Soviet bloc', seeking operating systems, programmed magnetic disks, microfiches, maintenance manuals and technical data sheets from embargoed Western equipment, siphoning them off in great numbers to the East. Their customers were at Elorg in Moscow and Intertechnika in East Berlin. All told, their sales and run into the millions. Buback termed the investigation 'a very significant case of industrial espionage', and indicated that an indictment on charges of espionage and high treason was in preparation.

Computer experts were baffled. Why would anyone go to such lengths to obtain ordinary repair manuals? The Neckermann computers – IBM System 360 and IBM System 370 – were standard commercial models widely available on the open market. Anybody could buy the manuals directly from the branch office of International Business Machines in Stuttgart. So why offer a $10,000 bribe to a Neckermann employee, as the burglars had, just to gain access to them? 'No one can be that dumb,' exclaimed one investigator. 'Absolute insanity,' concluded a computer expert at the department store. It just didn't make sense. Or did it?

It did.

The answer lay deep in the electronic innards of the IBM System 370 computer series, buried between the bytes and bits of a secret software protection program developed by 'Big Blue'. Sales strategists at the company's New York headquarters were then trying to secure an IBM monopoly over long-term service contracts for the new computer line. The way to do that was to block outsiders from gaining access to program details needed for maintenance jobs. In the 370 system, unlike earlier models, design architects had installed a new software scheme that allowed access only to the owners of that particular computer. The key to the program varied from machine to machine. Anyone seeking to break the supersecret IBM code would thus need to examine an entire fleet of IBM System 370 computers in order to compare results and, hopefully, unravel the program. One didn't need the actual computers, however. A close look at their individually coded manuals would suffice.

It was this piece of the puzzle, apparently, that the Neckermann intruders were seeking. It was needed in Moscow.

Serious Soviet interest in IBM products dated back to 1968. It was more than academic. Having great troubles with their own domestic electronics industry, Kremlin leaders had at that time decided to copy the successful American computer line IBM System 360. With considerable assistance from the East German Robotron computer works in Dresden, a top-secret engineering team in Moscow had proceeded to dismantle stolen IBM machines and reverse-engineer them for their own design. Their imitation, dubbed Ryad-1 (*ryad* means 'series' in Russian), appeared on the market in February 1972. It used the IBM operating system DOS, IBM peripherals, IBM software and was even being delivered to Eastern bloc customers complete with original IBM service manuals, translated verbatim into Russian. Competing only with primitive Soviet-designed equipment, the Ryad-1 had rapidly become the most popular computer model in the East.

At the time of the Neckermann break-in, Soviet and East German computer teams were designing a follow-up forgery. Experts at the 'Research Centre for Electronic Computer Technology' in Moscow were now dismantling stolen prototypes of the latest American computer generation, IBM System 370, in preparation for the Ryad-2. The new Soviet version was designed to be another carbon-copy IBM. But the complicated and tricky maintenance manuals were apparently still giving them problems.

Legally, there was no way for the Soviets to obtain the information they so desperately needed. Like the modern computers themselves, which were in extensive use at NATO military installations, the maintenance manuals also fell under the export restrictions of NATO (CoCom No. 1565), and export to the Eastern bloc was strictly prohibited. So the Soviets were resorting to covert operations.

West German counter-intelligence was well aware of Moscow's designs. Over the years too many cases had cropped up around the IBM offices in Stuttgart for it to have been an accident. The computer company had obviously become a major target of Soviet espionage efforts in West Germany. In 1970 IBM employee Gerhard Prager had been caught illicitly copying magnetic tapes and passing them on to the communist East German intelligence service *Staatssicherheitsdienst*. The tapes contained financial and private data from over 3,000 West German companies. Later an IBM manager named Arnold, also in Stuttgart, was exposed by an East German intelligence officer who fled to the West. Arnold had been secretly supplying the communists with internal designs, equipment, data sheets and software for over a decade. His intelligence, it was later learned, helped the East German Volksarmee ('People's Army') modernize its command structure, bringing it close to Western standards.

For Siegfried Buback the new case fitted this picture perfectly. Two employees of a reputable Stuttgart electronics company had initiated the operation. While servicing electronics equipment in Moscow, on assignment for a reputable Western company, they had been approached by Elorg officials much in the way Werner Bruchhausen was recruited. When the Soviets suggested they could earn more money merchandising directly for Moscow, they quickly left their well-paid jobs and formed their own company. Conveniently, the new offices were opened at Kleiner Schlossplatz in Stuttgart – right next door to the IBM building. The Soviets then helped them contact like-minded entrepreneurs in Düsseldorf, who in turn approached the two Frankfurt men later caught in white overalls at Neckermann's.

They had been pursuing their nefarious ends for over two years. Their sales – over a million dollars in hard Western currency – had been funnelled, typically, through 'a computer company operated by an Eastern espionage service'. In addition to Neckermann's, the group had also targeted the railway system and numerous computer centres of IBM. Several members of the group admitted serving as couriers, flying to Moscow to deliver their illicit wares personally.

The logic of the case was obvious: secret Soviet shopping lists, spy cameras, the exposed film – it was all there. Extensive written confessions had been recorded and signed. The indictment should have been child's play. But there was a hitch. The men had confessed only to business dealings with Soviets and East Germans. Their contacts, they insisted, had nothing to do with espionage. Confronted with evidence that their 'business partners' were known spies, the men simply replied that they hadn't known that. The Easterners had identified themselves as legitimate trade representatives and the Westerners had accepted them as such, closing their deals on a purely commercial basis. Criminal law on espionage, however, required proof of intent. It was not sufficient to prove the group had been co-operating with Eastern intelligence services. Buback had to prove they had done so knowingly. A dull feeling came over him as he realized he couldn't.

Within three months of the sensational press conference, the Attorney General quietly dropped the espionage and treason charges. Export violations, tax evasion and a little bit of embezzlement were what remained. The cases were handed down to the state government for further investigation, where they dragged on for several years.

Only one of the suspects was finally convicted: the Stuttgart businessman Peter Lorenz. He had funnelled some $3 million of strategic electronics out of the West through airports in Stuttgart, Frankfurt, Copenhagen, Amsterdam and Vienna. An IBM 360/S computer was part of one of his earlier packages, purchased for $1.5 million and sold to the Soviets for three times that price. IBM 370/S models were in later shipments. Both, authorities assume, were used in the clandestine Soviet reverse-engineering that led to Ryad. The Hungarian-born Lorenz had displayed several Ryads in his Stuttgart showroom, testing the Soviet machines with Western peripherals and software. The indictment accused him of 'using straw men, phoney companies, falsified contracts and manipulated bills to deceive the government'. He was convicted and sentenced to a fine of $60,000. Authorities withheld confiscated equipment valued at an additional $210,000.

But the Germans let the big one get away. At least that's what the Americans would soon be thinking.

By April 1975 all twelve suspects picked up in the Christmas dragnet had been released. Among those who stepped out of the state gaol into the wet morning air of Wiesbaden was a 34-year-old businessman whose high cheekbones and thin blond hair, complemented by a lean figure and a fat bank account, gave him the air of a European aristocrat. Within hours he had slipped out of his casual slacks into a well-tailored summer suit and was sitting on a plane to the Bahamas.

In prison he had lost his tan. But it would be back. He was now returning to the jetset life he had learned to live and love as a successful merchant for Moscow. It wasn't the last time that his name, which has been changed in view of his subsequent acquittal, would be mentioned in a case of illegal technology acquisition.

'Michael Gerkins' was born in the sleepy small town of Celle in Lower Saxony, located sixty-three miles south of Hamburg – which, in Germany, is the middle of nowhere. Celle had been a stronghold of Hitler fanaticism during the war and remained a centre for neo-Nazi die-hards in the post-war years. Gerkins began his professional career with a three-year apprenticeship as a paint salesman. But he found the town, and the job, dreary and soon moved south to Stuttgart to study electronics. There he attended computer courses at the offices of IBM and, later, at Memorex, where Belgian software smuggler Marc André DeGeyter had also been employed. Gerkins' first Eastern contacts came through IBM, when he handled East German and Soviet accounts at their Hamburg branch office. By 1971 he had made enough contacts to go independent. He moved to Freeport in the Bahamas and founded 'Michael Gerkins International Computer Consulting'.

Gerkins felt at ease in the social world he found there, where the motorboats were fast and so were the blondes. He talked smoothly, moved swiftly and liked to carry thick wads of banknotes wrapped in a rubber band. He lived in a condominium at the plush Harbour House Towers, one of three extravagant residences he soon owned. He drove a fire-engine-red Trans Am sportscar and a Yamaha 500 motorcycle and was known for his generous tips at the high-society bar of the Coral Beach Hotel. The German businessman could well afford the sunny side of life on the Caribbean island. His work in locating and procuring Eastern customers for interested US high-tech corporations was extremely lucrative in the détente of the mid-1970s, and like many others in his trade Gerkins became a millionaire.

In early April 1976, just a year after his release from the Wiesbaden state prison, the Federal Bureau of Investigation received a tip that Gerkins was back in the illicit high-tech trade business. Albert 'Poncho' Behar, a handyman at the Freeport yacht harbour and a neighbour of Gerkins', reported that the German businessman was involved in strange deals with microdots. Behar had heard the tales from Gerkins' partner, a high-living, fast-talking American playboy who will be called 'Robert Narges' here. Narges, a notorious drinker, had been shooting off his mouth at local bars about Gerkins and his big-time Soviet deals. Behar had heard, in fact, that Michael Gerkins was an alleged agent of the East German and Soviet intelligence services. The FBI assigned Behar the codename 'CI-1' and instructed him to keep his ear to the ground. His reports were entered in a newly opened file.

Two other informants – 'CI-2' and 'CI-3' – soon surfaced with additional incriminating information. The FBI office gave 'CI-2', a sharpshooting Texas businessman named Lloyd G. Williams, orders to accompany Gerkins on a business trip to Europe. On 8 September the two men flew to Wiesbaden, where they met a German industrialist wanting to buy aeronautics equipment for 'clients' in East Germany and Moscow. The purchase involved forty gyrocopes made by Litton Industries. The LTN-51s, navigational devices used in commercial aircraft, cost $119,000 apiece and were listed in strategic embargo regulations. 'CI-1' told of a visit to East Berlin, where Gerkins had rendezvoused with a Soviet named Yuri. FBI officials were later able to identify him as Yuri Federovich, a known KGB officer then posing as a representative of the Soviet Trade Mission in East Berlin.

Michael Gerkins and his American friend Narges were rumoured to be targeting IBM cards, manuals and problem-solving computer tapes, Bendex computer drive shafts, Memorex software systems, and even closely guarded nuclear fuels. Before long, 'CI-1' reported that Gerkins and Narges were planning a secret trip to Cuba to smuggle American cruise-missile secrets out of the country. On 25 March 1977 they purchased a 35-foot cabin cruiser for $23,000, paying in cash. The Chris Craft Commander, dubbed *Mi Toi*, was moored at Narges' private dock, ready to sail. When 'CI-3' announced that 'something really big was going down soon', the FBI decided to act.

The Bureau's Miami offices had had both Gerkins and Narges under round-the-clock surveillance for fifteen months. Undercover agents had trailed the two with everything the FBI could muster: federal helicopters had been hovering over them in the clear blue Caribbean skies, Coast Guard motorboats racing after them across the tropical waters; agents had been peering at them through infrared binoculars and telephoto lenses while eavesdropping on them with directional microphones and telephone taps. Their mail was opened, their movements to Berlin and Cuba closely followed. FBI special agent Bill J. Windland, who led the investigation, had spent a total of $3 million dollars on surveillance. When he was ready to move, Windland wanted the story of his success to receive appropriate public attention.

On 20 July 1977 Gerkins and Narges drove up to Fort Lauderdale International Airport in a Cadillac Eldorado and stepped into the waiting arms of an FBI stake-out squad. Shortly afterwards, television crews and newsmen were invited to photograph the suspects at their Florida arraignment. 'We have just arrested two enemy agents,' the FBI declared, hinting that espionage charges would be filed the next day. 'The Cruise Missile Spy Case,' showed the headlines in the *Miami Herald*. 'Atomic Spy Arrested', proclaimed the press in Germany. The FBI affidavit accused the two men of conspiring to smuggle vital defence components to Soviet agents in Cuba in their cabin cruiser. But the court indictment that followed made no mention of spying. Or treason. Instead, it accused them of the lesser crime of 'acting as agents of East Germany and the Soviet Union without prior notification to the Secretary of State'.

'It was just a normal business relationship,' Gerkins claimed at his trial. It had worked in Frankfurt. The American jury, however, didn't think it normal. They convicted him and he was sentenced to five years in prison. He had to sell his Freeport home. His million-dollar business in the Bahamas lay in ruins. Narges was sentenced to a year and a day.

But two years later a New Orleans appeals court reversed the decision, casting doubt on the reliability of the three key prosecution witnesses 'CI-1', 'CI-2' and 'CI-3'. Without their decisive testimony, the court concluded, the evidence was insufficient for a conviction. On 12 October 1979 all charges against Narges and Gerkins were dismissed.

When journalists called for comment, the two men answered the phone giggling. They were celebrating their acquittal with friends at a beer party. 'I have great faith in US justice,' Gerkins announced on the phone.

There were law officers in the United States who didn't share that opinion. The Soviet Ryad-2 computers, exact carbon copies of the IBM 370/S, were already on the market.

Source Notes

Neckermann burglary: *Deutsches Allgemeines Sonntagsblatt*, 26/1/1975; *Frankfurter Allgemeine Zeitung*, 17/1/1975; *Frankfurter Rundschau*, 6/5/1975; *Die Welt*, 16/1/1975; *Frankfurter Allgemeine Zeitung*, 16/1/1975; *Süddeutsche Zeitung*, 16/4/1975; 'Klopapier von IBM', *Der Spiegel*, 3/2/1975; *Handelsblatt*, 20/1/1975; *Frankfurter Rundschau*, 23/7/1977; 'Die roten Ideen-Diebe', *Die Zeit*, 19/11/1978; *Tagesspiegel*, 16/1/1975; *Die Welt*, 16/1/1975.

Lorenz: *Handelsblatt*, 28/11/1975; *Die Welt*, 7/12/1978; 'Re-exporting: How Peter Lorenz Shipped IBM Hardware to Russia', *Datamation*, January 1975.

Ryad: See Chapter Eleven.

Arnold and Prager: *Wirtschaftswoche*, 20/1/1985.

Gerkins and Narges: Since both were acquitted in court their names have been changed. Those interested can take a look in: *New York Times*, 27/7/1977; AP, 20/7/1977; *Washington Post*, 21/7/1977; AP, 21/7/1977; AP, 22/7/1977; AP, 27/7/1977; Facts on File, *World News Digest*, 30/7/1977; AP, 9/8/1977; AP, 23/9/1977; *Washington Post*, 12/11/1977; *Stern* magazine, 1/2/1979; *Miami Herald*, 13/10/1979; *Miami Herald*, 21/7/1977; Tad Szulc, 'To Steal our Secrets', *Parade*, 7/11/1982.

FIVE

Sitting Pretty in Switzerland:
The Elmont Case

On Monday 5 July 1982, when Günter Marwitz arrived in his office at the Munich freight company HAT-Express, it looked like the beginning of a normal week. Marwitz shuffled routinely through the papers on his desk. His first shipment of the day consisted of thirteen crates that had arrived the night before by truck via Frankfurt. His instructions were to forward them to Zürich without delay.

Marwitz didn't think it unusual that the receiver was a post office address in Switzerland (Box 6301 in the village of Zug), nor that his instructions had come from a fly-by-night entrepreneur named 'Herr Gessner'. Marwitz knew that Gessner had some strange habits, often ringing up from a hotel room in Zürich, Paris or Munich, never leaving a return address. That wasn't uncommon in the freight business, though. Gessner was a regular customer at HAT-Express, one who paid his bills promptly. Besides, he had informed Marwitz of the arrival of the shipment by telex and his name was listed in the freight documents. It looked legitimate enough.

The German freight agent had no way of knowing that Gessner's Munich address at Tassilo Platz 7 was fake. Nor could he have guessed that the thirteen innocuous-looking boxes contained embargoed strategic equipment that had been funnelled through an international maze of phoney addresses and middlemen on its way to secret recipients in Moscow. Ever since 1979, Gerald 'Jerry' Gessner (whose true address is Hirschgarten Allee 45 in Munich) had been registered in the official, but confidential, blacklists of German and American trade authorities as a known embargo-runner.

Even if Marwitz had become suspicious, he probably would have said nothing. Marwitz had learned early on in his trade that it doesn't pay to ask too many questions. But an hour later, as he was typing the final shipping papers, German customs agents burst into the airport offices of HAT-Express to seize the shipment – and Marwitz was asking plenty of questions.

Employees at Apollo Air Cargo in Frankfurt suffered a similar shock a few days later. A young man from the Trans Travel freight agency arrived on a motorcycle from southern Germany to pick up thirty-eight crates labelled 'computer equipment'. They, too, were bound for Switzerland. But before he could load the crates, and his motorcycle, into a rented truck, Frankfurt customs officials surrounded him and seized the shipment.

In both cases, German authorities were acting on American instructions. US law enforcement efforts to stop the illegal flow of sensitive Western technology to the communist bloc had made considerable progress since the Spawr, Bruchhausen and Gerkins cases had first drawn attention to the problem several years before. Realizing that only a co-ordinated international effort had a chance of success, the US Treasury Department had set up a special task force called 'Operation Exodus'. The confiscations in Munich and Frankfurt, announced in Washington by Customs chief William von Raab, were the latest in a series of successful actions by the specially trained smuggle squad. Since it was established in October 1981, the new customs team had seized a total of 1,400 shipments valued at over $80 million.

In this case, they bagged four complete PDP-11 computers from the Digital Equipment Corporation. The PDP-11 is a model useful in the design and construction of microchips, heart of all modern weapons systems. Computers of this type fall under NATO export restrictions (No. 1565 on the CoCom list), and cannot be exported without a licence. It was the latest indication that the Soviets were continuing to concentrate their efforts on obtaining American manufacturing equipment for their own computer industry.

Suspicion was first aroused when a small Canadian company, MLPI Business Systems of Toronto, ordered the PDP-11s in Phoenix, Arizona. MLPI slated the purchase 'for domestic use only', but they ordered the 220-volt version adapted to European power sources, instead of the standard 110-volt North American version. The Digital Equipment Corporation, who produce the PDP-11, reported the incongruity to customs. When the 4.6 tons of electronic gear (value $445,000) started to move, Operation Exodus agents were watching.

The crates were shipped from Phoenix to Toronto, where on 2 July they were loaded onto Air Canada flight 872 for Germany. The shipment had been divided into two sections – one for Frankurt (waybill number 014-8140-1003) and one for Munich (waybill number 014-8140-0012). The decision to confiscate was made just two hours before the computers were to cross the German frontier into neutral Switzerland. From there, according to US Treasury sources, they were to be forwarded to Czechoslovakia and on to the Soviet Union.

While United States, Canadian and West German investigators swarmed out with search warrants in their respective countries, two men in the small Swiss border town of Kreuzlingen were growing uneasy. Their shipment from Phoenix was overdue. Swiss businessman Freddie Schiavo and his partner, German physicist Dieter Enderlein, were wondering what had gone wrong. It wasn't until their freight representative – a certain 'Herr Gessner' – appeared at the offices of HAT-Express in Munich to pay the bill that they learned of the customs raid.

Had they been American citizens, Schiavo and Enderlein would have faced serious interrogation, at the very least. But their company, Elmont AG, was located in Switzerland, inaccessible to US and German customs authorities. Switzerland is not a member of NATO, nor of CoCom, which regulates strategic exports from the West. Thus I was the first to approach them, dropping by their offices in Kreuzlingen unannounced one quiet Saturday afternoon.

The town of Kreuzlingen is a popular holiday resort straddling picturesque Lake Constance which – weather permitting – can attract considerable numbers of tourists from both sides of the Swiss/German border. Its main street is crowded with overpriced cafés, small boutiques and souvenir stands. Elmont AG resides in a modest eight-room suite on the sixth floor of an inconspicuous office building, a stone's throw from the frontier. The steel and leather furnishings are, like the view of the lake, pleasant but not spectacular. Several computers are scattered about the various rooms. Hearing that a journalist was in the office asking questions, the two owners had abandoned their plans for a quiet weekend and driven over immediately. Freddie Schiavo, muscular and intense, sat stiffly in a leather armchair, very much on guard. Schiavo was the company president. The quiet-mannered German physicist Dieter Enderlein was slumped on a nearby couch, apparently wondering what he was doing there.

Schiavo took the lead. 'Yes, we ordered the computers,' he admitted almost offhandedly. 'MLPI in Toronto was acting on our instructions. But we didn't know the PDP-11s were on any NATO embargo lists.'

It's hard to believe him. Elmont AG was doing a good 40 per cent of its business with the East, much of it in computer electronics. Schiavo and Enderlein should have been intimately acquainted with US export restrictions, especially since, as Schiavo explained, they had been among the first to be hit when regulations were tightened during the Poland crisis a year before. Within twenty-four hours of the presidential announcement of the new restrictions on 29 December 1981, Elmont export licences had been cancelled by the American government. Schiavo seemed as unconcerned about the old case as he was about the new one. In Switzerland he knew he was immune to prosecution by either American or German authorities. Perhaps, after the US government's actions, he had simply raised his prices.

'CoCom regulations are outdated and useless anyway,' said Enderlein, joining the conversation for the first time. 'We know, in fact, that the Eastern bloc is already manufacturing its own version of the PDP-11.' To prove his point he produced a news clip on an Eastern computer from *Mini-Micro Systems* dated June 1982. The document was not convincing:

'The position of the SM4-20 mini from ZVT in Czechoslovakia is not yet clear. Like the mid-range East German Robotron machines, it is said to be compatible with the Digital Equipment Corporation's PDP-11.'

Small companies like Elmont AG are by no means the only ones illegally running strategic Western wares across Eastern borders. According to an investigator familiar with the case, a number of prominent European industrialists are tacitly involved in similar operations. He explained it this way:

'If a reputable corporation has a multimillion-dollar machine-tool deal with the East and the Soviets insist on a $15,000 embargoed computer as part of the package, that company will do everything in its power to get the computer through. Embargo-running, however, is risky business. So if they don't want to get their own hands dirty, they turn to a small Swiss outfit that's willing to run the risks for them. And they're willing to pay handsomely for it.'

On 29 March 1984, federal authorities in Miami arrested a 36-year-old Canadian businessman in connection with the Elmont case. Czechoslovakian-born Leslie Klein was indicted in Boston, where the case was being handled, on charges of conspiring with Elmont AG to smuggle strategic computers to the Soviet Union and East Germany. Freddie Schiavo and Dieter Enderlein were also indicted, but – being European – they were unavailable for arrest. The German Attorney General's office is now investigating them on espionage charges.

Schiavo and Enderlein claim that the seized shipment was not headed directly for the Soviet Union. But they are unwilling to say where it was going. Glen Langdon, president of the Canadian purchasing company MLPI in Toronto, also denied the Soviet destination. Langdon couldn't understand all the commotion. 'The PDP-11,' he claims, 'is about as strategically significant as a Dodge Dart.'

American authorities disagree. Among them is Assistant United States Attorney Robert S. Mueller, who handled the Elmont case from Boston. His New England office holds jurisdiction over all foreign cases dealing with smuggled equipment produced at the Digital Equipment Corporation in nearby Maynard. Mueller knew that DEC equipment had become a hardware and software standard at NATO installations. Their computers were cropping up in dozens of embargo seizures around the globe. Taken together, the new cases indicated the Soviets were in the process of switching gears from the IBM norms they had copied in the 1970s to DEC norms for the 1980s. According to intelligence reports reaching the Boston prosecutor, Moscow was now adopting DEC systems and software in its own industry to produce electronic weaponry for the Red Army.

But Soviet smugglers had run into a snag well known in Western commercial computer circles. It is called service. At the beginning of the 1980s this aspect of the computer trade had apparently become a major obstacle in the otherwise smooth-running acquisition apparatus of the KGB. Eastern purchasers, who used to buy blind from catalogues, were now insisting on seeing and testing equipment first-hand in the West, before committing themselves to a sale.

Two other cases on the desk of Robert S. Mueller documented these difficulties.

Source Notes

The research for this chapter is described in the introduction to this book.
Quote from *Mini-Micro Systems*: June 1982.
Arrest of Leslie Klein: AP, 3/4/1984; *New York Times*, 4/4/1984.
Quote from Glen Langdon: *New York Times*, 7/15/1982.
Other sources on the Elmont case: *ARD Tagesthemen*, German television, 15/7/1982; *Weltwoche*, 18/8/1982; Deutsche Presse Agentur, 14/7/1982; *Stern* magazine, 12/8/1982; Deutsche Presse Agentur, 3/4/1984; *Chicago Tribune*, 8/12/1984.

SIX

All Hands on DEC:
The Williamson Case

The motors of five cars purred softly in a sidestreet of Plymouth, Minnesota. It was shortly before seven o'clock on the morning of 17 February 1983 and the occupants – members of the special US Treasury task force Operation Exodus – were waiting to make their move. As the second hand swept the hour, they pulled up at 15350 31st Avenue and presented search warrants to the startled employees of a company called Computer Maintenance.

At the same moment in England, where Big Ben was striking 1 pm, British customs agents began sweeping through the offices of Datalec in Wimborne in Dorset, while colleagues in Cologne, where it had turned two, raided the German firm Datagon at Bühlerstrasse 2.

Preparations for the synchronized international customs bust had begun four months earlier, when a former Datagon employee tipped off German authorities that his company was in the business of East-West computer bootlegging. An initial investigation, conducted covertly, revealed a British-based network comparable in scale to that involved in the Elmont case and intertwined with other embargo-running operations dating back over fourteen years. Apparently, the organization received Eastern orders at Datalec in England, forwarding them to associates in Minnesota, USA and camouflaging the final destination through a complex resale/reshipment arrangement at the West German sister company Datagon in Cologne. The bounty, once again, was electronics equipment manufactured by the Digital Equipment Corporation.

The customs raid was sparked by a DEC deal concerning three

VAX-11-780 computers. The top-of-the-line machines – compatible with the PDP-11, yet far more sophisticated – were listed in US search warrants as having 'substantial weaponry and nuclear as well as normal and commercial applications'. Unfortunately, the customs raid came too late. The three VAX computers had long since reached their final port of call. The first machine (serial number IMP-25598 QC) had been purchased at the headquarters of Digital Equipment in Maynard, Massachusetts – ostensibly for a US company – and trucked by a freight company called Dave's Motor Transport to the offices of Computer Maintenance in Minnesota on 28 August 1982. Three days later it was sitting in the belly of a Lufthansa cargo plane bound for Cologne. It was the usual route, and this time the US Department of Commerce had issued a valid licence (No. A-6 37343) for the export to West Germany. But as is so often the case, the destination listed for 'end use' in the freight papers was false. The equipment was reshipped by Datagon in Cologne to its sister firm in Dorset. From there, the investigation revealed, it was forwarded to a scientific institute in Bulgaria in apparent violation of US and British export regulations. The two other computers followed a similar route a few weeks later.

Ivor Edwards, one of three British managers at Datagon, pleads ignorance of any wrongdoing: 'I had no idea that this equipment was on any embargo list.'

Edwards admits knowing that the customers were Bulgarian. He says he was afraid to report any suspicions to authorities because he feared his company might never see its money. The first VAX computer had been paid for in advance by the Eastern purchasers. But they had made only a down payment on the last two machines, claiming the computers were faulty.

As Edwards tells it, the VAX computers were not defective at all. The Bulgarians had been having immense difficulties operating them properly and simply began balking on payments. The British-based company had run into a problem that is common throughout the electronics business – legal or otherwise. The problem is service. When complicated computer equipment is put into operation, unforeseen complications – an operational malfunction, incompatible peripherals or a software snag – are almost inevitable. Although easily solved by experts, such problems can lead to enormous frustrations if a buyer is left alone with his machine. Inexperienced Eastern-bloc users, who were often confronted with such situations, had come to appreciate a favourite slogan of the Western electronics trade: 'There is no worse mess than a computer mess.'

The way to avoid that mess, for the Bulgarians, was hands-on training in the West. In the autumn of 1982 they dispatched a seven-man crew to the British Datalec offices to inspect the next shipment of VAX machines they wanted to buy – and to practise operating them. Edwards had bumped into the foreign visitors on one of his visits to England. At first, he was told the Bulgarians were there for some simple software exercises. He later learned that the courses were part of a sales package, which also included a German trouble-shooter flown in from Hamburg. The German was later sent to the Bulgarian capital to install the machines and instruct local operators. Today, feeling he was sent to the communist country under false pretences, he has decided to reveal his story.

It was 20 October 1982 when Uwe Schümann stepped off a Luft-hansa plane into the warm afternoon air at Sofia International Air-port. He was accustomed to the wet and windy climate of northern Germany and – thinking somehow it would be cold in the Eastern bloc – he had brought a fur jacket along for the occasion. The West German electronics specialist was relieved to feel the sun bearing down warmly on his skin, and he threw his jacket easily over his shoulder as he headed for his baggage and the Bulgarian official who would be waiting for him in the terminal.

Schümann had not been looking forward to this trip. He was a computer maintenance man. But his new employers at Datagon had sent him to Sofia to give a seminar. His protests that teaching was not his speciality had been politely ignored and, since the pay was good, Schümann had grudgingly consented to the trip.

But the German technician had serious misgivings, and the friendly handshake from the smiling Bulgarian who greeted him at the gate did little to dispel them. The two piled into an ancient Skoda and were soon jostling through the dreary streets of Sofia. The Bulgarian wasted little time with formalities.

'Did you bring the floppies?' he demanded, his voice roaring over the rattling valves of the car engine.

'Yes,' Schümann answered. He was sure that if they hit a pothole the vehicle would disintegrate on the spot. There was no more con-versation during the half-hour drive.

Schümann had received a call from Sofia shortly before his depar-ture, and had packed the floppies into his bag at the last minute. They contained electronic data from the Digital Equipment Corpo-ration that the Bulgarians needed for their maintenance work. They were also embargoed by the United States and export to the East was strictly prohibited. Getting them out of West Germany, however, had been no problem. It would have been an easy matter to conceal the flat wafer-thin magnetic disks (about the size of a 45rpm record) in his luggage. But Schümann had not even tried. In fact, he had openly drawn attention to them at the Cologne airport, asking security guards not to run them through their X-ray machines. It wouldn't be hard to smuggle out top NATO secrets, he mused, as the Skoda rolled into a parking lot in front of a large grey building just off the main highway.

Today, Schümann says he remembers the name of neither the institute nor its smiling director. But he does remember the seven faces that greeted him in the plain, somewhat dilapidated building he entered. It was the same group of technicians he had met at the Datalec offices in Dorset a few weeks before. At the time, Schümann had wondered why Datalec went to the expense of flying him to England from Germany, instead of simply calling the local DEC service department. Neither had he understood just quite what Bulgarian scientists were doing in an English computer facility.

But now, as he followed them up the bare concrete steps of that building in the capital city of one of Moscow's staunchest allies, he was beginning to understand. He was taken to a small cheerless room on the second floor of the building. The spanking new VAX-11/780 computer he saw looked strangely out of place in the drab Eastern bloc setting. And it looked familiar.

After examining it more closely, he discovered it to be the same machine he had worked on in England.

The man behind the Datalec/Datagon connection – the one who issued the instructions for Schümann's trip – was not unknown to international enforcement agencies. His name was Bryan V. Williamson. The British wheeler-dealer was manager of Datalec Ltd in Wimborne, part-owner of Datagon GmbH in Cologne and had a history of involvement in East-West electronics schemes dating back over fourteen years.

Williamson had first come to the attention of the authorities through the sale of restricted US oscilloscopes to Eastern Europe while working for a Dublin company called Bay Laboratories back in 1968. He was blacklisted for his participation by the American Department of Commerce. 'I was asked to buy equipment for my company, which I did,' Williamson explained at the time. 'It was then shipped unknowingly to a prohibited destination. When, in fact, it was discovered, all was admitted and that was the end of it as far as I was concerned.'

It was by no means the end of it. In 1976 Williamson hooked up with another outfit that was running microelectronics manufacturing equipment to East Berlin, Warsaw and Prague, via Amsterdam. The ring was operated by a notorious Israeli embargo-runner named Jacob Kelmer who worked out of Haifa. Kelmer, himself barred from directly ordering US goods, hired Williamson, who set off for the GCA Corporation in Bedford, Massachusetts. There Williamson familiarized himself with a delicate piece of restricted equipment called a 'photorepeater', which is used to etch integrated circuits onto semiconductor chips. The machine was then purchased by the group and shipped by truck to a company in Canada. It ended up in Prague. The funds were funnelled through an untraceable Swiss bank account. The company in Montreal existed only on paper.

'I was under the assumption that the equipment was to stay in Canada, where I was to be employed by them,' Williamson reported this time. 'When in fact it didn't come to fruition, I wanted to know what the hell had happened and found out it had been mis-directed.'

Once again, Bryan Williamson was blacklisted by American authorities.

The United Kingdom was long regarded by the Americans as the 'black hole' in NATO's security fence. Scores of English companies had been involved in major diversions of strategic technology to the Eastern bloc. Despite American indictments, British-based offenders were almost never prosecuted or extradited.

Within a year of the Datalec/Datagon bust, things began to change. Pressures from the Reagan administration were mounting in London, and by November 1983 a British-born equivalent to Operation Exodus had been established. Nine customs agents and three specialists from the Trade and Industry Department were assigned to a new Customs and Excise unit, 'Project Arrow'. Their sole job was to stop illegal technology transfer to the East. Within the first month of its existence, Bryan Williamson was arrested.

He was apprehended on Sunday, 11 December 1983. British and American customs officials found him sitting in a truck at the English Channel port of Poole, waiting to board a ferry to France. Along with two colleagues, Williamson was personally escorting a shipping-container full of embargoed electronics. The cargo – six complete PDP11-34 and PDP11-44 computer systems – was valued at $750,000. The three men were arrested and the electronics seized. Although en route initially to France, British customs spokesman Hugh Rogers announced the shipment was to continue to Czechoslovakia and from there to the Soviet Union.

Bryan V. Williamson and Christopher A. Carrigan, a forty-year-old engineer at Datalec, were charged in Poole Magistrates' Court on 12 December 1983 with exporting strategic goods to the Soviet Union. A year later, the two were indicted again, this time by an American federal grand jury. Timothy Dean Stelter, president and owner of Computer Maintenance in Minneapolis was also charged for his participation in the earlier Williamson operation, as were Ivor Edwards and Martin Coyle of Datagon.

New England prosecutor Robert S. Mueller, who was co-ordinating several American cases involving computers manufactured by Digital Equipment, was pleased but sceptical when the news reached him from Great Britain. Mueller regarded the KGB acquisitional apparatus as an octopus. If a tentacle was severed in one country, others would crop up elsewhere. The mounting pile of cases on his desk attested to that.

Mr Mueller knew that Eastern-bloc difficulties with servicing were continuing. In fact, in a number of cases their intelligence agents were using the same intricate embargo-running networks in the opposite direction to return malfunctioning computers to the West for repairs. Highly-paid clandestine maintenance teams, assembled in deserted warehouses near key Western airports, fixed the defects and then secretly returned the equipment to the East via the same route.

Strangely enough, the Boston prosecutor noted, the biggest illicit DEC dealer – and probably the most successful Soviet high-tech smuggler of all time – was a namesake of his: West German businessman Richard Müller. Locals in his hometown of Jesteburg affectionately called him 'Megabuck Müller'.

But intelligence experts from the British MI6, the German BND and the American CIA, who were soon hunting him around the globe, had other names for him.

Source Notes

The raid: Interviews by the author with investigators involved with the case, as well as with Ivor Edwards and Uwe Schümann.
Williamson's arrest: AP, 11/12/1983 and 12/12/1983; Reuters, 12/12/1983; UPI, 12/12/1983; *New York Times*, 13/12/1983; *Washington Post*, 13/12/1983; *Frankfurter Allgemeine Zeitung*, 13/12/1983; Peter Bartolick,

'DEC Gear Bound for Soviet Bloc Seized in UK', *Computerworld*, 19/12/1983.

Background on Williamson's past: *Sunday Times*, 5/6/1983; R. Jeffrey Smith, 'Eastern Bloc Evades Technology Embargo', *Science*, 23/1/1981.

SEVEN

Megabucks, Music and Moscow: The Müller Case

The Germans have a tradition of getting together with friends for *Kaffee und Kuchen* on Sunday afternoons. The setting at the home of Roland and Angelika Waidhas looked perfect for it: the sun shone brightly on the patio table where hot coffee, home-baked fruit pies and freshly cut flowers were spread decoratively on a neatly ironed white tablecloth. The attractive young married couple and their close friends gathered around the table. In the past their backyard terrace in the north German village of Mölln had been the site of much conversation and gaiety. But this fair and breezy May afternoon in 1982 the faces were filled with gloom, almost tragedy. Their company, The Gerland Orgelwerke GmbH, was broke. When the courts opened on Monday morning, they would be filing for bankruptcy.

The firm had been founded two years before and was a labour of love. Roland Waidhas and his friends were music fans, each with a knack for electronics. They had decided to combine hobby and profession and build musical instruments. Before long the robust sounds of Gerland home organs, complete with electric violins, automated rhythm section and synthesizer, were ringing from apartments and homes across the land. Within two years the young entrepreneurs had thirty employees working on their assembly lines, and the financial pages were running features on their up-and-coming company. But the unexpected success blinded their better senses – they found themselves financially overextended. Now they would have to pay the price.

One of their friends was absent that Sunday afternoon. Without telling anyone, Gerhard Schaal, a partner at the Gerland Orgelwerke GmbH, had departed on a secret mission to save the company. It was an insane idea, Schaal knew. But he figured it was worth a try.

Schaal had heard tales of a wealthy and free-spending businessman in the nearby town of Jesteburg, named Richard Müller. His fabulous estate had aroused wild speculation among the townspeople as to the source of his income. Surrounded by barbed-wire fences and tall hedges, guarded by trained dogs and video cameras, the extensive grounds had been designed to block the view of curious passers-by. The reclusive owner, when he wasn't on one of his countless trips abroad, was waited on hand and foot by a large staff of servants. In addition to an extravagant fleet of cars which included two Rolls-Royces, he maintained a stud farm with five dozen of the world's finest thoroughbreds. English royalty was said to send its mares over to the Müller stables for breeding. There was even a solarium – for the horses, which, as neighbours noted with envy, lived more luxuriously than many of the town's human inhabitants.

The interior of the main house was antique. Müller had had it removed from an old English mansion, shipped to Germany and re-assembled in his new home. The windows were shaded by giant copper-beech trees, transplanted from faraway forests to lend their gentle rustle to the millionaire's estate. Richard Müller's wife Sieglinde was said to like the sound. For her, too, the cellar rooms were lined wall-to-wall with mirrored wardrobes containing hundreds of fur coats.

Jesteburg was a millionaires' town, home of many of the affluent shipping merchants, corporate managers and insurance magnates working in nearby Hamburg. But despite the competition, it was Richard Müller who had earned the affectionate nickname *Moneten-Müller* – 'Megabuck Müller'.

It wasn't the fabulous wealth alone that prompted Schaal to seek him out. Müller was also known for his impulsive generosity. Local merchants told of him dropping $400 tips. Others related the story of how he had hired a local petrol-station attendant as bodyguard and chauffeur by offering the man an enormous lifetime salary if he would accept the job on the spot. Even if large portions of the legend had to be written off to the exaggerations of village gossips, there was little doubt in Schaal's mind that Müller was neither an ordinary man nor a poor one. He sounded like a fairy-tale prince and Schaal was determined to ask him for help. After all, there was little to lose.

Late that afternoon the phone rang at the Waidhas house. It was Schaal explaining, quite out of breath, that he had come straight from a meeting with the Jesteburg businessman and had a cheque for 20,000 Deutschmark in his hand! Müller had written it almost immediately, adding, 'I hope this will tide you over until Monday.'

When they heard the news, the sad Sunday coffee group turned into an outrageous party. Schaal had to repeat the story of his meeting with the mysterious millionaire again and again. Müller had asked for no documents, seen none of the company books. He had just pulled out his chequebook and the company was saved. At least, that's what everyone thought.

But the musical instruments from Gerland would soon be playing alien tunes.

Within weeks Richard Müller's accountants had examined the company's balance sheets and the ownership of the Gerland Orgelwerke GmbH was transferred to his international group. 'At first,' Roland Waidhas remembers, 'Herr Müller showed considerable interest in our instruments. But that turned out to be a ploy to win our co-operation. Later that year he relegated the organ business to a back corner of the shop, announcing that he would be needing the space. He then arrived with seven large trucks full of modern electronics equipment.'

Richard Müller had no intention of getting into the music business. His speciality was the computer trade, and his dealings had international flair. Müller had earned his millions, or at least large hunks of them, as a successful merchant for Moscow. Over the years he had been implicated in scores of illicit trading cases, indicted in one and blacklisted by the US Department of Commerce. His current companies were notoriously well known at Western law enforcement agencies. A new firm – one with legitimate reason to be purchasing electronics, yet involved in the unsuspicious business of manufacturing musical instruments – was perfect for his purpose: strategic smuggling.

The electronics equipment unloaded at the Mölln factory came from his other companies. It consisted of VAX-11/780 computers produced by the Digital Equipment Corporation. Much of the software being developed for the American military was orientated to the VAX computer line and DEC machines had already become a standard line at the Pentagon. Obviously, they were on CoCom embargo lists.

When the shipment arrived, the Gerland employees began to doubt the intentions of their new benefactor. They were asked by

Müller to repack the computers in plain, unmarked cartons and to destroy the original DEC packaging, especially telltale freight markings which might reveal origin or shipping route. The young entrepreneurs kept asking each other what the point of these mysterious doings might be. In the twilight hours of 29 October 1982 they got their answer.

That night, according to Roland Waidhas and other eye-witnesses, five heavy-duty trailer-trucks rolled on to the Gerland lot in Mölln. One was operated by the Hungarian trucking company Hungarocamion in Budapest and bore the licence number YP-40-56. Richard Müller had arrived to supervise the late-night loading personally, barking precise commands as the inconspicuous boxes disappeared into the backs of the waiting vans. They were then hidden behind other crates containing harmless, but heavy, wares, the view thus blocked from anyone curious enough to open the truck. Carefully prepared freight documents listed the shipment variously as 'air-conditioners', 'office furniture', 'linoleum' and 'lighting equipment'. The return address was a Müller company: Techimex Import and Export GmbH, Hauptstrasse 16, D-2101 Harmstorf.

But Techimex was then in the process of liquidation, as was Müller's other Harmstorf company, the Deutsche Integrated Time. Both had served their purpose in past operations. Müller no longer needed them. He now had the Gerland Orgelwerke GmbH in Mölln to use as a staging area and as camouflage for his Eastbound contraband. The freight labels were addressed to: Mahart Kft., Punto Franco u., H-1163 Budapest, Hungary.

The diesel motors of the heavy MAN trucks growled and the strategic computers rumbled out into the German night, travelling down the Autobahn, past inattentive customs guards in the nearby frontier town of Helmstedt and on into Eastern Germany. The shipment wasn't challenged.

The Mölln organ builders were horrified about what they saw happening with their company. But things were to get worse before they got better.

'One day Müller arrived at the company with an architectural drawing,' Roland Waidhas continues. 'Contrary to customary practices, however, the sketch was unlabelled – revealing neither the location of the building nor the name of the architect. It merely showed the shape and size of twenty-seven naked rooms. They were to be equipped as a modern electronics data centre, Müller told us. His shopping list included not only scores of specific pieces of equipment – all state-of-the-art – but also a large number of non-strategic items, including colour-coded office furnishings, air conditioners, carpets, lighting, even fire extinguishers. We later learned that the rooms were, in fact, located in Russia, near Moscow.'

Now convinced that Müller was bootlegging embargoed electronics equipment to the Soviets on a large scale, Waidhas and his friends balked. Although they did not grasp the full strategic significance of the operation – and neither did the German authorities who would soon be investigating the affair – they wanted no part of it. They told Müller as much, and he fired them on the spot.

Their claim that Müller was equipping entire electronics centres for the Soviets is supported by scores of documents that later fell into the hands of the German authorities, including correspondence with one Hamburg company describing 'data-processing air conditioners for a computer centre'. The Hamburg manager says Müller openly admitted that the equipment was destined for the USSR. There was also a delivery list for sensitive electronics gear shipped to Moscow on 27 December 1982. Written on the stationery of yet another Müller firm, the Swiss Semitronic AG in Zug, it bears the address V/O Technopromimport, 117330 Moscow, Mosfilmovskaya 35, USSR.

After firing Roland Waidhas and the others, Müller left the country. For his business associates and family the Jesteburg millionaire booked the entire first-class section of a jumbo jet to Cape Town in South Africa. There, tucked between the coastline slopes in the suburb of Constancia – with views of both the Indian and the Atlantic Oceans – another of his plush homes was waiting: the historic Buitenverwachting estate, one of the original five wine farms of South Africa. Müller had purchased it in 1980 for $2 million, adding acreage from neighbouring farms and renovating the premises as only 'Megabuck Müller' could. To his new neighbours, Richard Müller presented himself as a wealthy German philanthropist, spreading money generously to add credence to his story. He also quietly set up shop in a converted shoe factory, where an entire fleet of new VAX computers was soon installed.

Müller's rapid departure from Germany is not easily explained. Perhaps he had got wind of some activities at the Gerland Xerox machine, where the young entrepreneurs had been secretly squirrelling away incriminating documents for the police. Perhaps he feared his financial transactions had aroused suspicion: he was paying his staff from Switzerland, while claiming that his German companies were not earning any taxable income. He was ordering sensitive electronics with unusual plugs, large quantities of spare parts and no service contracts – all dead giveaways for a secret diversion. Indeed, West German counter-intelligence had been informed of his shady dealings. In fact, an undercover stake-out squad from Cologne actually observed one of the illicit shipments from the bushes. But things didn't get dangerous for the multimillionaire from Jesteburg until much later.

The events at the Gerland Orgelwerke GmbH expose but a small part of the worldwide operations of Richard Müller. The actual run across the frontier is only the low-risk grand finale of an embargo endeavour. It must be preceded by a complex zig-zag odyssey across continents to conceal origin and true destination – involving constant shipping and reshipping, labelling and relabelling of the contraband in much the way that illicit drug money must be laundered before it can be spent. The most difficult leg of the journey is the export from the United States, where regulations and penalties are stiffest. Müller learned the ropes early on.

Richard Müller was born on 25 April 1942 in the town of Giessübel, which was then part of the German Reich and now belongs to Czechoslovakia. After a troubled youth, he emigrated to South Africa, returning to Germany at the age of twenty-nine.

'Müller used to duck in and out of my office back then, trying to hustle up a deal, almost any deal,' says a former German business acquaintance. 'He was a rather pitiful sight in those days, with insecure eyes, soiled clothing and broken fingernails. He had big plans, a big mouth and little else to show. I was convinced he would never amount to anything.'

It is still unknown exactly when he first became involved in Soviet smuggling. Some say he was fired from his last place of employment in Hamburg, a freight company called Buhrmeister, after attempting to arrange an illegal West-East transaction involving lasers. Whatever happened then, it was soon clear that Richard Müller was moving swiftly down the high-tech trail.

He first caught the attention of authorities during an illegal caper at the Honeywell Corporation in Germany in 1974. The other players were Gerald 'Jerry' Gessner (whose later activities were discussed in the chapter on the Elmont affair) and a corrupt Honeywell worker named Lothar Hädicke, then associated with Müller. The three men were implicated in a scheme to purchase sensitive equipment for the Soviets from two Silicon Valley companies: I.I. Industries and Kasper Electronics. Hädicke placed the orders through Honeywell in West Germany – without bothering to inform his employers.

The Honeywell worker was arrested and later convicted in Stuttgart on espionage charges. The court concluded that, as a KGB agent working for Moscow, he had compromised West German security information. He was sentenced to four years in prison. With that, Lothar Hädicke was out of business for good. But Richard Müller – who was never charged – was just getting started.

Müller continued to cultivate his contacts with the two California companies and within a year he had established an international network that was to function considerably better than the simple one-man ploy attempted by Hädicke. His main customer was Technopromimport in Moscow. Before American authorities got wind of the scheme, he had slipped scores of shipments to the USSR from Silicon Valley through dummy companies, fake addresses and shady intermediaries in Canada, Holland, West Germany and Switzerland. In those years, Richard Müller was still an apprentice in the intricate reshipping racket of high-tech piracy, practising it much as Werner Bruchhausen and the others had. But Müller was later to become its true master, able to set up or close down one of his countless paper corporations at the drop of a hat. Or a dollar.

One of the first orders – $143,000 in photo-lithographic printers – came from a small company in Mays Landing, New Jersey, where Müller was posing as a West German intelligence agent. The devices were used to transfer highly complex circuitry designs onto silicon, a decisive link in the microelectronics production process.

The purchase itself went through without a hitch and export arrangements followed the familiar pattern: the equipment left the United States for Canada in May 1975, addressed to two companies in Montreal called 'USA Trade' and 'Semitronics'. Not surprisingly, neither company existed in Montreal. Müller was using a Hamburg freight company which maintained offices at the Montreal airport. On his instructions, the crates were reshipped to Zürich, where Müller's Semitronic AG passed them on to their true destination. The freight company was later fined by Canadian authorities for its participation in the deal. Müller was not.

Alternative routes were established through Kansas, Hamburg, Amsterdam and East Germany. An accomplice named Frederick Linnhoff had established himself in Kansas, renting warehouse space in the town of Overland under the aliases 'Paul Allen' and 'Allen Electronics'. Linnhoff's job was to receive the computer shipments ordered by Müller in California, declare them in freight papers as 'air-conditioners' or 'washing machines', and forward them to Hamburg in Germany. The address: Reimer Klimatechnik, Parallelstrasse 20, Hamburg/Norderstedt.

At 'Reimer Klimatechnik' (*Klimatechnik* is the German word for air conditioning), Müller's sidekick Volker Nast was waiting to pass the cargo on down the pipeline. The activities of Richard Müller were by no means limited to the diversion of American hardware. At the same time, he was using his Silicon Valley connections to recruit US experts for consulting ventures in the USSR. John Marshall, former owner of several high-tech companies and a leading specialist in his field, was one of them. Marshall described his recruitment by Müller at a US Senate Sub-committee hearing on technology transfer on 4 May 1982:

Marshall: 'He was trying to get me to supply some very sophisti-
cated mask-making equipment. He was saying he was going to
buy it from West Germany and then move it from West Germany
into the Soviet Union.'
Question: 'He was making no bones about that?'
Marshall: 'That's right.'
Question: 'Did he tell you it was illegal?'
Marshall: 'It was obviously illegal.'
Question: 'He knew it was illegal? No question about it?'
Marshall: 'Sure.'

Müller must have received enormous sums for his services. When he had purchased his first modest home in Jesteburg, neighbours recall, he was so heavily in debt that he couldn't afford furnishings. By the time John Marshall arrived – on a stop-over from their Moscow journey – Müller was strutting about the construction site of his new estate, where two shiny Mercedes-Benz limousines were parked and helicopters were airlifting full-grown copper beeches onto the grounds for his wife. The man with the soiled clothes and broken fingernails had been dry-cleaned and manicured. Müller was major league. 'I now belong to the upper class,' he declared to his friends.

John Marshall, who travelled to the USSR with Müller only twice, had been lured into co-operation with the tale that he was to help the Soviets construct an electronic watch factory. It was soon clear, however, that Müller had deceived him: 'They had in mind the manufacture of any number of high-technology products, including computers.' Marshall quit and he was never paid for his work. Owing to his intimate knowledge of Müller's dealings, he later became an invaluable witness for the United States Senate – and for the Federal District Attorney's office.

By late 1975, officials had got wind of Müller's dealings. In

Kansas City, US customs agents intercepted one of his shipments, removing the sensitive cargo and replacing it with sand, as Dr Theodore Wu had done in the Bruchhausen case. While the crates were allowed to continue on to their destination in Moscow, police raided the offices and homes of the Stateside participants. The evidence they seized was quite sufficient for a conviction – at least of the American participants.

At an interview with American officials at the US Consulate in Hamburg, Linnhoff later confirmed that the shipment did ultimately reach its destination, to the great displeasure of the paying customers. In the crates, overzealous customs agents had inserted in the sand a greeting with the words 'F*** you!'

On 1 February 1977, Robert Johnson of Kasper Electronics and Carl Storey and Gerald Starek of I.I. Industries were convicted of conspiring to ship $900,000 worth of semiconductor manufacturing equipment to the Soviet Union without a licence.

The three German participants, Müller, Linnhoff and Nast, were also indicted by a San Francisco grand jury. Of course they never had to face the charges, or worry about them. A local investigation, initiated by the Hamburg District Attorney's office in connection with the case, dragged on fruitlessly for many years before someone finally closed the file on 18 July 1981. The California indictment did, however, end Müller's Stateside travels and he chose to maintain a low profile for a while. It was Volker Nast who now came to the fore.

Nast was soon targeting a MSR-903 microwave receiver built by the Micro Tel Corporation of Baltimore. Capable of eavesdropping on military satellites, or even 'Air Force One' (the US presidential plane), the $45,000 device would have been a pretty prize for the Soviets.

According to a Senate investigation, two businessmen, a German named Rolf Peter Helms and an American named Werner Hilpert, made the purchase in the United States. Acting on Nast's instructions from Hamburg, Hilpert placed the order in June 1980 with Micro Tel in Baltimore. Company officials informed him on repeated occasions that its export was subject to the rules of the Arms Export Control Act and would need a licence. After checking back with Nast in Hamburg and Helms (who was also co-operating) in New Jersey, Hilpert proceeded with the purchase. He paid $10,000 down on the $45,000 purchase price. Hilpert assured Micro Tel that his friends would take care of the necessary export formalities. But, of course, no one did.

Hilpert and his wife appeared at the offices of Micro Tel on 19

January 1981 to pay the balance and pick up the 38-kilo machine. But when they packed the device into the trunk of their waiting car, they had more electronics in their suitcase than they had paid for. The Federal Bureau of Investigation had added a tiny transmitter to the package.

A team of eighteen men observed the Hilpert car as it pulled out of the Micro Tel parking lot in Baltimore and headed north on the New Jersey Turnpike. At the Hilperts' house in Princeton, FBI agents had installed two concealed video cameras. A helicopter hovered unnoticed nearby. Mr and Mrs Hilpert spent the night at their home packing and sleeping. They were planning a trip to Europe. As the two got back into the car after breakfast the next morning, the stake-out squad continued to track them: north on the New Jersey Turnpike to New York, east on the Belt Parkway to John F. Kennedy Airport, and – now on foot – over to the Pan Am ticket counter. When Rolf Helms checked the microwave receiver through to Munich with his luggage, he was arrested.

Both Helms and Hilpert were arraigned and gaoled in Maryland. And both confessed. In their statements, they incriminated Volker Nast of Hamburg, who was indicted by the court on 26 May 1981. But Nast was sitting in his comfortable Hamburg villa at Jägerdamm 17, immune again.

For American customs agents, who had gone to great effort and expense in both the I.I. Industries and the Micro Tel cases, the German refusal to release Nast and Müller was incomprehensible. They nicknamed the two 'The Untouchables'. US Senators, who came across the cases in their high-tech hearings in May 1982, shared their sense of outrage, asking their legal counsel again and again if there was no way to force an extradition and shaking their heads disbelievingly when the answer came. In the nine-page 'Findings, Conclusions and Recommendations' at the end of their investigation they bitterly mentioned the name of Volker Nast a total of six times!

The names of Müller and Nast were also repeatedly brought up at NATO meetings, as Washington tried to cajole its allies into a stiffer enforcement of embargo regulations. To little avail. For over a decade the two Germans continued their business with impunity. It wasn't until the evening of 9 November 1983 that they started to feel the heat.

German customs agent Peter Bohn was growing edgy. He had arrived at the Afrika Kai pier in Hamburg's harbour at 3:30 pm with instructions to stake out the Swedish freighter *Elgarin*. An illegal cargo of highly sensitive electronic equipment was supposed to be confiscated. It belonged to Richard Müller.

But Bohn had been sitting alone in his car in a shadowy corner of the docks for over seven hours and time was running out. As far as he could discern from the silhouetted figures moving about the spot-lighted deck, loading procedures would be completed within the half-hour. His colleagues with the court injunction were nowhere in sight.

Six days before, US Customs had received a confidential tip that three containers aboard the ship were on their way from Cape Town via Hamburg and Sweden to the USSR. The contents: several advanced VAX-11/782 computers made by the Digital Equipment Corporation. A special team of 'Operation Exodus' investigators had been assembled in Washington under Roger Urbanski to co-ordinate the hunt. It had taken them five days to find the freighter.

When the *Elgarin* was located that morning, several officials attached to the US Embassy raced up the Autobahn from Bonn to Hamburg to handle the case. They arrived, however, only to hear the local judge reject their last-minute request for seizure. Now, while German customs agent Peter Bohn continued his fretful watch in the harbour, telephone lines between Bonn, Washington and Hamburg were buzzing. Over twenty American agents and experts paced nervously through the halls of Hamburg's judicial building at Sieveking Platz. An appeal to the higher courts was their only hope.

When a hastily convened appeals court finally approved the seizure in a late-night hearing, the officials grabbed the papers and headed for the docks in squad cars, sirens screaming. At the water-front, they jumped into waiting speedboats and raced across the night waters to the Afrika pier. They arrived just seven minutes before the *Elgarin* was to steam down the Elbe River – out of Hamburg and out of NATO territory. The three twenty-foot ocean-going containers, weighing up to ten tons each, were hoisted by crane onto land and impounded. The startled Swedish crew, who had nothing to do with the affair, were allowed to continue their journey. The relieved and weary law officers headed for their hotel beds.

The next morning, a team of US electronics experts arrived to examine the bounty. They discovered to their horror, however, that only part of the embargoed equipment had been seized. Documents found in the crates indicated that the shipment consisted of a total of seven containers. The remaining four were still on board the ship now crossing the Baltic Sea on its way to Helsingborg in neutral Sweden. 'If I had been armed,' one US official exclaimed in disgust, 'I would have shot myself.' Diplomats in several Western capitals reached for their phones.

On 2 November the Swedish Government – under considerable pressure from Washington – agreed to seize the remaining containers. They were removed from the *Elgarin* in Helsingborg and placed under armed guard at a terminal in Malmö.

The strategic electronics gear was addressed to Swedish businessman Sven-Olav Haakansson, a Müller associate who himself had run foul of US regulations in the past. Approached by reporters, Haakansson claimed the computers were intended simply for a local data centre and pointed to a warehouse in the Stockholm suburb of Taby that had allegedly been rented for the purpose. The warehouse was deserted, without climate-controlled clean rooms, without offices, without much of anything but a couple of old paint-cans in the corner. It hardly presented a suitable environment for top-of-the-line VAX computers capable of calculating at a speed of 100 million transactions per second.

These, however, were not the only doubts cast on Haakansson's remarkable claim. In customary Müller style the original crates had been replaced with innocuous boxes and the serial numbers carefully filed off the machines to prevent identification. No one had arranged a service contract with the local offices of DEC, which would have been essential for the maintenance of the electronic 'superbrains' Neither was there a plausible explanation for the roundabout – and costly – shipping route Müller had chosen: from the New York Saxbo Corporation, where the computers had been purchased; to the South African firm Microelectronic Research Institute (owner: Richard Müller); to Optronix in Cape Town (owner: Richard Müller); to Integrated Time in Lucerne (owner: Richard Müller); to Deutsche Integrated Time in Harmstorf (owner: Richard Müller); and, finally, to his partner in Sweden.

Müller and Haakansson had been acquainted for over six years. The Swede had found Müller a seaside retreat on the Baltic island of Bjono, where he often docked his yacht – a three-masted schooner dubbed *Tonga* he had purchased from Prince Rainier of Monaco. From his island hideaway Müller enjoyed an unhindered view of a strategic Swedish navy base dynamited out of the granite cliffs of Musko. Soviet submarines often played cat-and-mouse there with the Swedish navy.

The raids in the harbours of Hamburg and Helsingborg were followed by an extensive clean-up operation. New shipments were being intercepted in Scandinavia almost daily. Crates of software arrived by ship in Malmö, boxes of hardware and peripherals by train and plane in Stockholm. It wasn't until the smoke had cleared that a full picture of Richard Müller's latest escapade began to emerge.

Experts puzzling over the pieces first noticed the pattern: the architectural drawings of a twenty-seven-room Soviet computer complex, discovered by the organ-builders in Germany; a former shoe factory in Cape Town Müller had converted into a modern electronics centre; two complete top-of-the-line VAX-11/782 computers on board the *Elgarin*; carpets, desks and fire extinguishers funnelled through East Germany. The extensive Soviet shopping lists found in the various operations, taken together, revealed a bold master plan to construct a factory of computer-designed and computer-constructed very-high-speed integrated circuits, or VHSICs – node of the ongoing electronics race between Japan and the United States. It was the razor edge of hot new technology.

The VHSIC is a highest-priority research offensive of the Pentagon – a $680-million project to develop faster, more reliable and radiation-resistant computer chips for military systems ranging from cruise missiles and anti-submarine warfare to satellite surveillance and communications. The strategic implications of the programme, initiated in 1978, were enormous. An F-15 fighter plane, for example, now carries 4,778 silicon chips mounted on over forty circuit boards. With VHSICs the same functions could be performed by forty-one chips on one board, cutting flight weight from 50lb to 31lb. Moscow had apparently hoped to leap-frog ahead, overcoming a ten-year US lead in this vital field.

Müller had painstakingly gathered the pieces of his puzzle from the far corners of the world, diverting them through his corporate maze and assembling the equipment at his Cape Town front company Microelectronic Research Institute (MRI). There, apparently, the equipment was plugged together for a test run to demonstrate to the Soviets the workability of the complete system. Then, with the same clockwork precision, it was dismantled and funnelled back through the maze – destined this time for the USSR.

According to American officials, Richard Müller had assembled the entire manufacturing package for the Soviets following their own technological specifications. They not only wanted him to acquire American know-how for design and compatibility of the entire system. They also wanted him to order luxurious Western furnishings suited to their high-tech élite in the secretive electronics city of Zeleenograd. Two Hamburg workers were flown there to install the anti-static flooring for the computer room.

'The case demonstrates how Eastern agents work,' American Customs chief William von Raab concluded. 'The acquisition of technologically advanced goods now has highest priority for the Soviets and other Eastern espionage services. According to our information, this has become more important to them than pure military data.'

News of the case was soon causing concern at the highest levels within the Reagan Administration. A postmortem on enforcement activities had revealed a devastating chain of botches, bungling and typical inefficient Washington bureaucracy. The Commerce Department, as it turned out, had long been aware of Richard Müller's South African scam. As early as May 1980 intelligence reports had been reaching its enforcement branch warning that MRI of Cape Town might be fronting for his notorious Swiss smuggling outfit, Semitronic AG. But instead of sharing the reports with other agencies, Commerce had hoarded them, proceeding to issue a total of twelve separate licences for the export of over $8 million worth of sensitive technology to MRI. The confusion at Commerce culminated in the December 1982 approval of the VAX computers. President Reagan decided it was time for a major shake-up of his Administration. It is described in Chapter Thirteen.

Politically, the Müller case came at an opportune moment. Over on Capitol Hill, debate was raging over a controversial government bill to renew the Export Administration Act. Industrial lobbies and several key Congressmen wanted to water down its stiff provisions. At a White House meeting, Reagan decided that the case should receive some high-level attention. Two cabinet members were dispatched to a large hangar at nearby Andrews Air Force Base.

On 19 December 1983, Secretary of Defense Caspar Weinberger appeared before the press with what he termed 'the single most significant confiscation of illicit electronics ever captured'. Surrounding him was an impressive display of DEC top-of-the-line VAX-11/782 computers. They had been flown in from Hamburg for the press conference, which was devoted entirely to the operations of a Jesteburg businessman named Richard Müller.

'We have prevented,' seconded Treasury Secretary Donald Regan, who was appearing with Weinberger, 'what would have been an espionage coup by the Soviet Union.' A spokesman from the Commerce Department was not present.

For the first time in his long and twisted career, 'Megabuck Müller' was in serious trouble. And other events in Cape Town were adding to his difficulties. He had shipped the VAX computers from South Africa on 20 October 1983 – coincidentally at a time when an acquaintance of his, German-born Dieter Gerhardt, had landed in court. Gerhardt, too, had skyrocketed to startling successes: as an Eastern-bloc spy.

Dieter Gerhardt was second-in-command at the strategic South African naval base in Simonstown, when, in one of the most spectacular espionage cases in recent times, he was exposed as a Soviet spy. Gerhardt had access to all significant NATO secrets for the defence of vital southern shipping lanes, from atomic submarines down to the supersecret listening and command post 'Silvermine' burrowed deep in the mountains behind the Simonstown base. As a commanding officer, Gerhardt was also familiar with new emergency defence plans for securing South African harbours against a new type of Soviet shipping mine.

Together with his wife Ruth, Gerhardt was convicted and sentenced to life imprisonment for espionage on 31 December 1983. During interrogation, Western intelligence sources report, he revealed the identity of his agent controller: Richard Müller.

Müller was indicted on export charges in Germany and again in the United States. Volker Nast and three other accomplices were later apprehended and received light sentences for their involvement in the affair from a Lübeck court. The primary suspect was not present – last seen in October in Durban boarding a plane for London.

On one occasion, British police were able to locate a hideaway in London where Müller had been living for a time with his wife Sieglinde. The German was gone. A few months later West German officials learned that the unabashed businessman was visiting his home town of Jesteburg. When they arrived with a warrant, Müller had vanished again.

Intelligence sources report that the fugitive tech-trader has since undergone plastic surgery to change his appearance and continues to operate from bases in the Eastern bloc. A Swedish businessman arrested in Germany on espionage charges revealed that Müller had approached him in early 1984 at Hotel Metropol in East Berlin, and persuaded him to obtain Western high technology through a small company in the North German town of Laatzen.

The West German intelligence service Bundesnachrichtendienst (BND), Great Britain's MI6 and the US Central Intelligence

Agency have long since joined the hunt for him. But 'Megabuck Müller' has remained elusive.

Source Notes

Möllner Orgelwerke: Interviews by the author with law enforcement officials, eye-witnesses and participants, as well as documents which the author was shown. The quotes from Roland Waidhas were recorded in a television interview on *Panorama*, NDR-German TV, 27/9/1983. See also: *Der Spiegel*, 26/12/1983; *Jesteburger Rundschau*, 2/10/1983; *Durban Sunday Tribune*, 9/10/1983; *Die Welt*, 5/12/1983.

Müller and Nast in USA: US Senate Subcommittee on Investigations, Washington DC 1982, pp. 71-80, 283-295. See also: 'KGB's Spies in America', *Newsweek*, 23/11/1981; 'Crackdown on Electronics Smugglers', *Business Week*, 31/2/1981; *San Francisco Chronicle*, 29/4/1976, 2/2/1977, 11/10/1978 and 2/5/1981; *San Jose Mercury News*, 19/1/1979 and 24/1/1979; *Boston Globe*, 9/10/1983; *Los Angeles Times*, 18/12/1983; *Sunday Times*, 20/11/1983; *Wall Street Journal*, 15/2/1984.

Star smuggler in Sweden: Largely interviews by the author. See also: *ARD Tagesthemen*, German television, 23/11/1983; AP, 15/11/1983; Reuters, 15/11/1983; *International Herald Tribune*, 16/11/1983; *Hamburger Abendblatt*, 17/11/1983; *Hamburger Morgenpost*, 17/11/1983; AP, 21/11/1983; *International Herald Tribune*, 21/11/1983; *Time*, 28/11/1983; Reuters, 23/11/1983; *Frankfurter Allgemeine Zeitung*, 23/11/1983; 'Foiling a High-Tech Coup for Moscow', *Newsweek*, 5/12/1983; *Neue Züricher Zeitung*, 8/12/1983; *New York Times*, 15/11/1983, 21/11/1983 and 25/11/1983; *Frankfurter Allgemeine Zeitung*, 1/12/1983; *Neue Züricher Zeitung*, 2/12/1983; *Observer*, 4/12/1983; *Frankfurter Rundschau*, 7/12/1983; *Handelsblatt*, 7/12/1983; *International Herald Tribune*, 16/11/1983 and 21/11/1983; *Hamburger Morgenpost*, 17/11/1983; *Hamburger Abendblatt*, 17/11/1983; *Frankfurter Allgemeine Zeitung*, 23/11/1983; *Rheinischer Merkur*, 7/10/1983; *Die Welt*, 22/11/1983; London *Times*, 21/11/1983; Agence France Presse 21/11/1983; *Computerworld*, 28/11/1983; *Aviation Week*, 28/11/1983; *Der Spiegel*, 26/12/1983; *PM Computerheft*, February 1984; 'Computer-Schmuggel', *Chip*, April 1984; Deutsche Presse Agentur, 7/6/1984; *Journal of Commerce*, 17/1/1984; 'The Customs' Catch', Jewish Institute for National Security Affairs Newsletter, January 1984; 'Moscow's Computer Capers', *Newsweek*, 1/2/1984.

Dieter Gerhardt: *Die Welt*, 25/4/1983; Guardian, 21/11/1983; *Mail on Sunday*, 20/11/1983; *Business Week*, 7/3/1983.

DEC fine: Reuters, 5/9/1984; Agence France Presse, 5/9/1984; AFP, 5/9/1984.

EIGHT

Shopping For the Source Code:
The DeGeyter Case

'Want a cheque from Zürich? You got it. It's yours. I couldn't care less. I'm not involved.'

John Maguire couldn't believe his ears. The Belgian sitting across from him at National Airport in Arlington, Virginia, was discussing the matter openly. He wanted to buy trade secrets from Maguire's company, Software AG of North America. Maguire was both president and chairman of the board of the company in Reston, Virginia, and he owned 80 per cent of the company stock. Now he was being asked to rob his own company of its most strategic secret, in return for $150,000. Maguire couldn't decide which was more repulsive, the idea itself or the Belgian businessman presenting it. The method of payment alone – Swiss bank accounts or hundred-dollar bills in cash – made his stomach turn. But Maguire remained silent. Under his suit, a hidden recorder was taping every word.

'It's a one-time shot,' the Belgian continued. 'No paper, no contracts. Nothing.'

Maguire took advantage of the opportunity to examine the man more closely. The Belgian was thirty years old, 5 foot 10 inches tall, and had a ruddy complexion and thick sideburns. The curly brown hair ended in a bald pate. He had a beer belly. Marc André DeGeyter – born in Teilt, Belgium, on 6 February 1949 – was not unknown to Maguire. Two years before, he had approached an employee from a neighbouring company and tried to talk him into stealing IBM technology. Before that, he had been caught in a similar attempt and fired from his former place of employment in Belgium. At least that was what the trade grapevine was saying. Whatever his past, one thing was certain. DeGeyter was not the kind of man with whom the president of a leading American computer company normally spent his time.

John Maguire had other reasons for talking with the Belgian. The FBI had asked him to. They wanted him to feign interest in De-Geyter's proposal while the body recorder provided by the FBI taped incriminating evidence for a later court trial. It was 20 July 1979.

DeGeyter had made his first contact with Software AG in May. He had approached James M. Addis, a salesman at Software offices in California, introducing himself as the president of a Belgian engineering company and asking for a list of the high-tech élite of the company. He later called Addis and arranged a meeting at the Sheraton Hotel in Reston to discuss a business proposition. DeGeyter had not shown much subtlety on that occasion either. He openly expressed his interest in buying company secrets and declared he was prepared to pay $150,000 for them. It was the same spiel he would later give John Maguire, with DeGeyter suggesting payment either through a Swiss bank account or in cash.

James Addis was shocked and said he would have to talk it over with the company management. While the Belgian jetted on to other appointments in Los Angeles, London, Amsterdam and Brussels, Addis informed John Maguire. Maguire immediately called the FBI. Why? DeGeyter had openly admitted he was acting as a representative of the Soviet company Techmashimport in Moscow.

Soviet interest centred on a computer program developed by Software AG called Adabas. Adabas is a data base management system used to enhance computerized information systems. It can increase the effectiveness of computer software technology by up to 1,000 per cent. To Moscow, Adabas would have been priceless. It was a standard program in many of America's strategic computer. The National Security Agency used it for electronic eavesdropping, the Pentagon for the planning and co-ordination of worldwide troop movements, the CIA in Langely to sort through top-secret intelligence.

Computer software is not like conventional military hardware. It cannot be easily reproduced from a stolen sample. To duplicate a sophisticated program one needs the secret source code – a series of ciphers and symbols that define its logic. The market value of the Adabas source code was estimated at about $10 million. Not a bad buy at $150,000.

The Adabas code was so sensitive that Software employees referred to it cryptically as 'The Source'. Only two top managers – John Maguire was one of them – had access to the 350lb. safe on the eleventh floor of the company building where it was secretly stored. Maguire explained all this to the FBI agents, who were inexperienced in the world of computers. Duly impressed, they fitted him with body monitoring gear and sent him off to his first rendezvous with DeGeyter at National Airport.

It was the unadulterated cynicism of the Belgian trader that irritated Maguire most. DeGeyter repeatedly emphasized that the deal couldn't hurt Software AG's market position. Apparently he thought the fact that his sponsors in Moscow would never reveal the trade secret to Maguire's Western competition was his strongest sales argument.

The Belgian pulled no punches. He openly admitted that Adabas had been on his Soviet shopping list for three years. At first, other technology had been more urgent. But now, DeGeyter explained, Techmashimport had changed its priorities and was insisting he secure Adabas as soon as possible. The precious Software source was so important that Moscow had threatened to cut him off from other lucrative Eastern deals if he failed to obtain it. In the long run, failure could cost DeGeyter millions of dollars. He was in a hurry.

Maguire stalled. The agents from the FBI wanted to know more. They had instructed him to play for time. The first meeting at National Airport in Arlington thus ended inconclusively.

Two weeks later, DeGeyter rang up Maguire from Brussels. The FBI was listening. The following excerpt from the conversation was recorded and transcribed by the FBI – secretly, but with court consent.

Maguire: 'You know, I'm a little bit nervous. I mentioned some of the concerns before. This source code, my understanding is, that as far as moving something out of the US, you know, it may be an administrative technicality. Do you know about the export licences and everything? What if you get caught with that source code?'

DeGeyter: 'I don't think there should be any problem on that. I would then take the whole responsibility for that. You are not supposed to know where it goes to and what I am going to do with it.'

Maguire: 'OK. Is there any way they can trace it. . . ?'

DeGeyter: 'No.'

Maguire: '. . . back to us?'

DeGeyter: 'No. No way whatsoever. There's really no way. Nothing. But, you know, you have to trust me on that. I'm telling
you there's no way.'

The Belgian Techmashimport representative and the American
computer executive spoke more than twenty times with each other.
The stakes were raised first from $150,000 to $200,000, then to
$250,000, and finally to $450,000. But there were still considerable
problems concerning the delivery. Maguire (and the FBI) wanted it
to take place on American soil, where the Belgian could be
arrested. DeGeyter wanted the exchange in Brussels, where a
Soviet expert could check the authenticity of the computer tapes in
a special lab. After the transfer, DeGeyter suggested, both men
should fly to Zürich, where Maguire would receive his money in a
Swiss account. Neither was willing to make concessions.

Their final meeting took place over breakfast at the Sheraton
Hotel in Reston on 3 October 1979. It was clear to both that the deal
was not going to come off. The Belgian and the American parted
company. After seven months of intensive planning and expensive
observation, the FBI had failed to lure Marc André DeGeyter into
the trap. The Bureau had gathered a tremendous quantity of information on the case, but a legal violation had not occurred. As in
the illicit drug business, the law requires an actual purchase. Intent
is not sufficient for an arrest.

A few months later, the FBI, fearing their investigation might
otherwise be totally wasted, sent two agents to New York to interro-
gate DeGeyter in his hotel room. The Belgian admitted everything,
including his job as Techmashimport representative. But he
described his dealings with Moscow as a perfectly normal business
association. After close questioning, the lawmen issued DeGeyter a
stern warning and left – convinced he would never attempt a similar
deal again, and certainly not on American soil. They were wrong.

On 6 February 1980 – just two days after his encounter with the
FBI – DeGeyter was back in the black-market business. This time
he approached Charles Matheny, board chairman of another company that maintained offices in the same building as Software AG.
DeGeyter told Matheny a long, fantastic tale of Arabian banks, oil
sheikhs and megabuck accounts. His sponsors, DeGeyter claimed,
were setting up a super-modern computer centre and had expressed
special interest in programs from Software AG. If Matheny could
help him find a suitable informant, DeGeyter was prepared to pay a
finder's fee of $25,000. Referring to the sensitivities of his 'Arabian'

sponsors, DeGeyter stressed the importance of discretion. There was one person who under no circumstances should be permitted to find out about the deal: a certain John Maguire from Software AG.

To DeGeyter's surprise, Matheny quickly agreed. And his help came more quickly than expected. On 16 April DeGeyter finally found his man. The informant was a man named Timothy Klund, a Software employee who was prepared to steal the secret of the Adabas source code. Both men negotiated at length on an appropriate price for the precious computer tapes. Finally, during a transatlantic call, they agreed on half a million dollars, payable in cash. The two arranged to meet at Kennedy Airport in New York on 18 May.

But when Marc André DeGeyter arrived at 2 pm on Sabena flight 581, he was not carrying the cash the two men had agreed upon. Instead, he had a cheque for the $500,000. It was later revealed that the balance in his account at the Brussels Kredietbank (No. 473-2084381-06) was only $800. DeGeyter was apparently planning a double-cross.

Timothy Klund wasn't playing straight either. Instead of the super-sensitive computer code, he was carrying two carefully prepared dummy tapes in his attaché case. Klund had told DeGeyter his real name, but he had lied about his employer. He was not an employee of Software AG at all. His true employer was located at Constitution Avenue in Washington – Klund was a special agent of the Federal Bureau of Investigation. The moment DeGeyter handed over the cheque he was arrested.

In DeGeyter's black leather briefcase, a search warrant revealed was extensive evidence of participation in widespread illegal dealings in US strategic technology for the Soviet Union. Among the items listed in the FBI inventory were:

* one business card in the name of Yuvenaliy A. Seelakov, Vice-President, Novoexport, Moscow, USSR
* one handwritten list consisting of ten items beginning with 'Adabas' and ending with 'Adabas basics, V 4 1'
* two telexes to a Mr Belsyakov at Techmashimport. For example: 'Money has been received by my bank this morning. I need money for item 6 as agreed in Switzerland no later than May 8 in order to guarantee the replacements by May 11. Best regards, Marc'
* a ten-page contract (No. 46-04/91122-113) between Techmashimport and DeGeyter's company Cesa in Brussels
* a Cesa packing list for part of the material. Value: $250,000

* one credit document from the Swiss Volksbank in Zürich showing a payment of $450,000
* one seven-page project offer proposing the sale of short- and medium-wave radio broadcast systems to Iraq
* a valid Soviet travel visa, destination Techmashimport
* a bundle of airline tickets for flights between Los Angeles, Tehran, Washington, New York, Brussels, Athens, London, the Isle of Man, Vienna and Moscow – all within a period of one month

In the original indictment, DeGeyter could have been sentenced to a total of forty years in prison. Although he was convicted of violations of the Export Administration Act and bribery, charges were later reduced from a felony to a misdemeanour. In the end, his punishment consisted of four months in gaol, a civil penalty of $10,000 and a fine of $500. The mild sentence, as well as his early release from prison, were the result of behind-the-scenes negotiations. 'Significant governmental considerations' were said to be involved.

Shortly before his release, the federal prosecutor in the case, Theodore Greenberg, had received a confidential tip from the New York office of the FBI. DeGeyter had revealed to an informer that he was an operative of the KGB and would flee the United States if he was able to raise bail. Greenberg rushed to the court in a last-ditch effort to prevent DeGeyter's release. The prosecutor was unsuccessful. In a Congressional hearing, Greenberg later described the reaction of the judge:

Sen. Nunn: 'What happened after he was told that you had the informant or confidential source revealing DeGeyter himself was a KGB agent?'
Greenberg: 'We had a hearing on that. I put on an FBI agent who related that information to the court.'
Sen. Nunn: 'Before he got out?'
Greenberg: 'Yes. DeGeyter took the stand and denied making the statement. The judge let him go.'

The hands of the prosecutor were tied. The FBI couldn't reveal the name of its informant. Even details had to be held back, according to court documents, because 'such revelations will probably result in the death of the informant'.

The outcome of the court case was hardly suited to serve as a deterrent for future technology-smugglers and Soviet agents. It was more likely to discourage well-meaning citizens like John Maguire. The patriotic American corporate executive had sacrificed over seven months of his time and energy to the FBI investigation – at considerable personal risk. Maguire commented bitterly on the results of his efforts in Senate hearings two years later:

'I read newspaper reports of a Celanese Corp employee who in June 1979 was convicted and sentenced to a term of forty years for selling trade secrets to Mitsubishi Plastics Co., a Japanese competitor. From the scant newspaper reports, I can glean no evidence of national security interests or Soviet involvement. In sum, a businessman receives forty years for selling trade secrets to a competitor while a Soviet agent receives four months for attempting to transfer one of our most guarded technology secrets to the USSR. It is a sad state of affairs, if these cases accurately reflect this country's priorities on technology transfer.'

John Maguire decided to chalk it up to experience. He asked his public relations department to run a series of advertisements – 'Adabas: The Russians weren't smart enough to invent it, but they knew enough to want it' – and then tried to forget the whole affair.

But the Soviets wouldn't let him. They did, indeed, 'know enough to want Adabas' and had no intention of abandoning their efforts. They picked up where they had left off – at the headquarters of Software AG in Reston. This time they made their approach without a middleman.

In 1981, Geogiv V. Veremy, a Soviet diplomat later identified as an officer of the Soviet military intelligence service GRU, was observed inquiring about Adabas at several trade shows in the Washington area. On 25 September, he appeared unannounced at the headquarters building and asked for documentation on the Software AG product line. A secretary gave him a few standard flyers and sent him on his way. But Veremy returned.

On his second visit he was more insistent. When he wasn't granted an immediate appointment, the Soviet spy began wandering in and out of the offices. He simply ignored the repeated requests from the receptionist to be seated. When he was finally admitted to see a senior executive, Veremy declared that he wished to purchase all available Software AG documents – an order which would have filled twelve large cardboard boxes and cost $400. The executive turned him down.

But the Soviets just wouldn't take no for an answer. They asked their friends for help. Soon Hungarian and Polish representatives were beleaguering the Reston headquarters with requests for information on Adabas. Reports from the overseas branches of Software AG in Japan and Germany started arriving, where Eastern-bloc agents were also swamping company officials with inquiries.

Among the potential buyers was an employee of the Soviet Trade Mission in Cologne named Guennadi Batachev.

Source Notes

Telephone conversation between John Maguire and Marc DeGeyter is quoted from FBI protocols, which are cited in statements of Federal Attorney Theodore Greenberg on 23/6/1980, US Senate Subcommittee on Investigations (hereafter Senate Hearings), Washington DC 1982, p. 459, in Greenberg's statements on 5/5/1982, Senate Hearings, p. 437, and in the sentencing memorandum of 31/7/1980, Senate Hearings, p. 466. The rest of the chapter is primarily based on other information in the US Senate Hearings. See also: *New York Times*, 23/7/1980; *New York Times*, 2/8/1980; *Washington Post*, 8/7/1980; *Washington Post*, 19/6/1983; *Weltwoche*, 17/11/1982.

NINE

In the Shadows of the Cathedral:
The Batachev Case

It was a quiet winter day in Cologne, Germany, and the towering 500-foot spires of the city's historic cathedral threw long shadows across the bustling plaza. Commuters and shoppers darted like ants across the busy square below on their way from jobs and department stores in the inner city to the central railroad station across the way, while small groups of tourists gathered for a snapshot in front of the 700-year-old church, trying their best to muster a warm smile in the biting cold. An unschooled eye would have taken no particular notice of two well-dressed businessmen conversing quietly at the north end of the square – or guessed they were involved in a high-level espionage operation that was about to make front-page international news.

But on this winter afternoon there were a number of highly trained professionals watching who knew exactly what the two men were discussing: the sale of plans for a sophisticated voice-scrambler in use at key military and intelligence installations around the world. Observation teams from the West German federal police force Bundeskriminalamt peered down on the scene through binoculars from clandestine look-outs; heavily armed agents mingled inconspicuously with the passers-by. And when an envelope exchanged hands between the two men, the police pushed their way through the startled crowd to make the arrest. A number of Soviets, who had been lingering nearby, scattered in the ensuing confusion.

Often, Soviet intelligence agents participating in illicit embargo deals prefer to operate on their side of the East-West divide, approaching potential smugglers at trade fairs or business offices within the refuge of their own territory. That was the case with former GRU officer Viktor Kedrov, who purchased embargoed electronics from Werner Bruchhausen through the Moscow company Elorg, as it was with KGB resident Yuri Fedorovich, who conducted clandestine transactions with 'Michael Gerkins' while posing as a businessman at the Soviet Trade Mission in East Berlin.

The cover granted to Soviet spies by organizations such as Mashpriborintorg, Lizenzintorg, Elorg and Techmashimport is dual-purpose. Obviously, it is designed as a smoke screen for KGB and GRU involvement in the East-West electronics racket. But, more importantly, it protects willing Western helpers who might otherwise by exposed to arrest and prosecution on espionage charges. Should a businessman be caught red-handed on one of their deals, he can deny any knowledge of espionage, claiming he thought the sale was a normal business transaction with a legitimate company. Since criminal law in most NATO nations requires proof of intent for a conviction on spy charges, prosecutors are forced to indict on the lesser charge of embargo violations. The punishment, as documented in previous chapters, is generally mild.

This was not the case on 17 February 1983. The man netted by the West German sting operation in the shadows of Cologne cathedral was none other than Guennadi Batachev – citizen of the USSR and a high-level operative of the KGB's special department for high-tech piracy, Line 'X'.

Batachev had arrived in Germany on an official tour of duty two years before. Officially, he was listed as an employee of the Soviet Trade Mission. Although internal records showed no previous indication of an espionage career, authorities had kept an eye on the slick 42-year-old engineer right from the start. It was known that Soviet trade missions in the West are commonly used as a clearing house and staging area for Soviet smuggling operations. One branch had a particularly shady reputation for covering spies: the tightly guarded complex of the West German mission at Friedrich-Engels-Strasse 3 in Cologne, where Batachev was based.

The initial activities of the Soviet spy began with harmless inquiries. After roughly six months on the job, he rang up a sales manager at Racal-Milgo GmbH in Frankfurt, a local branch of an American company which does extensive US defence contracting. On the phone, Batachev introduced himself as a purchasing agent for the Moscow-based trade companies Technopromimport and Lizenzintorg. He expressed interest in a few general research reports, which he allegedly wanted to pass on to experts in Moscow for reference. Although the sales manager, a German electronics expert, responded that another Racal office handled all business for the USSR, Batachev insisted on a personal appointment. His request seemed innocuous enough. The material was not classified and, after all, Batachev was the registered representative of legitimate Soviet organizations. Finally, the sales manager consented to a meeting.

The man who walked into the Frankfurt offices of Racal-Milgo a few days later hardly seemed the type who would feel comfortable in the rigid military discipline, stiff green uniform and drab hallways of the KGB. As with most of the agents from Line 'X', the well-groomed Soviet did not fit the stereotype cliché of the crude KGB traditionalist. Guennadi Batachev belonged to a new breed of sophisticated professionals specializing in Western technology – smooth, cultivated, and often in possession of a disarming charm. He was sporting a well-tailored Western suit and a wide grin.

As the two men sat down for a talk, the KGB agent went into specifics. His company, Batachev said, was seeking information on a voice and data coding machine called Datacryptor. The Racal-Milgo device, which garbles computer communications during transmission and decodes them upon reception, is used primarily by large American and European banks to protect the sensitive financial data of their customers. It is intended to prevent anyone who might tap into data-lines from manipulating confidential electronic files. Obviously, that was exactly what the KGB had in mind.

Although the Racal-Milgo decoder is no state secret, its use is not limited to the commercial sector. Among others, the highly secretive intelligence service Bundesnachrichtendienst in West Germany also employs Datacryptors to protect its top-secret transmissions. It was later revealed that the USSR was already in possession of a prototype, spirited to the East through Austria by a KGB smuggling team. Apparently, either the Soviets had been unable to reverse-engineer the electronics of the device, or they needed more original machines for direct use. Whatever the case, Guennadi Batachev was extremely interested in any and all information he could obtain on Datacryptor.

The Racal-Milgo sales manager, who had no idea he was talking to a spy, gave the Soviet a few brochures and sent him on his way.

The Soviet businessman, however, proved to be quite persistent. By January, his calls and visits had become regular occurrences at Racal and the German sales manager began to notice a disturbing pattern. Batachev had switched their meetings from the office to swanky, but out-of-the-way, restaurants. He insisted on paying all the bills himself and was soon leaning across the table, patting the German on the arm and suggesting the two address each other on a first-name basis. The sales manager found the chummy overtures vulgar and, taken together with the Soviet's unrelenting interest in sensitive technology, he sensed a conspiracy brewing. After a night of deliberation, he decided to report the incident to the American manager at Racal, John Barnes.

Barnes called the police.

When news of Batachev's behaviour reached the headquarters of the West German security authority Verfassungsschutz in Cologne, it created quite a stir. For over a decade, officials of the counter-intelligence department had been tracing the murky activities of the Soviet Trade Mission in Friedrich-Engels-Strasse. In fact, a 1981 government report had publicly identified the institution as an espionage den. West German agents had pursued a good dozen of the KGB and GRU spies planted there. But most of them had proved elusive.

In 1972, a Soviet Trade Mission employee had successfully recruited a West German student who served as a reliable source of sensitive scientific intelligence for over four years. The fledgling recruit was started off with a monthly retainer fee of $30 and encouraged to visit seminars that would grant him access to research projects, technology and scientists targeted by Moscow. He was taught all the necessary tricks of the trade, including the ground rules for clandestine meetings, the use of dead drops and microfilm techniques. When his Soviet recruiter was recalled in the spring of 1976, the young scholar – who was by now financing his studies with KGB money – was simply passed on to a KGB successor at the Trade Mission. The student met with his masters on a total of sixty-one occasions before the ruse was finally exposed on 25 November 1976. When police caught up with the young German and arrested him, his Soviet controllers were already home free in the East.

At the time of Batachev's arrival in Germany in the summer of 1981, Verfassungsschutz agents were occupied with a colleague of his from the Cologne Trade Mission. They were stalking a Soviet spy who had approached a German electronics manager and offered him several thousand Deutschmarks for the acquisition of illegal equipment. 'The manager, who was well aware of embargo restrictions, was apparently lured by the attraction of big money,' a government report states. 'In the end, he consented to the deal.

When federal authorities finally arrested him, he was in possession of the embargoed equipment and a bill which explicitly referred to the legal restrictions he was violating.' The German was thus unable to plead innocence and a local court convicted him of export violations. But his KGB controller, who had got wind of the arrest, headed East on an unexpected 'holiday' before he could be apprehended.

That same year, Viktor Shepelev was exposed as a high-level intelligence officer of the GRU. As deputy director of the Soviet Trade Mission in Cologne, Shepelev had recruited yet another West German citizen at an electronics fair and won him over for a large-scale smuggling operation. On Shepelev's instructions, embargoed equipment had been ordered by a West German company abroad and funnelled through the usual maze of European freight agents to Moscow; payment was made in cash. Law enforcement agents managed to surprise Shepelev at a secret meeting with his Western business partner. Large quantities of incriminating evidence were confiscated. But Viktor Shepelev's status as second-in-command at the Trade Mission protected him from prosecution. The Soviet spy had diplomatic immunity and had to be released.

The Batachev case was welcomed as a breakthrough. For the first time, counter-intelligence officials at Verfassungsschutz had a realistic prospect of putting one of the spies from the Soviet Trade Mission behind bars. Their information was fresh; the Soviet was as yet unaware of law enforcement activities and – best of all – he did not possess diplomatic immunity. They asked the Racal-Milgo sales manager to co-operate in the extensive sting operation that was soon unfolding. He consented to the ordeal and was given detailed instructions on how to spark Batachev's interest without arousing his suspicion. Under police guidance, he began showing sympathy for the Soviet. What followed was a textbook recruitment.

The Soviet spy began by warming up the personal side of his relationship with the German. He brought along small personal gifts – a cigarette lighter, a jar of caviare, a bottle of Russian cognac. At the same time, he began introducing clandestine procedures into their meetings. Guennadi Batachev asked his new friend not to call him on the office phone or write to his business address. To reduce the necessity of other forms of communication, each future appointment was to be agreed upon in person at the previous meeting. Slowly and methodically, the Soviet began to broach the real issues.

There was a lot of money to be earned, Batachev said, if the German could help him gain access to certain electronics systems. Such transactions, however, could not be allowed to appear in any company books. Their dealings would be on a cash-down basis. He never mentioned the fact that they were also illegal. That was understood.

The shopping list presented – in writing – by the high-tech Soviet spy came as no surprise to the Western counter-intelligence experts who were soon poring over it. Batachev sought details on APX-432, a brand-new Intel microprocessor not yet available on the market, and on IBM Series 3081 main-frame computers, which were in use in a number of sensitive projects, including NASA's space-shuttle programme. Computer-aided design and computer-aided manufacturing (CAD/CAM) systems were also on the list, as were plans for A European computer project called EEC Esprit. At the top of his priorities, however, was the data base management system Adabas from Software AG in Reston, which the KGB had been pursuing relentlessly ever since the unsuccessful attempt by Marc André DeGeyter in 1980.

The German was instructed by the police to stall. He told the Soviet that the information requested was not available at the office of Racal. He would need time to acquire it. Batachev countered by suggesting they start off with data sheets and schematic drawings of the Racal decoder Datacryptor. He handed the German an envelope containing 1,000 DM and promised five times that amount as soon as the first delivery was made.

Verfassungsschutz observation teams tracked the movements of the two men as they rendezvoused discreetly a total of twelve times at small restaurants between Frankfurt and Bonn. The Western agents had to be extremely cautious. As it turned out, they were not the only ones showing inconspicuous interest in the table talk between Guennadi and his new western friend. The other side was also watching.

'It is not unusual for the KGB to send additional agents into the field to cover such meetings,' reports one official involved in the case. 'Obviously, they are there to keep a look-out for us. But that is not the sole reason. They also want to be sure that their man does not succumb to the lures of Western capitalism – and make a break for it.'

On one occasion, Batachev's KGB shadows were also visible to the German sales manager. He was driving his car through the exit of an underground garage in Cologne, where he had just parted from the Soviet, when he noticed Batachev conversing intently with another man on the street. The German honked his horn and waved. When Batachev realized that he had been observed in a conversation with his KGB contact, he froze in his tracks. His conversation partner hid his face from view and ran from the scene.

As events converged – and an exchange of documents became unavoidable – the two arranged the final meeting in the cathedral square, where the Soviet spy was to return a set of schematic drawings which he had borrowed from the German for copying. Guennadi Batachev had just passed a plain white envelope containing 1,500 DM in small bills when he was arrested. The two Soviets who scattered in the confusion were KGB agents there to cover Batachev. They had apparently been unable to warn him.

For the German electronics expert a gruelling two-month ordeal had finally ended.

The defendant flashed a sheepish grin to waiting press photographers as he stepped in handcuffs from a green police van and marched into the Düsseldorf federal court building for his trial on 6 July 1983. Four representatives of the Embassy of the USSR were on hand to monitor his trial. Batachev adamantly denied any espionage activities, claiming in a prepared statement that he had 'fallen victim to a planned provocation aimed at worsening relations between our two countries'.

The proceedings were held under tight security in hearing-room A-01 located in a specially constructed basement complex of the court building designed for terrorist trials. The room is surrounded by a steel and wire cage to thwart eavesdroppers. When the court went into closed session, armed guards swung a heavy insulated door closed, sealing off the courtroom from the outside world. A total of twelve witnesses testified.

In the end, Batachev was found guilty of espionage activities 'threatening the vital interests of the Federal Republic of Germany'. Since no damage had actually been inflicted, presiding judge Klaus Wagner announced a lighter sentence than might otherwise have been issued. The Soviet spy was condemned to two and a half years in a West German high-security prison.

As the sentence was delivered, Batachev didn't bat an eye. Being a highly trained specialist in the illegal acquisition of Nato know-how, he knew he would not have to endure the hardships of his drab Düsseldorf prison cell for very long. The mild-mannered man from Moscow knew his experience in the capitalist West would be an invaluable asset at home. Within five months of his conviction Guennadi Batachev was quietly put onto an eastbound Aeroflot plane.

The trial of the KGB agent had received front-page attention in a number of Western newspapers outside Germany. Within the country, reporting was limited to small back-page blurbs. Soviet espionage is not regarded as an important issue in the editorial offices of most newspapers there.

There was no news coverage at all of his release. Details of the discreet diplomatic arrangement between Moscow and Bonn are a state secret.

Source Notes

Batachev's trial: Largely based on personal interviews by the author. See also: press release of the Düsseldorf state court (Oberlandesgericht) of 28/6/1983; *International Herald Tribune*, 6/7/1983; *Hamburger Abendblatt*, 27/11/76; Deutsche Presse Agentur, 29/6/1983; *Tagesspiegel*, 7/7/1983; 'Moskauer EDV-Spione', *Computerwoche*, 6/5/1983; *Süddeutsche Zeitung*, 9/7/1983.

Other cases from the Soviet Trade Mission in Cologne: Annual reports of the German federal counter-espionage authority Verfassungsschutz, Cologne, 1977 to 1983.

Part III

CONSEQUENCES

TEN

With a Little Help From Your Enemies: Western Technology in Eastern Weaponry

New England fishermen working out of Providence, Rhode Island, were the first to see it one windy autumn day in late 1982: a strange cylindrical object glistening amongst the silvery fish in their haul. To them, it was just another piece of man-made refuse fouling the nets. But to specialists soon examining the find in a secret Pentagon laboratory, it was the biggest catch in a long time. The machine was an unknown type of Soviet eavesdropping buoy. In the electronic brain of the 800 lb. ocean-going detection device they discovered a Soviet-made computer chip (series 133). It was a circuit-for-circuit, pin-for-pin replica of an American chip – Texas Instruments Series 5400. In fact, when the TI chip was plugged into the Soviet reconnaissance system, it functioned flawlessly. Without Western technology – 'made in the USSR' – the Soviet buoy, designed to monitor the underwater movements of NATO submarines, would never have worked.

Across the continent on the sandy shores of the Pacific, a group of young boy scouts made a similar discovery only a few months later. On the beaches near Bangor, Washington, where Trident atomic submarines dock at a secret Navy installation, a Soviet acoustic collection device had washed ashore, apparently dropped by a Soviet trawler in the vicinity. It bore the inscription of the Soviet Academy of Science. But the device was clearly military. Once again, it contained reverse-engineered US electronics – pirated this time from the RCA Corporation.

Both cases presented new and frightening evidence that the Soviets not only possessed highly sophisticated Western electronics; they were reproducing it on factory equipment from the

West. The discovery came as no surprise. Intel chip-designer Peter Stoll stumbled across one example while leafing through a Soviet magazine: "That's not theirs, it's ours," he exclaimed when he examined a microprocessor shown there. "There's an Intel chip that looks just like that one. Every piece of it is the same – small details, right down to the last wiggle. It is an exact copy. Stolen."

US intelligence experts made a similar discovery when they dismantled an air-to-air missile captured in Syria. On a circuit board in the guidance system of the Soviet rocket they discovered a screw which served no purpose. The superfluous screw, which rotated counter-clockwise, turned out to be the personal trademark of the American engineer who had designed the original chip. Soviet copycats, apparently unable to tell the useful from the useless, had simply copied the nonsensical screw along with the rest of the electronic design.

For years, experts high in NATO circles had been warning that the Warsaw Pact was bolstering its massive arms build-up with NATO know-how. "More than 160 Eastern weapons systems include Western technology," US Undersecretary of Defense Richard Perle warned. "We are literally exporting the means they use to arm against us."

Perle was playing on a quote from Vladimir Ilyich Lenin: "The capitalists," the Russian revolutionary had said, "will sell us the rope we need to hang them."

Upon assuming office in January 1981, one of President Reagan's first actions was to assign the Central Intelligence Agency to investigate the strategic effect of legal and illegal technology transfers to the Soviet Union. By autumn of that year, preliminary results were reaching the White House. The theft of top technology, analysts at Langely had concluded, was saving the Soviet military establishment billions of dollars on research and development (R & D) and had already caused a significant shift in the balance of power.

The Red Army had trucks built with European manufacturing equipment in Naberezhnye Chelny in the Urals; the Red Fleet was repairing Kiev aircraft-carriers at Japanese dry docks in Vladivostok; and the Red Air Force was shooting down cruise-missile targets with American radar systems at a test-flight facility in Vladimirovka. According to the CIA report, large Western mainframe computers co-ordinated Soviet troop movements in East Germany; tiny Western microcomputers guided Soviet missiles in

Syria. In everything from spy satellites and supersonic fighters to artillery and atomic submarines, the communists were using technology begged, borrowed or stolen from their capitalist opponents.

The USSR is not only deploying Western systems in its own weapons, pointing them back across the border at the capitalists; Western technology is also being pitted against itself. IBM 360/S and 370/S computers stand guard in the air defence ring around the Soviet capital and Soviet concrete ICBM silos are constructed according to Western plans, X-rayed with Western quality-control devices and tested for hardness with Western hydraulics. Intelligence consultant Miles Costick of the Washington-based Institute of Strategic Trade, who has debriefed over 150 Soviet defectors, estimates the value of Western technology borrowed over the past twenty years at a total of $100,000,000,000. German East-West expert Heinrich Vogel of the Bundesinsitut für Ostwissenschaftliche und Internationale Studien in Cologne believes that up to 70 per cent of all new Warsaw Pact weapons systems are based on pirated technology.

One such weapon is the SS-20 – a mobile intermediate-range nuclear missile full of Western technology. The launch vehicles trucking them from site to site in East Germany, Czechoslovakia and the eastern regions of the Soviet Union were designed on IBM computers from New York using software from the Massachusetts Institute of Technology. The nose cones are tipped with a carbon-fibre heat shield developed in New Jersey and – should they ever be fired in anger – their three nuclear warheads will be guided into Western cities by a gyroscope system constructed with the help of machine tools delivered from Vermont. Between 1977 and 1983 the Warsaw Pact fielded over 300 SS-20 missiles, 243 of them aiming at Western Europe and the rest at targets in the Far East. The story of their deployment tells a revealing tale about Soviet military intentions.

In the 1970s, the West had taken no steps either to increase or modernize its European nuclear force. Détente was in full swing; peace and reconciliation were in the air. In 1979, NATO member states had committed themselves to a voluntary reduction of their atomic arsenals, withdrawing a total of 1,000 tactical warheads from Western Europe within a twelve-month period. Tactical weapons were not part of superpower negotiations. The step, taken unilaterally, was conceived as a 'confidence-building measure' to demonstrate Western goodwill for the Geneva disarmament talks.

Needless to say, the Soviets did not respond in kind. For ten years they had been expanding their own European nuclear forces at an unprecedented rate, increasing dramatically the quantity, speed and accuracy of their missiles. In the intermediate range, they had scrapped outdated SS-4 and SS-5 missiles, introducing the sophisticated SS-20 and increasing total payload effectiveness threefold. In the short-range arena, they had replaced their Frogs, Scuds and Scaleboards with new SS-21, SS-22 and SS-23 fleets, raising total force levels as they went.

Hoping to quell Soviet anxieties and promote progress at the Geneva negotiations, NATO leaders announced a further reduction of their atomic arsenals at an Ottawa meeting in November 1983, unilaterally proclaiming that an additional 1,000 tactical warheads would be removed from West European soil within two years. The decision meant a net reduction in the total number of Western warheads deployed on the continent from 6,000 to 4,000. Still the Soviets refused to budge. In the media they denounced the NATO reductions as a cheap propaganda ploy; at the conference table they continued to reject serious disarmament proposals. The West was compelled to retaliate with the stationing of cruise missiles and Pershing 2s. The Soviets had apparently been betting on the nuclear-freeze movement to block the NATO deployment. But, despite two years of heated public controversy – with mass demonstrations sweeping Europe and some coalition governments trembling – the alliance remained steadfast. The NATO missile plan was sealed when the West German Bundestag, where debate had raged intensely, approved it with a solid majority on 2 December 1983. Moscow responded with a further expansion of its European atomic arsenal. And the weapons it used were Western copies.

On 5 December – at an unusual Western-style press conference in Moscow – then Deputy Minister of Defence Nikolai Ogarkov appeared before journalists and announced that the USSR was accelerating the deployment of tactical nuclear weapons in East Germany and Czechoslovakia. But he had another surprise up his sleeve. Russian engineers had come up with a new underwater nuclear missile system whose aim, the Soviet Marshal declared, was to bring the threat of nuclear annihilation closer to the American homeland. The actors in Ogarkov's ugly scenario are nuclear-tipped SSN-19 cruise missiles designed to be fired from the torpedo tubes of Soviet Oscar submarines lingering close to American shores. Intelligence sources report that the sleek 26-inch turbo-fan motors powering them, and the computerized Tercom navigation system guiding them, are both of Western origin – designed by General Dynamics for the US naval missile Tomahawk. The Soviet copycat cruise missile was christened by NATO experts 'Tomahawk-ski'.

The SSN-19 and the SS-20 are by no means the sole Soviet atomic weapons systems supported by NATO know-how. According to the CIA report, they have also improved the accuracy of their long-range intercontinental ballistic missiles, or ICBMs, 'through the exploitation and development of good-quality guidance components – such as gyroscopes and accelerometers. The quality of these instruments, in turn, depends to a considerable degree on the quality of the small, precision, high-speed bearings used.'

The Soviets purchased the machines they needed to make them in Vermont.

In August 1972, the Bryant Grinder Corporation sold 168 ball-bearing grinders to the USSR. The Centalign-B machines were not a military secret. They had been widely available on commercial markets for two decades. Switzerland, Italy and Japan had since begun producing similar equipment. But the patented high-precision Vermont grinders, able to exact tolerances of 0.000025 of an inch, were unknown in the East. The Soviets had been pursuing them ever since 1961. At that time, their request had been rejected by President Kennedy, who feared the sale would contribute to the advancement of Soviet missile capabilities.

But twelve years later the Nixon White House took a different view of the matter. If America didn't make the sale, proponents argued, foreign companies would. It wasn't a weapons deal, they said, or even sensitive dual-purpose technology. The US President, who had rung in détente at an affable summit meeting with Leonid Brezhnev three months before, decided to ignore warnings from Congress and the Pentagon and approve the export licence.

Two of the Centalign grinders were installed at the Ilyich Machine Tool Factory in Leningrad, prime Soviet producer of ball-bearings. At the time, the plant was semi-artisanal. It was described in *Pravda* as being 'closer to the preparation of simple grindstones and breechblocks for machine guns than to the inconceivable precision of instruments'.

'My impression?' the president of Bryant Grinders remarked to his Soviet hosts after touring the Leningrad facility. "I could give you all our machine tools, but you would gain nothing. You cannot make machine tools for manufacturing instrument bearings with such technology, with such equipment and materials, and with such personnel." He was happy to sell 168 of his machines – at a price of $74,000 each – and the Soviets were happy to buy them. Micro-ball-bearings played a crucial role in the three-gimbal high-speed gyroscopes of a missile system they didn't have – but envied.

Until then, the technology of missiles with multiple warheads, called MIRVs (multiple independently-targeted re-entry vehicles), had been a monopoly of the United States. With MIRV technology, a single rocket booster can launch several nuclear devices in an extraterrestrial trajectory; each then switches to its own guidance system and begins seeking its own target. When accompanied by metallic decoys, the approaching bombs are difficult for an opponent to track and nearly impossible to intercept. The MIRV system multiplies the lethal potential of a missile fleet several times. With it, the USA held an important strategic edge over the USSR.

Within twelve months of the Bryant Centalign-B sale, the first MIRV missiles were seen rising from Soviet test sites. Each of the new Soviet rockets was tipped with several nuclear warheads. Their SS-18 monster missile, NATO experts observed, could carry a total of ten atomic bombs, dropping them with lethal precision to within only 100 metres of their targets. Their explosive power (measured in megatons) was eight times that of comparable American payloads.

The Bryant president had seriously misjudged Soviet proficiency at copying. In spite of all their limitations, they had proved quite capable of duplicating his equipment. Managers at the Ilyich plant, ridiculing the predictions of their American visitor, boasted about their accomplishments in *Pravda*: 'At the factory there soon stood six machine tools: two Bryants, two of the first domestic [Soviet] ones, and two exact copies of the American ones.' Perhaps the Soviets could have made their MIRVs on their own. Perhaps not. The Bryant equipment certainly helped them improve their manufacturing prowess in this vital strategic field.

The high-precision micro-ball-bearing machines from Vermont were but one stone in a vast mosaic of nuclear weapons technology pirated from the West and integrated into Soviet missiles. Heat shields, microelectronics, computer software and hardware, solid-fuel propulsion systems and – last but not least – the atomic warheads themselves have all been developed using some degree of Western know-how. The plans delivered by nuclear physicist Klaus Fuchs formed the corner-stone of the Soviet nuclear weapons programme. The secrets turned over by German spy Peter Thiessen helped them produce enriched weapons-grade U-235 uranium fuel. Eastern theft of Western know-how is nothing new; but the dimensions have changed.

American know-how acquired legally by the USSR during the Second World War contributed to the impressive Soviet radar capabilities of today. 'This, along with the unclassified MIT radiation laboratory volume on radar theory, were the basic ingredients for the early generations of Soviet radar design,' claims Jack Vorona, chief of the Defense Intelligence Agency's Science and Technology Department. Vorona adds: 'The Soviets are excellent radar theorists and have since added their own refinements. I would note, however, that the acquisition of US microcircuitry very probably enabled them to package sophisticated radar concepts into a weight and volume suitable to the militarily critical airborne application.'

Nine motors built by Rolls-Royce (model RD-45) were delivered to the Soviets by the British Labour Government in 1946 and installed in their post-war MiG-15 fighter-interceptors. The US B-29 Flying Fortress of Second World War fame served as an involuntary model for Tupolev TU-4 long-range bombers. While such replicas remained well behind Western technology, they did enable the Soviets to cut R & D expenditure considerably. At the same time, Soviet engineers proceeded with their own ventures – often crude in design and construction, but not necessarily backward.

Western experts were quite amused when the clumsy-looking Tupolev TU-95 turbo-propelled bomber (NATO name: Bear) first took to the air in 1954. But it was soon flying 160 kilometres per hour faster than anyone had thought turbo-props could travel. Today, it carries the largest radar and the largest air-to-surface missiles in the world. The Soviet SA-6 (NATO name: Gainful) surface-to-air missile uses a unique integral all-solid rocket/ramjet propulsion system described by the respected London military publication *Jane's* as 'a decade in advance of comparable Western technology'.

Jane's also reports that the Red Air Force flies 'the fastest armed combat aircraft ever introduced into squadron service'. The MiG-25 Foxbat surpasses Mach 3, or three times the speed of sound. On 17 May 1975 an E-266M version of the MiG-25 recaptured two time-to-height records from the McDonnell Douglas F-15 Streak Eagle, pride of many NATO air defence squadrons.

Two years later, a modern-day Soviet imitation sent shock waves through the executive offices of the Boeing Corporation. Just fourteen months before, the Seattle company had introduced its new YC-14 V/STOL (vertical/short-take-off-and-landing) aircraft which was able to utilize extremely short airstrips. On 22 December 1977 a Soviet twin took off. The AN-72 Coaler was such an exact copy of the Boeing YC-14 that without painted identification it could be easily mistaken for the American plane.

Boeing is convinced that the resemblance is not a coincidence. Early in the 1970s, while their engineers were still tinkering with top-secret YC-14 plans on backroom drawing boards, numerous Soviet delegations were wandering freely through other parts of the plant. Understandably, the Soviet visitors showed keen interest in all projects at the US facility, which was doing heavy defence contracting. They were ostensibly there to buy civilian aircraft for Aeroflot, but Boeing managers are now convinced that the Soviets took advantage of the opportunity to steal the YC-14 blueprints. How they did it, no one knows. But the planes themselves are proof enough that it happened.

In another incident at Boeing, the Soviets were caught red-handed. During a tour in 1973, Soviet delegates were caught picking up metal shavings from the factory floor with special shoes and putting them into their pockets. Boeing representatives observing the incident were infuriated, fearing the metallurgic samples would be used to identify US lightweight alloys. But the State Department pooh-poohed the affair. The gum-shoed, sticky-fingered delegates were allowed to keep their find.

Defence contractors at the Lockheed Corporation, which also hosted countless Soviet delegations in those years, suffered similar experiences. The methods applied were less sneaky, but the results were equally devastating. 'Soviet military aircraft designers have "ordered" documents on Western aircraft and gotten them within a few months,' the CIA confirms, 'including plans and drawings for the [Lockheed] C-5A giant transport aircraft early in its development cycle. These plans, although dated now, have contributed to current Soviet development of a new strategic military cargo plane.'

By far the most sophisticated military electronics on board any plane these days is carried by NATO's AWACs. The early-warning aircraft is the backbone of airborne reconnaissance. Inevitably, the Soviets have their own early-warning system, which is carried by the Tupolev TU-126 Moss. Mounted on its fuselage, the TU-126 carries a mushroom-shaped turntable remarkably similar to the structures on E-3A AWACs from Boeing. The only visible difference is that the Soviet turntable is two metres larger than the American version. Military experts, however, are less concerned about external similarities than about the performance of the electronics inside. According to CIA Director William Casey, they are identical.

A follow-up model, the Ilyushin IL-76 Candid, was developed in the early 1970s by a team headed by C.V. Novozhilov and entered squadron service in 1984. The Soviet reconnaissance plane is modelled after Lockheed's C-141 transports. Aircraft experts at the Pentagon and at *Jane's* agree that Candid is not a duplicate – at least aerodynamically – but the electronics are described in the CIA report as 'nearly identical'.

Nearly.

The acquisition of classified aeronautical plans has long been a priority of traditional Soviet intelligence-gathering. But the job isn't done with the theft of secret blueprints alone. Western contractors working in a free-market system tend to produce a colourful variety of designs, models and prototypes. While appealing to the various companies and countries involved, this has complicated the job of standardizing weapons systems for wartime requirements. For their part, the Warsaw Pact allies choose to concentrate on the long-term development of a few basic lines, producing them in huge quantities and cutting R & D costs. Thus, when they wish to introduce a hot NATO innovation into their own systems, the Western technology must first be adapted to existing mass-produced Soviet lines.

Top-of-the-line main-frame computers are quite suited to this type of job. One application is in the field of aerodynamics. Fed with proper data, a high-speed computer can simulate test-flights of theoretical aircraft designs. In a matter of days, thousands of different wing shapes, jet motors and construction materials can be paired with one another, analysing stress, speed, air-resistance and manoeuvrability. The computer then picks the ideal combination. Electronic 'test flights' of this nature serve as a high-tech substitute for costly and time-consuming model-building and wind-tunnel tests.

This, US National Security Adviser Zbigniev Brzezinski feared, was why a Univac 1100-10C computer was openly purchased by the West German branch of a Swedish company and – with permission of Western governments – resold to the Soviets. The Soviets claimed the machine would be installed in the State Institute of Synthetic Rubbers Giprokauchuk outside Moscow and used to calculate chemical formulae. But, according to Brzezinski, the computer was diverted to the nearby Tupolev aeroplane factory where, along with Western-designed software for stress-analysis, called Aska, it helped create the supersonic Soviet Backfire bomber.

Brzezinski was an Administration hardliner, once described by the *Washington Post* as 'the most often out-voted man in the White House'. His warnings about the computer deal were ignored.

Most probably the Univac computer also served in a later development from the Tupolev engineers: the Blackjack bomber. The Blackjack flies at Mach 2.3 and can travel 15,000 kilometres without refuelling. A first prototype was photographed in the air over the Ramenskoye test-flight centre on 25 November 1981. Although the Blackjack imitates the supersonic, swing-wing design of NATO's B1-B bomber, the Soviet copy, which is 20 per cent longer, will see regular squadron service first.

Another civilian sale by a Swedish electronics company was also quickly diverted to the Red Air Force. The sophisticated flight-control radar system from Datasaab was originally intended for Moscow airport. It was integrated into the Soviet capital's air defence system, along with several pirated IBM 360/S and 370/S computers.

The deadly consequences of bootlegged Western weaponry were first felt by American soldiers in Vietnam, where Soviet SA-7 surface-to-air missiles killed scores of American pilots. The SA-7 Grail, which was fired by Vietcong and North Vietnamese anti-aircraft units, is labelled by *Jane's* as 'counterpart to the US Redeye missile'. A sister system called the SA-3 uses the propulsion, guidance and electronics of the American ground-to-air missile Hawk.

The technology of the US Sidewinder missile is also in use by both NATO and the Warsaw Pact. The Soviet AA-2 Atoll is a one-to-one replica of the Sidewinder system, a perfect carbon copy. It is standard equipment under the wings of the MiG-21 fighter-interceptor. It was an Atoll missile that Red Air Force pilot Colonel I. Shchukov fired into Korean Airlines flight KE-007 when the civilian plane strayed into Soviet territory on 1 September 1983. Two hundred and sixty-nine innocent people died in that crash (and Shchukov was awarded a medal for heroism).

The Sidewinder was stolen by a KGB agent and unwittingly spirited away to Moscow by the West German postal service. All too often, strategic technology appears to be civilian – at least to the unschooled eye – and its sale has been officially sanctioned by Western governments.

When the Red Army crossed the southern border of the USSR at Termez and invaded Afghanistan on 26 December 1979, it was riding in Western transport. Many of the spanking new trucks carrying the invasion forces had been produced in a giant factory at Naberezhnye Chelny in the Urals. The truck factory, located on the Kama River, was designed and equipped by Western companies and financed to the tune of $1.5 billion by Western banks.

The very latest in automotive manufacturing technology, including automated casting works, assembly-line robots and computerized quality control, had been installed over a seven-year period. The general contractor was Mack Trucks, USA. Fiat of Italy and Mercedes-Benz of West Germany contributed expertise and equipment of their own, while IBM supplied 370/S mainframe computers. In the end, the plant was equipped to produce up to 250,000 diesel trucks, many of them designed to military specifications.

Lawrence Brady, licensing chief at the Department of Commerce under Jimmy Carter, was opposed to the Kama River project from the start. When the contracts for the plant were negotiated, the Soviets gave assurances that all vehicles produced there would be used solely for civilian purposes. At least nineteen of the 150 Kama-related contracts contained written 'end-use' clauses to that effect. But Brady was suspicious. He reminded the Administration of other broken Soviet promises, like the ZIL-131 trucks, built with the help of the Ford Motor Company, which were carrying war equipment down the Ho Chi Minh trail to the Vietcong. Soviet assurances hadn't prevented them from delivering roughly one quarter of their production to the Red Army then. The same, he warned, could happen at Kama River. But Brady's criticism, which he took to the media, was not appreciated in the Carter White House. The inconvenient export chief had to leave.

In the end, Brady was proved right. The Soviet assurances were meaningless. By the summer of 1977, while the plant was still under construction, Kama trucks were already being sighted among Soviet units in East Germany.

Afghanistan marked a turning point in public thinking on the issue of technology transfer. Enraged politicians pointed to the Soviet invasion of Czechoslovakia in 1968, when chronic transportation shortages had forced the Warsaw Pact to requisition public buses from Moscow to move its forces. In Afghanistan, the Red Army was invading with a large and modern vehicle fleet, including rocket-launchers and troop transports. For the first time, officially condoned Western-supplied civilian technology was being used in a fighting war.

President Carter reacted with sanctions. On 21 January 1980 he ordered the Department of Commerce to cancel all licences for Kama River computer components. On 11 May delivery of the assembly line was also stopped.

If the United States delivered the wheels, Austria supplied the cannons. Rotary forges sold by the state-owned Gesellschaft für

Fertigungstechnik und Maschinenbau (GFM) were used to produce gun barrels for Soviet T-72 tanks and several navy war ships. The smooth-bore barrels, which Soviet industry had been unable to manufacture on its own, were capable of piercing the latest armour shields developed by NATO. The Warsaw Pact managed to deploy the new weapons system before the West could, using – as some experts believe – the greatest gun-barrel manufacturing capacity in the world. Ironically, the same GFM equipment is used to manufacture cannons for the General Motors army tank M-1.

Proponents of both deals had argued that diesel motors and forging machines could hardly be categorized as strategic technology. Are we going to prohibit the export of a button factory, they had asked rhetorically, simply because its products might be used to hold up a soldier's trousers in time of war? But much of the technology sold to the East during détente was far more significant to the Kremlin's armies than buttons.

The Red Navy was once an almost laughable force, consisting largely of coastal patrol boats. A glance at a map reveals the natural handicaps it confronted. Soviet harbours are either ice-locked in winter on the Arctic coasts, or bottle-necked behind strategic cut-off points in the Baltic, by Japan, or in the Black Sea. Soviet fleets suffered devastating defeats in the Russo-Japanese War of 1904 and in the First and Second World Wars. Joseph Stalin once stated flatly: 'The Soviet Union has no navy.' On a visit to the United States, Nikita Khrushchev was prepared to scrap 90 per cent of the Soviet naval cruisers: 'They're just used to ferry admirals back and forth.'

But Khrushchev's only admiral of the time disagreed. Sergei Gorshkov managed to save six cruisers from the old Second World War stocks. Soon after the Cuban crisis Gorshkov was given a sweeping mandate to build up Soviet sea power. Under his skilled and aggressive leadership the Red Navy has since grown to a fully fledged blue-water navy capable of challenging Western control of the seas. Today, some NATO naval experts believe, it may even be superior to Western forces.

With a total of 350 ships, the Soviet submarine fleet is the largest in the world and new models created at the shipyards on the Black Sea continue to amaze Western military observers. The hunter Alfa is constructed with the use of a titanium alloy as yet unknown in the West. Early models, in service since 1970, were short and stunted, but nevertheless able to establish a world record in deep diving (in excess of 2,000 feet) – out of reach of even the most sophisticated NATO anti-submarine weapons. On 8 June 1983 an advanced model was photographed at the Sudomekh shipyards in Leningrad. It is said to be the fastest attack submarine ever built. The new elongated Alfa generation reaches top underwater speeds of 40 knots, being able to outrun not only comparable NATO hunters of the Los Angeles class (35 knots), but also their torpedoes.

A new Soviet underwater launching platform for strategic missiles has generated even more concern in Western naval circles. It is called 'Typhoon'. Built at the Severodvinsk shipyards, this 180-metre monster submarine displaces 30,000 tons when submerged and is the largest underwater vessel ever built. Twin hulls, separated by a water cushion, render it practically immune to attacks by conventional torpedoes. Powered by a double nuclear reactor, it is mighty enough to crash through the Arctic ice. Armed with no less than twenty SSNX-20 missiles (each tipped with twelve atomic warheads), it can sit on the sea floor for months on end – silent, mobile, submerged. *The Guinness Book of Records* has awarded Typhoon the title of deadliest single weapons system on the face of the earth – and most serious naval analysts agree.

In the CIA's presidential report, released to the public in a censored version in April 1982, experts warned that future Soviet acquisitional efforts would be concentrating on three strategic areas of submarine warfare where the West was still leading: acoustic sensoring, submarine silencing, and underwater navigation. The clandestine operations of the KGB and GRU were soon proving them right. By October of that year, the USSR had begun a major Kosmos space initiative with a global positioning system, called Glonass. The Russian navigational system, nicknamed 'Navstarski' in the West for its resemblance to the US Navy Navstar programme, was registered at the International Telecommunications Union in Geneva as a civilian programme for the Soviet Merchant Marine. Western experts are convinced its primary purpose is underwater orientation for submerged submarines. Documents submitted in Geneva reveal that the Soviet satellites not only possess orbital parameters virtually identical to those of the American Navstar spacecraft; but also transmit on the same frequencies (140 and 400 megahertz).

The list does not end here.

Computerized seismic listening devices called 'array processors' were installed in Soviet ships by experts from Texas. But it was soon discovered that the Soviets were not searching the seabed for natural resources, but rather hunting the hidden movements of NATO submarines.

Cargo ramp technology developed in England, France and Finland was sold by Finland to the USSR. The eager purchasers were quick to note, however, that the highly sophisticated roll-on/roll-off (ro-ro) technique, which stabilizes loading ramps between ship and either dock or beach, was not only useful for unloading automobiles and bulky machine crates. It was also good for tanks and heavy artillery. The Finnish equipment was installed on the *Ivan Rogov*, a new type of amphibious warship that carries both helicopters and high-speed air-cushioned landing craft and is capable of disembarking 550 naval infantrymen in the furthest corners of the world.

Japan sold a giant 1,000-foot floating dry dock to the Soviets in 1978 for $42 million. The Swedes followed suit three years later with a similar set-up. In the contract, the Soviets assured the sellers that the equipment was needed for their Merchant Marine. But the ceremonial ribbons were hardly cut when the Japanese dock was diverted to the Pacific Fleet at Vladivostok, the Swedish one to the North Fleet in Murmansk on the Arctic Sea. Both docks, the only ones in the USSR capable of handling the V/STOL aircraft-carriers of the Kiev class, are today servicing Soviet warships. Their primary purpose, however, is yet to come, when the first large-scale Soviet aircraft-carriers (nuclear-powered and weighing 60,000 tons) go into service in the 1990s.

The Soviets possessed the technological proficiency to build similar dry docks themselves, had it been necessary. But it wasn't, and they were thus able to avoid large-scale re-tooling of their own industry and interruptions of other priority armaments programmes. As a bonus, the naval-yard equipment was financed with generous low-interest loans.

Western research facilities are a major source of vital strategic information for the Soviets. 'In fact,' Jack Vorona of the Defense Intelligence Agency (DIA) exclaimed at a US Senate hearing, 'they tap into US research and development so frequently that one must wonder if they regard it as their own national asset. They have enjoyed great success in this endeavor with minimal effort, primarily because, as a nation, we lack the awareness of what they are about.'

Western Technology in Eastern Weapons

Warsaw Pact Weapons System	Western Technology	Origin
SS-18 ICBM	micro-ball-bearings for multiple warheads	Bryant Grinder (USA)
SS-18 ICBM	silo design	unspecified (USA)

Warsaw Pact Weapons System	Western Technology	Origin
SS-18 ICBM	silo testing equipment	unspecified (USA)
SS-20 nuclear missile	carbon-fibre heat shield	unspecified (USA)
SS-20 launch vehicle	design hardware	IBM (USA)
SS-20 launch vehicle	design software	MIT (USA)
AA-2 rocket (Atoll)	seeker/navigation/ propulsion	Sidewinder air-to-air missile (USA)
AN-72 STOL (Coaler)	aeronautical design	YC-14 STOL, Boeing (USA)
Ivan Rogov amphibian warship	roll-on/roll-off loading system	unspecified (Finland)
Kiev aircraft-carrier	dry dock construction	unspecified (Japan/ Sweden)
Backfire bomber	computer-aided design (CAD)	1100/10-C computer, UNIVAC (USA)
MiG-15 fighter-interceptor	jet engines	Rolls-Royce (Great Britain)
sonar listening device	chip design	TI-5400, Texas Instruments (USA) CD 4000 Series, RCA (USA)
SSN-19 cruise missile	turbo-fan motor, Tercom navigation	Tomahawk, General Dynamics (USA)
TU-126 AWACs	design, electronics, radar turntable	AWACs E-266M, Boeing (USA)
T-72 tank cannon	rotary forges for production	GFM (Austria)
Glonass submarine navigation	orbital parameters/ radio frequencies	Navstar satellites (USA)
air defence system in Moscow	computer guidance	IBM 370/S (USA), Datasaab (Sweden)
space weapons	hardened laser mirrors	Spawr Research (USA)
missile-launchers, transports	truck factory	Mack Trucks (USA), IBM (USA), Fiat (Italy), Mercedes-Benz (West Germany)

(Author's note: some of the above technology was supplied legally and illicitly diverted by the Soviets, some was pirated. In none of the above cases did a Western company knowingly supply know-how or equipment for an Eastern-bloc weapons system.)

Obviously there are many fields where the USSR still lags significantly behind the West. This is no reason, however, to underestimate its technological capabilities. Western experts were amazed at the rapid deployment of the MiG-15 shortly after the Second World War. The Soviet atomic bomb was constructed far faster than Western intelligence had predicted. The USSR was the first nation to explode a hydrogen bomb dropped from an aircraft. The first ICBM ever to fly was Soviet and a month later it boosted Sputnik into orbit, putting the American space programme to shame. In all decisive strategic technology – from the atomic bomb and MIRV to solid-fuel propulsion and strategic submarines – the Soviets have managed to close the gap faster than anyone thought possible.

Where the Soviets are unable to match Western quality, they outrun Western quantity. In 1982, for example, their factories produced 30 long-range bombers, 1,300 fighter planes and helicopters, 200 ICBMs, 175 intermediate-range missiles and 53,000 surface-to-air missiles. Recent US Defense Department estimates indicate that the Warsaw Pact is continuing to outdistance NATO production in these areas at a rate of more than two to one.

Americans may have put the first man on the moon, but in the vital military orbits closer to home it is the Soviets who enjoy a clear edge. Their boosters have more thrust, their manned space stations are bigger, their cosmonauts stay up longer. In the early 1970s, the USA temporarily abandoned its research in laser weaponry, while Soviet scientists at the secret laser centres in Saryshagan and Samipalatinsk continued full steam ahead. By 1977, intelligence services were reporting that Soviet lasers were ten times more potent than American weapons. At that time, the United States had orbited only 348 satellites. The Soviets possessed twice that number. In 1982, the USSR fired 101 satellites into space, the USA a mere 19. Since then, the Soviet launch rate has continued to outpace the American by five to one.

In the early hours of 18 June 1982 aerospace technicians scurried about the Baikonur Space Centre in final preparation for the launch of a Soviet satellite named Kosmos-1379. Punctually at 10:00 am its booster ignited. US sensory satellites picked up the launch immediately and radar stations tracked the Soviet rocket as it rose to an orbit 1,000 kilometres over the earth. By 14:23 hours Greenwich Mean Time, Kosmos-1379 was approaching its target: another Kosmos satellite, number 1375.

US Air Force experts, who monitor all space activity from a secret command post deep in the Cheyenne Mountains of Colorado, quickly classified the event as a killer-satellite test – a rocket rendezvous for self-destructing mini-bombs. The rocket approaches an enemy satellite and detonates, blowing itself and its neighbour to smithereens. The men had seen such kamikaze manoeuvres before. Soviet killer-satellites were nothing new. But the blips that came flying across their radar screens this June day were more than they had ever witnessed. Between the launch of Kosmos-1379 and its lethal appointment with Kosmos-1375, a total of ten additional Soviet missiles took to the air.

The 100-foot-high US radar tower on Shemya Island in the outer Aleutians detected two ICBMs as they parted from concrete silos in eastern USSR, only to be intercepted by Soviet ABMX-3 anti-ballistic missiles. US spy-satellites tracked one SS-20 and two SS-11s as they soared from their land-based launching sites, while a sea-based missile crashed through faraway ocean waters. Soviet technicians in Plesetsk fired the navigational satellite Kosmos-1380 into orbit while their colleagues back at Baikonur readied the medium-resolution reconnaissance orbiter Kosmos-1381 for its start. Both were apparently intended as substitutes for the victims of the war game raging in the heavens.

It was over within hours. Instead of moving infantry and tanks, frigates and fighter planes in a conventional military manoeuvre, Moscow's high command had chosen to fire space weapons and nuclear missiles, testing operational co-ordination and communication lines under the realistic conditions of a global war game. The outer-space operation, described in an account in *Air Force Magazine*, amounted to no less than a fully fledged rehearsal for the Third World War.

The incident may have been the most dramatic Soviet space event of the year. It was by no means the only one. Soviet reconnaissance satellites are undergoing a process of continual adjustment and readjustment, as engineers direct the remote-controlled cameras and antennae of their countless vehicles – searching for strategic signals in an enigmatic choreography of the heavens.

The arrival of the British fleet at the Falklands during the 1982 war with Argentina was followed promptly by the launch of the sea-monitoring satellite Kosmos-1355. It immediately took course for a low-altitude pass across the area of conflict. A few days later, HMS *Sheffield* was sunk by the Argentine navy. The radar receivers on board Kosmos-1355 were capable of locating the *Sheffield* and it is still not known whether the Soviet satellite played a role in the sinking.

In the early hours of 25 March 1982 the orbital jets of Kosmos-

1343 burned briefly. The high-resolution photo-reconnaissance vehicle rose to a slightly higher orbit, carrying it over White Sands, New Mexico. There, the American space shuttle was approaching for a landing. On 30 March the jets ignited again, dipping Kosmos-1343 to a lower orbit, passing this time across Fort Irwin, California, where 2,300 US soldiers were about to be airlifted in the Gallant Eagle exercises of the Rapid Deployment Force.

Satellites are the eyes and ears of a modern military power. They would be vital in war, and are also essential in the everyday job of peacetime intelligence. Both the superpowers are continually observing each other's army, navy and air force – monitoring movements, eavesdropping on communications and checking on the observance of disarmament accords. Hovering in geostationary orbits over foreign territory, satellites can detect secret weapons development, reconnoitre Third World arms sales or track distant troop deployments.

American reconnaissance satellites may not be able to read the small print in *Pravda* from outer space, but the high-resolution cameras and films aboard the US vehicle 'Big Bird' can identify objects measuring only fifteen centimetres across. Its films are parachuted back to earth in special capsules. Lockheed's fourteen-ton, bus-sized KH-11 'Keyhole' satellite transmits its images in real time. At receiving stations in Cheltenham, England, and Fort Meade, Maryland, analysts can thus follow Soviet events 'live' on television – including the movements of individual people. During the Polish crisis, the US satellite was stationed over Brest on the USSR/Polish border, keeping Soviet troop activities under surveillance.

For many years, the Soviets underestimated American capability in the field of photo-reconnaissance. They tried to camouflage their ICBMs with painted patterns on the rocket tips. They drew designs that would resemble industrial smokestacks when seen from the air. Air Force experts were quite amused by this, and US disarmament delegates relished revealing the pitiful attempts to their embarrassed Soviet counterparts. The Americans even named specific sites where paint was peeling from the missile cones, and recommended a touch-up. The Soviets quickly abandoned the scheme.

The remarkable capability of American space surveillance was a direct result of the enormous advances made in miniaturized computers. But the military potential of microelectronics goes far beyond the video-imagery of reconnaissance satellites. In the mid-1960s, fighter aircraft carried heavy black steel containers about the size of a shoebox to produce head-up radar displays in their cockpits. Each contained 48,000 pieces of information, or bits. Today, the same functions are performed by a single microchip. The average price for a bit of electronic information has dropped from four cents to under one-thousandth of a cent. Had the automobile industry made similar progress, a Rolls-Royce today would measure 4 millimetres and cost $2.23.

Highly sophisticated computer systems which used to fill entire office suites can now be packed into a jeep, or even on the back of an infantry soldier. Shoulder-fired heat-seeking missiles track and destroy fighter planes; air-to-surface missiles home in on the beams of ground radar and take out radar stations. And both can be misled by a wide variety of decoy and jamming techniques. The world of warfare has become a jungle of electronic measures, counter-measures and counter-counter-measures. Its combatants sit at computer screens and terminals, fighting unseen foes in scenarios remote from reality. Much of the mind-boggling gimmickry is straight out of James Bond.

Battery-operated radio transmitters the size of a packet of cigarettes beam messages to satellites – relaying news from troops behind enemy lines to command posts on the other side of the world.

Mile-long underwater chains spiked with listening devices trawl inconspicuously behind ocean-going freighters – monitoring the movements of unseen enemy submarines.

Radar-guided television cameras pick out the painted markings on the tail-fins of faraway aircraft – identifying friend and foe at distances of up to eighteen kilometres.

Ground-based Doppler radars analyse the technical characteristics in engines of low-flying jetplanes – peering into their spinning turbines during the split-seconds of a supersonic fly-by.

Naval radar detects and identifies approaching missiles, while chaff machines automatically cut and disperse metallic clouds of aluminium snips, individually tailored to confuse the homing system of the attacking missiles – all within seconds.

'The miniaturization of microelectronics is by far the single most significant military development of the past two decades.' This statement, made in a special issue of the *Economist* devoted to defence technology, is as simple as it is irrefutable. Inevitably, computers have assumed a central role in the operation of almost every conceivable weapons system of the 1980s – with the exception of the simple infantry rifle. Computers dominate not only the complex command centres of nuclear-missile fleets and space missions, but also the small conventional weapons of army, navy and air force.

During combat in the Bekaa Valley in the summer of 1982, Syrian and Palestinian forces were baffled by what appeared to be Israeli telepathy. Whenever Syrian armoured divisions began to advance – even under circumstances of the utmost secrecy – an Israeli counter-attack was launched almost simultaneously. Whenever Palestinians abandoned the safety of their sandbagged shelters, they found themselves the centre of an intense barrage of heavy artillery fire. Even sites of the awesome Soviet SAM-7 missile had been struck with apparent impunity by the Israeli air force.

The secret of their success, Israeli officials later revealed, was a remotely piloted vehicle (RPV) called 'Scout'. A simple two-stroke combustion motor carried the propeller-driven drone deep into Syrian-controlled territory, where it could be parked at an altitude of 3,000 feet for nearly seven hours without refuelling. Its twelve-foot fibreglass frame – hardly larger than a child's model plane – was virtually indetectable by radar. Scout's remote-controlled, high-resolution video cameras instantly transmitted intelligence back to the Israelis, including stunning aerial footage of the PLO withdrawal from Beirut. When armchair generals in Scout's truck-based ground-control station noted a target of interest on their television screens, Scout was instructed to mark them electronically, guiding 'smart' bombs from distant Israeli artillery to an unerring bull's-eye hit.

Great Britain, France, Germany and the United States are all financing advanced RPV programmes. In addition to battlefield reconnaissance, drones can also be deployed as disposable attack aircraft. Tipped with explosive warheads, the Minidrone system from Dornier of West Germany, for example, homes in on targets in a self-destructing kamikaze flight. Literally thousands of the inexpensive wooden throw-away drones can be purchased for the price of a single modern fighter-interceptor.

Other RPVs are launched by conventional manned aircraft. Fired many miles from the target, these 'stand-off' weapons fly the risky leg of the mission on their own – guided across alien territory and through enemy anti-aircraft fire by lasers, television cameras, 3-D satellite maps and a host of other sophisticated systems. The pilot simply points them in the general direction and pushes a button, returning with his multimillion-dollar machine to the safety of his home base.

Most stand-off weapons are conventionally-armed cruise missiles. Instead of carrying a nuclear warhead, the flight vehicle serves as a container for scores of tiny computerized mini-missiles armed with low-yield conventional explosives. Messerschmitt-Bölkow-Blohm's Apache, for example, flies a fifteen-mile solo approach. When it reaches the target area, it spits out forty-two miniature mines which then burrow deep into the ground and detonate at irregular and unpredictable intervals. They are designed to halt approaching armoured divisions or destroy airstrips. Hughes Aircraft has developed another anti-tank submunition called 'Wasp' which also disperses scores of tiny missiles. Each of the radar-guided Wasps is programmed to home in on its own target, dive-bombing from above, where armour is thinnest. A computerized guidance system ensures that no two missiles attack the same vehicle.

In addition to cutting anti-aircraft risks for pilot and plane, such systems have another all-important advantage over all previous weapons: they raise the threshold of nuclear war.

One of the first high-level officials to recognize the long-term strategic implications of stand-off missiles, drones and convention-ally-armed cruise missiles was General Bernard Rogers. As Supreme Allied Commander of NATO's forces in Europe, Rogers realized that the old numbers game – the mere addition and subtraction of cannons and cruisers, squadrons and submarines, weapons and warriors – was becoming less meaningful by the day. 'Thinking weapons' had given East-West statistics an entirely new dimension. In a battlefield situation, their ability to stop a single ammunitions delivery could be more important than twenty cannons firing on the front; their ability to destroy a single tanker bringing fuel to an armoured division more important than forty fighting tanks.

At his instruction, the first in a series of secret strategic studies was commissioned by the NATO high command to evaluate the options created by advanced conventional weapons. The conclusion reached was that in fleets of hundreds, the remotely piloted vehicles were capable of overwhelming Warsaw Pact radar and penetrating deep into its staging areas. Armed with sophisticated new submunitions, a single missile could execute surgical strikes on targets such as bridges, airfields, ammunition depots or fuel-storage tanks, inflicting military damage equivalent to a one-kiloton atomic warhead. Nearby cities, however, would not be devastated – with luck, not even touched – by the low-yield pinpoint precision weapons. If adequate money was invested in research and development, the internal NATO reports concluded, and adequate numbers eventually deployed, third-generation 'thinking weapons' could replace tactical nuclear arms in Europe almost entirely by the mid-1990s – with no loss of defence capability.

On this basis the NATO commander developed a new strategy for the defence of Europe without tactical nuclear weapons. It soon bore his name. The 'Rogers Plan' was a revolutionary idea, born of revolutionary technology, and it was hailed with relief at almost all levels of the Alliance.

Obviously, the reduced dependency on nuclear weapons – and with it, the reduced risk of annihilation in time of conflict – was the major attraction for European leaders. But there were other more immediate considerations. The technology envisioned – cruise missiles, drones, submunitions and lasers – was in areas in which local industry could compete, which had not been true in the field of ICBMs, strategic submarines or spy satellites. The Rogers Plan would be an expensive undertaking, but the chances were good that a large proportion of the money spent would remain in Europe.

With the advent of the Rogers Plan, which today is already in preliminary stages of implementation, computer electronics have become more than ever the nub of the East-West arms race. The struggle for the strategic edge is a scramble for smart bombs and stand-off missiles, a battle of the bits and bytes. In his book *Always in Readiness to Defend the Fatherland*, Marshal Ogarkov addresses the military issues posed by electronic innovations in the field of conventional weaponry. Ogarkov's conclusion – when seen in the light of his rank as second-in-command in the Red Army – indicates a significant shift in Soviet strategic policy: 'A profound and – in the full sense of the word – *revolutionary* change in military affairs is now taking place.'

Ever since the Second World War the nations of NATO have relied on superior technology to offset the greater numbers of Warsaw Pact weapons and troops deployed in Europe. The security of the West is founded in the conviction that manpower and mass of equipment can be compensated by ever-improving weapons systems. The fate of the West, which is unwilling to accept the burdens associated with a complete militarization of society, matching the East tank for tank and man for man, continues to rest on the superiority of NATO know-how.

But how about the Soviets? How have their industries and armaments been faring in the great superpower scramble for electronics? Can they meet the challenge?

Source Notes

Submarine buoy: 'Technology Transfer: A Policy Nightmare', *Business Week*, 4/4/1983; *New York Tribune*, 11/7/1983; 'Some of Our Chips are Missing', *Time Magazine*, 14/3/1983; *New York Times*, 2/1/1985.

Quote from Peter Stoll: BBC *Panorama*.

Captured rocket from Syria: *Die Welt*, 5/7/1984.

Heinrich Vogel: *Der Spiegel*, 26/12/1983.

Richard Perle: US Senate Subcommittee on Investigations (hereafter Senate Hearings), Washington DC 1982, p. 114.

Tomahawk-ski: *Business Week*, 4/4/1983; 'Internationale Presse-konferenz in Moskau', *Sowjetunion heute*, 1/1/1984.

Heat shields: Ralph Kinney Bennett, 'The Great Russian Raid', *Readers Digest*, March 1984.

Bryant Grinders: This classic case of legal technology transfer is discussed in numerous articles on the subject. The most complete account (including *Pravda* quotes) was compiled by Thane Gustafson, *Selling the Russians the Rope*, Rand Corporation, Santa Monica, CA, April 1981. See also: 'How Russia steals US Defense Secrets', *US News and World Report*, 25/5/1981; Miles Costick, 'How to Stop US Technology from Building Soviet Military', *American Sentinel*, 12/12/1983.,

MIRV capability of the Soviets: Richard Head, 'Technology and the Military Balance', *Foreign Affairs*, April 1979; Jack Anderson, 'High-Tech Pipeline', *Washington Post*, 26/12/1982; 'The High-Tech Secrets Russia Seeks', *US News and World Report*, 3/5/1982; Arnaud de Borchgrave, 'Selling Russia the Rope', *The New Republic*, 13/12/1980; *International Herald Tribune*, 28/2/1976.

Ogarkov in the *Kommunist* on new offensive capabilities: 'Zwischen den Klippen', *Der Spiegel*, 28/11/1983.

Vorona on radar capabilities: Jack Vorona, Senate Hearings, p. 112; *Die Welt*, 29/4/1982.

Red Air Force: John W. Taylor, 'Gallery of Soviet Aerospace Weapons', *Air Force Magazine*, March 1983 and March 1984; Clarence Robinson, 'Soviets Deploying New Fighters', *Aviation Week*, 28/11/1983; 'Cutting Russia's Harvest of US Technology', *Fortune*, 30/5/1983; Senate Hearings, pp. 9-20, 112-15; 'Russia's High-Tech Heist', *Life*, April 1983; Donald Goldstein, 'Technology Transfer from a Defence Perspective', *Signal*, August 1983; Reuters, 4/4/1984.

Boeing visit: Ehud Yonay, 'Sticky Shoes and other Stories', *New West Magazine*, September 1983; Ulrich Schiller, 'Arroganz des Pentagons', *Die Zeit*, 14/10/1983.

Brzezinski: The *Guardian*, 24/12/1979.

Kama: Kenneth Tasky, 'Soviet Technology Gap and Dependence on the West', *Soviet Economy in a Time of Change*, US Congress, 10/10/1979; 'Double Dealing', *Reason*, February 1983; *Neue Züricher Zeitung*, 13/5/1980; 'Trading with the Communists', *The Review of the News*, 6/7/1983; *Frankfurter Allgemeine Zeitung*, 13/5/1980.

130 Consequences

Canons: *International Herald Tribune*, 10/11/1979 and 19/11/1979; 'Höchst befremdlich', *Der Spiegel*, 3/1/1983.

Eavesdropping devices: *Boston Globe*, 5/4/1983; *Christian Science Monitor*, 28/10/1982.

Red Fleet: 'Les nouveaux Monstres Soviétiques', *L'Express*, 22/7/1983; 'Eine gewaltige Herausforderung', *Der Spiegel*, 2/6/1980; '*Militärmacht UdSSR*', *Der Spiegel*, 11/4/1983; Jack Anderson, *Washington Post*, 26/12/1982.

'Navstarski': 'U-Schiffe', *Marine Rundschau*, November 1977; Rüdiger Proske, *Auf der Suche nach der Welt von Morgen*, NDR German television, 24/10/1978.

Datasaab and seismic equipment: 'How Russia Steals', *US News and World Report*, 25/5/1981; Arnaud de Borchgrave, 'Selling Russia the Rope', *The New Republic*, 13/12/1980; *Die Welt*, 10/4/1984.

Roll-On/Roll-Off technology: Caspar Weinberger, 'Technology Transfer Control Program', Report to Congress, February 1983.

Dry docks: 'Soviet Industrial Espionage', *Signal*, March 1983; US Department of Defense, 'Technology Transfer Control Program', Report to Congress, February 1983.

Brezhnev quote: 'Moskaus Griff nach Afghanistan', *Der Spiegel*, 7/1/1980.

Vorona quote: Senate Hearings, p. 114.

Der Spiegel quote: Issue no. 2/1980.

Kosmos: Nicholas L. Johnson, 'Soviet Strides in Space', *Air Force Magazine*, March 1983; Rüdiger Proske, *Auf der Suche nach der Welt von Morgen*, NDR German television, 24/10/1978.

Quote from the *Economist*: 'Marching Forward', 21/5/1983.

New conventional weaponry: 'Israel develops new tactical Weaponry', *Aviation Week*, 4/7/1983; 'Beam Weapons Advances', *Aviation Week*, 18/7/1983; 'Israelis Use Bolsters', *Aviation Week*, 18/7/1983; 'Israel Inventory', *Aviation Week*, 4/7/1983; 'Paper Planes', *Forbes*, 26/9/1983; *New York Times*, 23/5/1981; 'Unbemannte ferngelenkte Fluggeräte', *Soldat und Technik*, March 1977; 'USAF Shifts View', *Aviation Week*, 4/12/1978; 'US, Germany press Drone Development', *Aviation Week*, 28/8/1978.

Espionage satellites: 'Hey Ivan, Say Cheese', *Washington Post Magazine*, 4/12/1983.

Rogers Plans: Erwin Horn, 'Defensive konventionelle Verteidigung', *Sozialdemokratischer Pressedienst*, 8/9/1982; press release of the CDU/CSU Bundestag minority, 21/5/1982; *Hamburger Abendblatt*, 23/10/1982; *Frankfurter Allgemeine Zeitung*, 11/10/1982; 'Finstere Gedanken über Rogers', *Die Welt*, 19/10/1982; *Frankfurter Rundschau*, 9/10/1982.

Ogarkov on conventional weapons: Edgar Ulsamer, 'Will Economic Weakness Increase Soviet Militancy?' *Air Force Magazine*, March 1983.

ELEVEN

Univac – A Sputnik Shock For Moscow: The Eastern Electronics Industry

The fourth of October 1957.

Most Americans remember the day well. There was a strange peeping sound on the radio that morning. It came from outer space, the announcer said, broadcast by the first man-made satellite ever to orbit the earth. The 168 lb. basketball-sized device bore the Soviet name 'Sputnik' and was an achievement of the USSR. Citizens across the country – whether managers in Michigan or truckers from Tennessee, farmers or physicists, plumbers or politicians – recoiled with a sense of shock. It was a day of defeat for their proud nation.

The trauma that shook America's breakfast tables that day would later be recorded by historians as the 'Sputnik shock'. Until then, most Americans had regarded space travel as a God-given heritage of their homeland. Now the Soviets, of all people, had got there first. The political consequences followed three years later when President Kennedy announced his historic commitment to put a man on the moon by the year 1970. The efforts and achievements that followed were without precedent in peacetime.

Little-known to the West, the Soviets at the time were suffering their own superpower shock – caused by a piece of American equipment that emitted peep tones similar to Sputnik's. It wasn't registered in the official press reports of Tass and Novosti. In fact, the average Soviet citizen probably noticed nothing at all. But behind the Kremlin walls a shock wave was reverberating through the power élite in Moscow that wouldn't quickly be forgotten. The machine emitting the tones was called Univac and its existence signalled that the United States was on the threshold of a new technological breakthrough – in the field of computer electronics.

In the early post-war years, there had been little indication of a Soviet electronics lag. Soviet universities and research institutes, physicists and engineers were among the world's finest. The computer science of cybernetics, spurned in the dark years of the Stalin era as a 'bourgeois folly', had since been rehabilitated and was enjoying unprecedented popularity in the Soviet Union. The USSR was the first European nation to construct a digital computer. It was known as MESM (Malaya Elektronnaya Schetnaya Mashina) and an initial prototype went on-line in 1951. A large scientific-research computer called BESM (Bystrodeistvuyushchaya Elektronnaya Schetnaya Mashina) followed two years later.

By today's standards the computer technology of the 1950s was not spectacular, in either East or West. MESM calculated at a speed of about fifty transactions per second (today's personal computers can do two million). Like early radio and television receivers, they ran on old-fashioned vacuum tubes. In some cases they even used mechanical relays. The primary beneficiaries of the new electronic brains were scientists. Architects and aeronautical engineers used them to calculate stress factors, physicists and mathematicians for their complicated theoretical models. Obviously the military, too, was using them for its designs. But widespread civilian applications were unknown then. As was the case elsewhere in the world, the Soviets thought computers had been invented solely for computing.

During the rest of the decade there were no significant developments. But at the outset of the 1960s two parallel developments were soon demanding a radical reorientation in Politburo thinking about computers. On the one hand, the Soviets observed that data-processing was being implemented with increasing success in the West. On the other hand, their own bureaucracy was being smothered by the mass of raw information involved in a centrally planned economy.

Economists at the planning ministry Gosplan had to cope with data from some 40,000 industrial plants, as well as from the countless thousands of farms and agricultural collectives, mines and mass-transportation companies scattered across the vast land. Apparatchiks equipped with little more than cardboard filing cards and cumbersome accounting books were making vital economic forecasts of production goals and raw-material needs for entire sectors of Soviet industry. Marxist theory did not recognize white-collar workers as part of the productive economy. Yet their ranks were swelling by the day. The more administrators were employed, it seemed, the less the institutions of the land were able to cope with the information flooding in from the expanding Soviet economy. Railways, the postal system and other national organizations were in a state of total chaos. Accurate statistical data, a rarity in the USSR under the best of circumstances, had become so scarce as to be almost non-existent. Gosplan planning had been reduced to little more than guesswork.

Computers offered a perfect solution. The needs of a centrally planned economy made the USSR an ideal user of electronic data-processing. To this end the Soviets developed two all-purpose machines called Ural and Minsk.

Minsk is a smoky, industrial city in the heart of European USSR about halfway between Warsaw and Moscow. Because of its armaments industry, it is closed to all foreigners. The Ordzhonikidze electronics plant – named after Serge Ordzhonikidze, a comrade-in-arms of Joseph Stalin – developed the first Minsk machines in 1962 under the direction of the Radio Ministry. The all-purpose Minsk-2 and Minsk-22 were the first Eastern-bloc computers to be produced in large quantities. The Ural series, tailored specifically to the needs of state planners, was developed three years later in Penza, also under the direction of the Radio Ministry. Between 1962 and 1975, some 2,000 Minsk and roughly 500 Ural computers were produced in the USSR. Most of them are on-line today.

Both computer lines, however, soon developed serious flaws. In comparison to Western products, the electronics were primitive, susceptible to breakdown and cumbersome to operate. The Minsk computers, for example, could process words only in predetermined 37-bit combinations, which prevented the use of versatile software. Memory storage was severely limited and difficult to access. Brand-new computers were often discovered to be defective before they were even installed, returning to the factory never to be seen again.

Unable to get satisfaction from plant management, computer-users often took their criticisms to the Communist Party and numerous articles were soon appearing in Soviet trade journals and magazines criticizing the Ural and Minsk machines. It was difficult to feed information into them, they complained, and information once stored was nearly impossible to retrieve. One article in the economic magazine *Sotsialisticheskaya Industriya* described the chaos caused by a Ural computer at the Charkover Kirover Turbine Works, where 'as a result of poor preparation the computer was on-line for a total of only 1½ hours a day'.

When complaints in the Soviet Union hit the public press, things are bad. And they were. *Pravda* compared the Ural-14 computers delivered to the Moscow Transportation Ministry to a six-cylinder engine that has four malfunctioning cylinders: 'Some computers have two memory circuits, others only one; some are delivered with a magnetic drum, others without a magnetic drum. It is not even possible to develop common programs that can be used interchangeably between the different machines. Is this what they call effective technology?'

Magnetic tapes were so unreliable that important data had to be recorded three times – an original plus two safety copies – thereby ying up limited computer capacity more than ever. Even then, information could not be stored for more than a month without loss. To avoid these problems technicians generally reverted to old-fashioned punch cards to feed data into their computers. Due to poor-quality Soviet paper the cards often got stuck in the sorting machines. The rough-hewn raw material was quickly dubbed 'Russian birch bark' by East German technicians. Magnetic hard disks and floppies were then unknown in the East.

Meanwhile, in the West the electronic age was rapidly becoming reality. The stars of Silicon Valley were making their products smaller, faster and cheaper by the day. Everyone in America – from multinational banking establishments down to small-town hardware stores – was getting into the computer swing. International Business Machines had already produced 35,000 units of their IBM-360 series. Their engineers, too, had run into countless quirks and quagmires while developing the new computer line. But IBM research teams profited from the flexibility of the free-market system. Their field representatives were in constant contact with buyers – reporting operating deficiencies and customer suggestions back to the home office, where corrections were incorporated immediately into the design of future models. Under heavy pressure from growing and aggressive competition, Western managers were forced to streamline manufacturing processes, improve product reliability and reduce customer costs.

The Minsk and Ural computer plants had no comparable system. In fact, under normal circumstances their managers never even learned whether customers were satisfied or not. A Soviet buyer, who generally has to endure a very long wait before he receives his purchase, is not likely to complain about poor quality. He knows that to return faulty equipment means an even longer wait. If the worst comes to the worst, his complaint – and his purchase – could disappear for ever in the Soviet bureaucracy. In the USSR it is better to keep what you have and make the best of it.

Even if a user suggestion did reach the company – or a plant engineer recommended a cost-cutting manufacturing improvement – the chances were that the suggestion would go unheeded. Innovations meant nothing but headaches for Soviet managers. They orientated themselves on the rigid production goals set down by the central authorities at Gosplan. The Soviets did have a bonus system established to motivate plant managers. But owing to the Soviet obsession with statistics, the system rewarded only the quantities produced. Quality didn't count, at least financially, so a Soviet plant manager would tend to ignore it. He did not care if his computer developed a flaw within months of leaving the plant, as long as his production statistics looked good. He may not even have cared if it worked at all. Changes, even minor but essential improvements, only threatened to disrupt his pre-set production schedule – and that could cost him his Gosplan bonus.

The centralized distribution of raw materials and resources, which could function reasonably well in some areas of the economy, was having disastrous effects in the rapidly growing electronics industry.

By the middle of the 1960s, the failure of the Minsk and Ural computers could no longer be ignored. In the official Soviet press, which otherwise took every opportunity to praise the glorious achievements of the socialist state, Party apologists were sent scrambling for excuses: 'The construction of electronic computers,' A. Dorodnizhyn was soon explaining in *Pravda*, 'began with a lag of five years as compared with the United States. This was caused by losses and difficulties incurred by us during and immediately following the war.'

Up to this point, the Soviets had relied on their own resourcefulness. Software specialists had developed programs like Lyapas, Refal and Epsilon, which in Western estimates were not without promise. Hardware was based entirely on original Soviet designs. A total of sixty different computer models came out of Soviet electronics plants between 1959 and 1970, so statistics were looking good. The trouble was, most of them were handmade prototypes that functioned poorly. Less than twenty models were mass-produced (in quantities of more than 100).

Hopes that Soviet science would somehow bridge the technology gap with the West had foundered miserably. The Soviets were missing one of the most significant revolutions of the time, and the military implications were enormous. The Kremlin leadership pondered the problem at the highest level. Several leading scientists were dismissed from their posts. But the search for scapegoats wouldn't suffice. Something had to be done.

On a cold winter afternoon in 1968 the top members of the entire Soviet electronics industry gathered in the computer metropolis of Minsk. It was 14 February and Aleksei Kosygin was about to make a speech. The Soviet Prime Minister had recently returned from a visit to the factories of Elliot Computer Limited in London. In fact, he had been intensively studying the ways of the West for several years. Kosygin had decided on a bold course of action. What he was about to say would not be popular, especially among the electronics bosses assembled before him. More importantly, he knew his speech would stir great controversy in the Kremlin. But he saw no alternative. He stepped before the communist managers and praised the achievements of the class enemy.

'In the capitalist system,' Kosygin began, 'monopolies are forced to wage a sharp fight for profit, to react quickly to the demands of the consumer, to introduce modern technology and to seek the most rational forms of productive organization. On our side, it would be short-sighted not to make use of the most modern foreign developments in science and technology. We should take every opportunity to acquire licences and work at intensifying the use of those licences we possess in order to further the progress of our own industry.'

Kosygin, who later became a principal architect of the policy of détente, was the first Politburo member openly to advocate increased dependence on Western technology. At the time, the Politburo was undertaking a high-level review of the scientific and technological situation of the Soviet Union for its new Five-Year Plan (1971-5). The debate sparked that winter day in Minsk continued at the 23rd Party Congress in Moscow a few months later.

'We could profit from the purchase of licences, instead of solving the problems ourselves,' the pragmatic Prime Minister argued again. 'The acquisition of patent rights would help us save hundreds of million roubles on scientific-research costs in the coming five years.'

Kosygin's move challenged functionaries with vested interests in the Soviet bureaucracy, awakening old prejudices and injuring the national pride of many Party members. Some rose to debate him. The policies he was advocating, they contended, had a high price. Copying Western technology meant limping behind it. If the USSR were to consent to such a scheme, it could cost Soviet science a decade. Among Kosygin's vocal opponents was his Politburo rival Leonid Brezhnev.

'Certain officials clearly underestimate the achievements of scientific-technological thought in the socialist world,' Brezhnev countered. 'And the same people are inclined to exaggerate the achievements of science and technology in the capitalist world.' Appealing to the entrenched Stalinists of the old guard, the square-faced Soviet leader argued that the period of Western economic expansion had peaked. A capitalist crisis of major proportions was approaching. Within a few years, he hoped, Soviet science would be able to bridge the gap with America on its own.

His arguments were popular and they carried the day. But Brezhnev would soon be forced to recognize the wisdom of the course plotted by Aleksei Kosygin, and he would later follow it down the road to détente.

The Soviet Union not only had the technological prowess of the West to fear. Its Eastern partners had developed impressive computer projects of their own, which were threatening Moscow's position of leadership within the Eastern bloc. Czechoslovakian and Romanian industry had advanced to being net exporters of electronics equipment. Considering the strategic and economic implications of this vital industry, Moscow was growing increasingly uneasy. This, combined with the arguments outlined by Kosygin, gave birth to the largest and by far the most successful line of Soviet computers, later dubbed Ryad.

The plan called for a unified computer concept throughout the Eastern bloc, and with it Moscow wanted to kill two birds with one stone. By binding its allies to a Soviet computer line, Moscow hoped to stifle the neighbouring competition and strengthen its own economic position within the Eastern bloc. At the same time, the standardization was aimed at re-enforcing military ties within the Warsaw Pact.

But this time, instead of relying on Soviet science for a solution, the USSR turned its attention to the capitalist camp, where IBM was enjoying such eye-opening success with its 360 series. They decided to steal it. The Ryad project was entrusted to a renowned and loyal Soviet scientist named A.M. Larionov. The Soviet electronics industry entered phase two.

When he took charge of the Ryad programme, Comrade Larionov was well aware that duplicating the American system would cement the US lead for years to come. But the advantages were enormous: there were no research risks, since the system had been tried and proven in the West; development costs had already been paid (by IBM); and should Soviet science have difficulty developing peripherals (printers, monitors, disk-drives, etc.), they could always buy them in the West.

The biggest savings, however, were to be made in the software field. Western companies had already developed computer programs for the S/360 valued at billions of dollars. And software at that time, stored on magnetic tapes and disks, had a very attractive technical trait: just like a tape cassette, it could be easily copied. One had only to 'borrow' the originals, which should be easy for the KGB and the GRU.

The Eastern bloc standardization programme was first mentioned publicly in the trade magazine *Woprossy Ekonomiki* in 1966: 'Soviet economists face a grandiose task: the creation of an automated system for the optimal control and planning of the nation's economy. The technical basis must be a standardized state network of computer centres.' At a secret electronics institute not far from the shipyards of the Red Fleet in Severodonetsk, work was soon under way on the first IBM imitation.

The upwardly compatible M-1000, M-2000 and M-3000 Soviet computers developed there in 1966-7 by Minpribor used IBM-like 8-bit bytes. Technicians translated the original IBM instruction manuals verbatim into Russian for distribution to the users of the new Soviet machines. But the computer copies didn't work as well as their American counterparts. The integrated circuits built by Minpribor were deficient and the project in Severodonetsk ended in failure.

In 1968, after the sad demise of its own national project, Moscow turned to the expertise of its communist partners. Each member country in the Eastern trade association Comecon was asked to contribute research time and personnel to the Soviet initiative. But the satellite states balked and negotiations turned turbulent. Language barriers, wariness of new technology and the usual political sensitivities all played a role. But there was another snag. Considerable vested interest was at stake: Moscow's neighbours were all profiting from a booming co-operation with the West.

Hungary: in the 1960s, the French Compagnie Internationale de l'Informatique (CII) sold licences for its Iris-50 and Iris-80 computers to the Videoton factory in Budapest. The Videoton versions, dubbed IMG-810 and IMG-830, were built with 90 per cent Western components. A later model, introduced in 1973, was a licensed version of the French Mitra-15 computer.

Romania: Bucharest had also received French help for its computer industry, and was busily building the Iris-50s and Iris-80s in its Cietc plant. Under the Romanian name Felix, the computers were selling well in the Eastern bloc. A joint venture, Rom Control Data, was founded together with the American electronics giant CDC on 4 April 1973.

Bulgaria: The Bulgarian company ZIT had started producing electronic components in 1964, also with French support. Additional licences for a Japanese computer line were obtained in 1969.

Czechoslovakia: with help from Bull/General Electric the Czech ZPA electronics works at Cakovice were building the US-designed Gamma-140/145 computer. They called their version Tesla.

Poland: International Computers Limited of Great Britain had trained 5,000 Polish technicians at the Mera-Elwro plant in Wroclaw, where the Polish Odra computer was rolling off the assembly lines – built with Western hardware and designed for Western software. The Merex-100 was equipped with a Honeywell keyboard, microprocessors from Intel and Texas Instruments and a mosaic printer from Logabox.

East Germany: specialists at the Robotron computer works in Dresden were intensively investigating the compatibility of Western integrated circuits and their own Eastern hardware. In 1976 they published numerous studies involving Intel-8080, Intel-8008, Texas Instruments TI-7400 and Zilog Z-80 microchips, which by then had already been integrated into East German computer systems on a large scale.

Obviously, these countries were less than enthusiastic about the Soviet overtures. They did not want to sarifice their promising lines, outdated by Western standards but considerably better than many roughshod Soviet electronic wares. Nor did they wish to give up their modest export earnings which allowed them room to manoeuvre within the Comecon association. But that was, of course, the Soviet intention: 'brotherly solidarity', Moscow emphasized, required that the new computers be built under Soviet direction.

Resistance to Kremlin coercion is traditionally short-lived in the Eastern bloc, and so it was in this case. Despite strong protests, the Ryad norm was adopted in 1968.

The interest of Comrade Larionov and his Ryad computer team centred on East Germany. At the Robotron computer works in Dresden, diligent German experts had been working on a copy of the IBM System 360 for some time. The Dresden design thieves had already succeeded in producing a passable copy of the IBM-1401 computer and their chances of success looked considerably better than at Severodonetsk, where the Soviets themselves had failed.

The German Robotron model R-40, then under construction, was completely IBM-compatible: from architecture through peripherals right down to the IBM operating system DOS. Most of the integrated circuits used were German-made TTL types duplicated from Texas Instruments originals (series TI-7400). In the late 1960s East German spies had been systematically smuggling IBM System 360 prototypes out of the West. Several examples of these operations are described in Chapter 5. By 1970, according to N. C. Davis of the CIA's Office of Scientific Intelligence, the East Germans had acquired, dismantled and reverse-engineered a good dozen of them.

Soviet engineers at the Ordzhonikidze works in Minsk, who had continued their own efforts to produce a passable IBM imitation, came up with yet another computer model. Only a few, however, were actually built, and in 1972, when the first German Robotron machines began hitting the market, most of the Soviet models were already back at the factory for 'adjustments'. They had failed again.

By 1973 the Robotron machines were in mass production, rolling from Dresden assembly lines at a rate of 80 to 100 units per year. They weren't about to overtake IBM, but it was a reasonable start. The East German computer was assigned the Soviet type number 'ES-1040', and quickly became a key machine in the Ryad series.

The American company Control Data later managed to purchase one of the East German Ryads and sent it to their Minneapolis laboratories for testing. Their analysis provided the first close look at the internal workings of an Eastern-bloc computer. Unsurprisingly, it was discovered to be fully compatible with the IBM model System 360-50. In fact, it was a copy – if an imperfect one. The power demands of the memory system were roughly double that of the original, so that the computer had to be run way under capacity to avoid overheating. Storage and peripheral capabilities were well below US standards.

Despite all its limitations, the Ryad-1 received rave reviews in the Eastern press. By 1974 production was in full swing and dozens of units were going on-line throughout the East. But while Soviet science was basking in the success of their somewhat dated coputer copy, IBM managers in New York were enjoying their fourth successful year with the next generation of machines. And Eastern agents were hard on their heels.

The phone rang at the State Department in Washington.

Soviet Ambassador Anatoli Dobrynin was on the line, asking if he could bring a 'personal guest' over. According to Dobrynin, the Soviet visitor just happened to be in the United States seeing his daughter and would like to discuss the use of computers in the American foreign service. US diplomat Nathaniel Davis, who arranged security clearance for the unexpected visit, would later remember the astute attention paid and the sharp questions asked by the white-haired Party functionary he escorted on a brief tour of the State Department facilities: 'He impressed me as being an influential man.'

Indeed he was. His name was Konstantin Chernenko.

At the time of his inconspicuous appearance in Washington, no one could have guessed that Chernenko would one day assume command of the Soviet Union. Nor could anyone have guessed the importance Moscow attached to its newest computer development – a Soviet carbon copy of the latest IBM line. 'Big Blue' called its US original the IBM System 370; the Soviets dubbed their copy simply 'Ryad-2'. Moscow knew that the new IBM computer would become a standard machine of the Pentagon. The Red Army wanted it as well.

Again it was the counterfeit specialists at Robotron in Dresden who were entrusted with the project. By the time the new American model had been introduced in June 1970 they had already gathered enough contraband to start their work: prototypes of the IBM System 370 models 125, 135, 145, 155 and 158. They also had large quantities of peripherals, spare parts, software and maintenance manuals. Again they painstakingly dismantled the original machines, carefully analysing and reverse-engineering them for their own design. Again they translated original IBM manuals verbatin into Russian and German, distributing them with their imitations. By mid-1978, Ryad-2 was ready for the market.

The following table shows the Ryad machines and their IBM counterparts in detail:

Copied Computers and their Western Originals

C-256 (Romania)	Licence: Iris-50/80 (France)
IMG-810 (Hungary)	Licence: Iris-50 (France)
IMG-830 (Hungary)	Licence: Iris-80 (France)
Felix C-256 (Romania)	Licence: Iris-80 (France)
Tesla-200 (Czechoslovakia)	Licence: Bull-GE Gamma-140 (France)

Odra-1300 (Poland)	Licence: ICL-Software (Great Britain)
ES-1010 (Hungary)	Licence: Mitra-15 (France)
ES-1020 (USSR and Bulgaria)	Copy: IBM 360 (USA)
ES-1030 (USSR)	Copy: IBM 360 (USA)
ES-1040 (East Germany)	Copy: IBM 360-50 (USA)
ES-1050 (USSR)	Copy: IBM 360 (USA)
Robotron 300 Series (E. Germany)	Copy: IBM 1401 (USA)
Robotron R-21 (E. Germany)	Copy: IBM 360 (USA)
ES-1025 (Czechoslovakia)	Copy: IBM 370-125 (USA)
ES-1035 (USSR and Bulgaria)	Copy: IBM 370-135 (USA)
ES-1065 (USSR)	Copy: IBM 3033 (USA)
ES-1055 (East Germany)	Copy: IBM 370-158 (USA)
SM4-20 (Czechoslovakia)	Copy: PDP-11 from DEC (USA)
SAM-80 Minicomputer (Hungary)	Components: Intel 8080 A (USA)
EMU-11 Minicomputer (Hungary)	Components: Intel Series 3000 (USA)
Fellas-Systems (Romania)	Components: Intel-8080, Signetics 2650 (USA)
Inteldigit PI (Poland)	Components: Chip Intel 8080-A (USA)
Mera-2500 (Poland)	Components: Chip Intel 8008 (USA)
Merex-100 (Poland)	Components: keyboard from Honeywell (USA); mosaic printer from Logabox (USA); chips from Intel and TI (USA)

From a Soviet viewpoint, the advantages of the new system were obvious: spare parts were interchangeable should Soviet ones fail; peripherals could be purchased in the West should Eastern designs prove inadequate; and software could be begged, borrowed or stolen at will. If need be, the entire system could be replaced with a US substitute, for example in the strategic air defence rings surrounding Moscow, where IBM 370/S computers – not Ryads – today stand guard.

Despite all the secrecy shrouding its acquisition, once the Soviets possessed the new computer line they displayed it with pride. They were hoping to sell over 500 units to Eastern bloc and Third World customers, and Ryad machines were shown at every opportunity in electronics exhibitions and trade fairs around the world. At the extravagant Exhibit of Economic Achievement – a Smithsonian-like museum in Moscow – the Soviet electronics industry proudly displayed dozens of new computer desk-top calculators, available in the West for a few dollars, and the Ryads on display were little more than a shell. Western businessmen noted that the internal electronics had been replaced by IBM equipment. Moscow's faith in its own engineers had limitations.

Long before the first Ryad models appeared publicly Kremlin strategists had begun quietly plotting the next phase of their operation.

In 1971 at the electronics trade fair Systemotechnika in Moscow, Eastern managers surprised their Western colleagues with unusually frank remarks about the inadequacies of their own products. They openly admitted an enormous technology gap and acknowledged that it could be bridged only with widespread Western imports. Before this time, Westerners had heard similar admissions only at hotel bars after heavy vodka consumption. Now they were being made publicly in the speeches and talks of official industry spokesmen.

The candid comments of the Soviet electronics representatives were no accident. They were the first step in a carefully orchestrated foreign-trade offensive that had been approved at the highest levels within the ruling Communist Party of the Soviet Union.

'Comrades,' Leonid Brezhnev announced to members of the 24th Party Congress on 3 March of that year, 'we now face a task of great historical import: we must combine the accomplishments of the scientific-technological revolution with the advantages of the socialist economic system and develop our own socialist forms of combining science and production.'

Brezhnev had come a long way since the 23rd Party Congress five years before, when he had violently opposed increased dependence on Western technology. Majorities had shifted within the Kremlin leadership and the great computer debate had long since decided in favour of the Kosygin faction. By March 1971, when Brezhnev proclaimed the 'historic task', expansion of East-West trade had become an official Party objective. Nikita Khrushchev's old battle-cry, that the Soviet Union would economically bury capitalism by 1980, was discreetly forgotten, echoing hollowly through the halls of the Kremlin along with other obsolete socialist slogans of the past. Western technology was to assume an ever larger role in the Five-Year Plans of the Soviet Union, and 1971 marked a turning point.

At the time of the 24th Party Congress, the Kremlin had come to appreciate capitalist computers and the vital role they played in Soviet industry and the army. But the painstaking process of stealing and reverse-engineering them was proving inadequate. Not only was the illegal acquisition of prototypes an expensive affair – drawing heavily on precious hard-currency reserves – but besides, Soviet engineers were unfit for the task. A number of them had been demoted or dismissed after the Severodonetsk fiasco but there was no assurance that future efforts would be any more successful. The technology of the 1970s could not be mastered simply by reading foreign patent-applications or twiddling the knobs on a smuggled machine. Manufacturing in microelectronics was too exacting, the equipment needed too delicate for the roughshod Soviet industry of the time. State-of-the-art machines had become so sensitive that vapour from the floor wax could cause a breakdown; components were so tiny they were measured in microns (a micron is approximately one-hundreth the width of a human hair).

To keep abreast of developments, the leadership concluded, the time was ripe for phase three of the electronics industry of the USSR: the manufacture of Western forgeries on original Western equipment – to be purchased outright on the open market. The Soviets needed direct access to the all-important know-how. The capitalists, Lenin had taught, would sell the rope with which to hang themselves. To buy that rope, the Kremlin needed détente – and the road to détente led through Western Europe.

'There can be no doubt,' Kosygin explained to the assembled delegates, 'the conclusion of the Conference for Security and Co-operation in Europe will build confidence and smooth the way for widespread scientific and technical co-operation.' Moscow was prepared to make human-rights concessions in Helsinki in order to gain access to desperately needed Western equipment.

Fourteen months after those words were spoken 'Air Force One' touched down at Moscow's Vnukovo II Airport carrying the President of the United States. West Germany – with the approval of both superpowers – had already signed a whole string of trade accords with Eastern bloc nations, including the USSR. Chancellor Willy Brandt's Ostpolitik, aimed at reconciling the two Germanies, had proved susceptible to the rewards offered by Moscow and had already secured itself a place in history. Richard Nixon was coming to the Soviet capital to usher in the détente era at summit level.

Under an ostentatiously dignified glass chandelier in the Vladimir Hall of the Kremlin, Nixon and Nikolai Podgorny put their signatures to the first of several historic trade documents that were to be signed during that visit. Soviet officials present at the ceremonies applauded enthusiastically. Those who wouldn't have applauded, like the Ukrainian Politburo hawk Piotr Shelest, were absent. Brezhnev had banished his sceptics to the provinces shortly before Nixon's arrival. Crimean champagne was soon flowing generously, as American and Soviet leaders mingled, patting backs and smiling for the photographers. At one point, after a chat with Henry Kissinger, Leonid Brezhnev turned to look for other partners to toast – and collided with a waiter, spilling his drink and soaking his elegant black dinner-jacket and trousers. After a second's pause, the Soviet leader broke into a hearty Russian laugh, and those around him joined in. They had reason to: 23 May 1972 was an important day for the USSR.

As Western correspondents reached for the phones to report the results of the historic East-West summit, they noticed the words 'Feuer/Notruf', which is German for fire/emergency, on the dials. The newly installed telephones at the Intourist Hotel in Moscow had been imported from West Germany – a symbolic precedent for the age that had just begun.

Before the year was out, the USSR had nearly tripled its legal imports of Western computers – from $10 million worth in 1971 to $27 million worth in 1972. In that single year it imported more electronics than in the two decades of the 1950s and 1960s combined. Their Eastern bloc neighbours contributed an additional $52 million of business (including eleven main-frame computers at an average price of $1.5 million each). And things were just getting started.

In 1973 total Eastern computer imports rose to $92 million, and by 1975 they had skyrocketed to over $200 million. Staansaab of Sweden sold electronic radar systems to Moscow airport (price: 300 million Swedish krona); CIT-Acatel of France sold computer-guided oil-distribution systems to Rostock in East Germany (price: 100 million French francs). In Britain the Soviets purchased fifteen Argus-700 computers for a truck factory in Nizhnekomsk, and in West Germany they bought an entire centre for automated technology. But the Europeans weren't the ones who profited most.

At the advent of détente, the embargo policies of NATO were undergoing a major review. The Paris-based Co-ordinating Committee for East-West Trade (CoCom), established by the Alliance in the Cold War to protect sensitive technology, was under heavy pressure from the Europeans to relax its restrictive trade policies. At first, Washington resisted. But soon American companies were scenting the sweet smell of big money in the virgin and virtually insatiable markets of the East. When things started to soften, they pushed forward with aggressive marketing strategies of their own. Within a few short years, over half of all computers going to the Soviets went directly from the United States. An additional 30 per cent were US-made computers routed through other countries, bringing the total American share of the Eastern electronics trade to an unbelievable 80 per cent!

IBM, obviously, attracted the most interest and 'Big Blue' eventually opened its own offices in the Soviet capital, delivering an IBM 370-145 computer to Intourist and an IBM 370-158 to the Kama River project. Thomas J. Watson, who was chairman of the board at IBM, was named US Ambassador to Moscow.

Sperry Rand also maintained offices there, signing a trade agreement with the State Committee for Science and Technology and even training Soviet technicians on modern computer units. One Univac-1106 was sold to the Ministry of Civilian Aeronautics, another to the Giprokauchuk Institute for Synthetic Rubber.

Control Data delivered Cyber-73 computers to, among others, the Institute for Geophysical Exploration and the Soviet Ministry of Technology.

International Telephone and Telegraph (ITT) contributed satellite technology and electronics components. Honeywell, National Cash Register, Hewlett-Packard, CBS and General Electric were all in business with Moscow, as were Marconi in England, Nippon Electric in Japan, CII in France and Siemens in Germany.

By 1978 the Eastern bloc had acquired some 1,300 Western computer systems valued at a total of $639 million – and the acquisitions were all absolutely legal.

Computer Imports to the USSR and Eastern Europe between 1972 and 1978 (in $ millions)

1972

USSR:	27.2
Eastern Europe:	51.8
total:	79.0

1973

USSR:	19.3
Eastern Europe:	72.5
total:	91.8

1974

USSR:	22.5
Eastern Europe:	96.9
total:	119.4

1975

USSR:	63.9
Eastern Europe:	148.7
total:	212.6

1976
USSR:	49.0
Eastern Europe:	86.7
total:	135.7

1977
USSR:	63.1
Eastern Europe:	109.1
total:	172.2

1978
USSR:	100.0
Eastern Europe:	119.1
total:	219.0

(*Source*: Kenneth Tasky, 'Soviet Technology Gap and Dependence on the West: The Case of Computers', *Soviet Economy in a Time of Change*, Joint Economic Committee of Congress, Washington DC, 5 October 1979.)

Dramatic as they are, the figures in the table reflect only a fraction of the total West-East electronics trade actually taking place. Aside from KGB and GRU black-market dealings which continued unabated, other Western companies preferred not to have their Eastern business recorded publicly. Since no regulations required them to register their transactions with the authorities, they do not appear in official statistics.

In spite of the enormous quantities of modern computers imported by the USSR, shopkeepers and accountants across the land continued to tally their receipts on primitive wooden abacuses. Neither electronic games nor quartz watches, video recorders nor modern kitchen appliances were made available to the average Soviet consumer. Those experts familiar with Moscow's system of priorities (*Zelenaya Ulitsa*, or 'the green street') had few doubts about where the most sophisticated Western equipment was going.

But in the West, the military potential of the now booming Soviet high-tech trade was either played down or completely ignored. Optimists of the day hoped that exposure to the comforts of modern-day Western products would awaken Soviet desires, forcing more money into the consumer industry and somehow arousing irresistible grass-roots pressures for greater freedom. The two opposing political systems would grow closer together. A serious examination of internal Soviet thinking of the time should have discouraged such ideas. The ink on the Nixon/Brezhnev trade documents had hardly dried when ideologists at the official Party newspaper *Kommunist* began beating their drums:

'In the West, there are those wishing to confuse the international policy of détente with a merging of the two political systems. This fashionable ploy, taken in the evil intention of influencing uneducated and naïve people, is founded in lies. No! Communists will never sacrifice their ideals. We have always fought for them and will continue to do so – until the worldwide triumph of communism.'

By the middle of the 1970s, Western trade had become a cornerstone of economic planning in the USSR. The increase in high-tech imports permitted drastic reductions in Soviet research and development budgets. Growth of scientific and technological expenditure dropped from 17 per cent in 1970 to under 5 per cent by 1974 – the lowest in over two decades. Despite these enormous savings some voices were heard, especially within the ranks of the Red Army, expressing concern that the USSR was risking its strategic independence. In April 1976 Brezhnev felt compelled to speak a reassuring word to the military. In a rare appearance before Warsaw Pact senior officers he explained:

'We communists must co-operate with the capitalists for a while. We need their agriculture and we need their technology. But we shall continue our massive armaments build-up and by the middle of the 1980s we will be able to return to a much more aggressive foreign policy, in order to win the upper hand in our relations with the West.'

But inevitably co-operation leads to some degree of dependence, and the Soviet shopping spree was exacting a high price at home. Necessary investment in a number of industries was being either postponed or cancelled entirely. By 1978, for example, nearly a quarter of all Soviet money for the machine-tool sector was being spent in the West. Other high-trade areas such as oil-prospecting and petrochemicals were also being neglected. But the protests of worried critics in the Kremlin were quickly overruled, primarily because the purchases were being financed with generous government subsidies and low-interest bank loans from the capitalists. In the view of most Soviet planners, it was just too good to be true.

By 1980 *Pravda* was boasting that the USSR produced 'hundreds of thousands of microprocessors in ten different designs, as well as thousands of microcomputers and millions of components in thirteen different types'. *Pravda* neglected, however, to mention the origin of this technology: built under Western licences, often under Western supervision and using Western components. Eastern bloc engineers were being trained by Control Data and Sperry Rand. They were using designs from Honeywell and IBM, chips from Intel and Texas Instruments, peripheral equipment from Motorola and

Logabox and software from the Digital Equipment Corporation or Micropro. Some of it was stolen; much of it was purchased openly; all of it was of foreign origin.

In the end, the Soviets had become, as one Western expert put it, 'computer junkies', hopelessly dependent on imported technology. The more they got, the more they wanted.

The commotion when the supply lines were severed was considerable.

The first signs of change came with the warm summer breezes of 1978 when Jimmy Carter cancelled export licences for a Sperry Univac main-frame computer. The Univac-1100 had been ordered by Tass for its press centre at the Olympic Games. But, according to the White House, there were insufficient guarantees that the machine would not later be diverted to the military.

The cancellation was serious news for the Soviets. They had been banking on Olympic goodwill for permission to import an entire fleet of new Western computers, hoping that CoCom would relax regulations even further for the international sports event. They needed Western electronics to cope with some 200,000 Olympic guests expected in Moscow for the games – and for the $200 to $300 million in coveted hard currency they would be bringing. The Soviet Ryads available on-line would hardly do the job. As with many foreign-policy decisions of the Carter White House, this one, too, was reversed. Within months the President had reviewed his decision and approved the computer export.

For Moscow, it was a first warning. In the autumn of 1979, when Kremlin leaders were planning the invasion of Afghanistan, they must have realized what consequences their action could have for trade with the West. Perhaps Politburo hawks, long opposed to détente, wanted to provoke a break. Aleksei Kosygin had not been seen publicly since October of that year. Whatever the case, the Soviets decided to launch the Christmas attack and nine days later, on 4 January 1980, Jimmy Carter appeared on US television to announce that embargo regulations were being immediately tightened. When Ronald Reagan took office a year later it was abundantly clear that Western supermarkets for sophisticated technology would be closing their doors to the Soviets – perhaps for ever.

The year 1981 was one of hectic activity within the Eastern bloc. At the 10th Party Congress of the East German Communists, for example, Erich Honecker proclaimed an ambitious ten-point programme intended to enable his country 'to draw the bulk of its microelectronic needs from domestic production by 1985'. Honecker's list of goals was long, his deadline short: within five years, East Germany was expected to double its production of electrical components and triple its production of integrated circuits. The production of industrial robots was to increase from 9,000 to 45,000 and, at the same time, a new computer generation was to be developed. It was a desperate programme with no realistic chance of success.

Other Comecon nations announced equally ambitious, and equally illusory, programmes. In Moscow, a high-level government comission was established to seek answers to the Washington freeze. Despite public statements to the contrary, US high-tech trade embargoes had hit hard. By the middle of the year, Western visitors to Moscow were witnessing a heated dispute within the electronics industry. Officials wanted to drop Western architectural models as quickly as possible. The German trade paper *Computerwoche* reported: 'When they speak of dropping Western architecture, they mean – above all – abandoning IBM.'

Easier said than done. With the Ryad line they had committed their commercial electronics industry to the American design, and not only with their Ryad-1 and Ryad-2 computers. A new Ryad-3, also based on IBM, was so far down the road that an architectural about-face was practically impossible. A sudden switch from IBM hardware and software to another system would cost the Comecon countries years, probably decades.

News from New York was soon compounding the Soviet predicament. Engineers at 'Big Blue' had just completed development of a new series: The 3081 Series. As a result, management at headquarters was announcing that they would be discontinuing the Systems 370 and, at the same time, the IBM operating system DOS/360. The consequences for Moscow were no less than catastrophic. DOS/360, or the Soviet carbon copy thereof (dubbed DOS/ES), was the basis of Ryad programming. Without IBM up front, socialist countries would be on their own for all future software developments, working with an alien system that the West had declared obsolete.

Ten years before, Leonid Brezhnev had termed the scientific-technological revolution a main battlefield in the class struggle with imperialism. 'We stand at the beginning of a long and hard struggle,' he had said. 'And we are determined to fight it earnestly, proving the superiority of the socialist system.'

The victory of socialism had fizzled. Instead of battling the capitalists, the Kremlin had gone shopping in their supermarkets. The computer gap was greater than ever before: between 1974 and 1981 the Soviets had managed to increase the number of computers installed from 12,500 to 20,000. But in the same period, US on-line machines had grown from 207,000 to 325,000. When the large-scale Soviet purchasing offensive came to a screeching halt, old-guard Stalinists saw their worst fears verified. They demanded a return to methods and means that the Soviet state mastered better. The hour of the agents had struck.

Source Notes

MESM and BESM: S.E. Goodman, 'Computing and the Development of the Soviet Economy', *Soviet Economy in a Time of Change*, Joint Economic Committee of Congress, Washington DC, 10/10/1979.

Ural and Minsk: *Frankfurter Allgemeine Zeitung*, 2/11/1982; *Pravda*, 5/1/1971, as quoted in *UdSSR*, January 1971; 'Ein Jahrzehnt hinter dem Westen', *Der Spiegel*, no. 52/1975.

Charkover Kirover Turbine Works: *Sotsialisticheskaya Industriya*, 20/10/1973, as quoted in *UdSSR*, November 1973.

Pravda on electronics gap: Klaus Krakat, 'Die Entwicklung der elektronischen Rechentechnik in den RGW Ländern', *FS-Analysen*, Forschungsstelle für Gesamtdeutsche Wirtschaftliche und Soziale Fragen, West Berlin, March 1982, p. 63.

Andropov's speech 1983: *Neues Deutschland*, 16/6/1983.

Eastern software: *Dallas Times Herald*, 18/8/1983; *Business Week*, 4/4/1983; Dorothy Nelkin, 'Intellectual Property: The Control of Scientific Information', *Science*, 14/5/1982; *New York Times*, 27/11/1983.

Kosygin in Minsk: Kenneth Tasky, 'Eastern Europe: Trends in Imports of Western Computer Equipment and Technology', *East European Economic Assessment*, Joint Economic Committee of Congress, 10/7/1981, Washington DC.

Infighting between Brezhnev and Kosygin: a complete collection of publicly available quotes can be found in Bruce Parrott, *Politics and Technology in the Soviet Union*, MIT Press, Cambridge, MA, 1983. See also: Holland Hunter, 'Soviet Economic Problems and Alternative Policy Responses', *Soviet Economy in a Time of Change*, US Congress, Washington DC, 10/10/1979.

Brezhnev's answer in *Pravda*: Tasky, 'Trends', *op. cit.*; Paul Cocks, 'Rethinking the Organizational Weapon', *World Politics*, January 1980.

Kosygin at the 23rd Party Congress: Eugene Zaleski, and Helgard Wienert, *Technology Transfer between East and West*, OECD, Paris, 1980, p. 158.

Ryad: N.C. Davis, and S.E. Goodman, 'The Soviet Bloc's Unified System of Computers', *Computing Surveys*, 2 June 1978; S.E. Goodman, 'Computing and the Development of the Soviet Economy', *Soviet Economy in a Time of Change*, Joint Economic Committee of Congress, Washington DC, 10/10/79; Kenneth Tasky, 'Soviet Technology Gap and Dependence on the West: The Case of Computers', *Soviet Economy in a Time of Change*, Joint Economic Committee of Congress, Washington DC, 5/10/1979; Richard Judy, 'The Case of Computer Technology',

East-West Trade and the Technology Gap (ed. Stanislaw Wasowski), Praeger Publishers, New York 1970, pp. 43-72; Klaus Krakat, 'Die Entwicklung der elektronischen Rechentechnik in den RGW Ländern im Zeichen der Messen in Leipzig und Hanover', *FS-Analysen*, Forschungsstelle für Gesamtdeutsche Wirtschaftliche und Soziale Fragen, West Berlin, March 1982; *Neue Züricher Zeitung*, 12/9/1981; 'Blick durch die Wirtschaft', *Frankfurter Allgemeine Zeitung*, 23/9/1982; *Tagesspiegel*, 7/8/1981.

Czechoslovakia: 'Co-operation, not competition, in the East', *Mini-Micro Systems*, June 1982; 'Some E. European Firms Woo Western Markets', *Mini-Micro Systems*, June 1982.

East Germany: Klaus Krakat, 'Die Produktion und der Einsatz von Mikroprozessoren in der DDR', *FS-Analysen*, July 1981, p. 82; 'Some E. European Firms woo Western Markets', *Mini-Micro Systems*, June 1982; *Frankfurter Allgemeine Zeitung*, 17/10/1980; 'Einsatz von Robbies', *Computerwoche*, 18/3/1983.

Chernenko in Washington: 'The Quiet Siberian', *Time Magazine*, 27/2/1984.

Systemotechnika and Krakat quote: Krakat, 'Entwicklungen', *op. cit.*

Brezhnev on 3/3/1971: Paul Cocks, 'Rethinking the Organizational Weapon,' *World Politics*, 1980.

Kosygin at the 24th Party Congress: Tasky, 'Soviet Technology Gap', *op. cit.*

Western trade with computers: Klaus Krakat, 'Einseitiger West-Ost Technologie-Transfer zum Vorteil für den Comecon', *FS-Analysen*, West Berlin, April 1981; 'US finds E. Germany a tough market to crack,' *Mini-Micro Systems*, June 1982; Robert J. McMenamin, 'Western Technology and the Soviets in the 1980s', USSR in the 1980s – Economic Growth and the Role of Foreign Trade, NATO Colloquium, Brussels, 17-19 January 1978; John P. Hardt, 'The Role of Western Technology in Soviet Economic Plans', East-West Technological Co-operation, NATO Colloquium, Brussels, 17-19 March 1976, p. 315; Peter Wiles, 'On the Prevention of Technology Transfer', NATO Colloquium, Brussels, 17-19 March 1976. Directorate of Economic Affairs, NATO Information Service. Bruce Parrott, 'Technology and the Soviet System', *op. cit.*

Kommunist: Zaleski et al. *op.cit.*

Brezhnev speech to military: 'Moskaus Griff nach Afghanistan', *Der Spiegel*, 7/1/1980.

Pravda 1980: Krakat, 'Einseitiger', *op.cit.*

Univac–1100: *New York Times*, 3/1/1980; Juliana Geran Pilon, 'Double Dealing', *Reason*, February 1983.

Honecker's list: Krakat, 'Mikroprozessorenin der DDR', *op.cit.*

Abandoning IBM: 'Harte Zeiten für IBM-Nachbauer', *Computerwoche*, 7/8/1981.

Brezhnev's main battlefield: Krakat, 'Einseitiger', *op.cit.*

TWELVE

The Hour of the Agents:
Inside the Machine

'My name is Josef Arkov.' The voice came from an unseen witness behind a smoked-glass screen. It was lying, and the Senators gathered in Room 3302 of the Dirksen Building on Capitol Hill knew it. They listened intently. The man appearing before a Congressional inquiry on technology transfer was a Soviet refugee hiding his true identity to protect his family. He had been warned that Soviet officials from the nearby Embassy occasionally dropped in on public hearings dealing with strategic issues. It was 4 May 1982 and Arkov was the first witness.

'In my plant, as in many other engineering research and development facilities in the Soviet Union, the major emphasis is on military pursuits.' For ten years Arkov had been employed as a high-level engineer in the Soviet military establishment. He was last assigned to a plant where the guidance systems for Soviet missiles were built and his task was to reverse-engineer Western electronics. 'My supervisors made no attempt to be deceptive about what they wanted me to do. I was not to conduct any original research. I was given components and told to copy them.'

While the Western defence industry is widely known to the public, and even photographed by television crews and magazine photographers, comparable institutions in the East are shrouded in secrecy, hermetically sealed off from the rest of Soviet society. In the West, almost nothing is known about the armaments works, laboratories and think-tanks where plans and prototypes for MiG fighters or Backfire bombers, SS-18 nuclear missiles or Typhoon atomic submarines are developed. The activities of the Warsaw Pact war-machine were once described by dissident physicist Andrei Sakharov as 'events unseen by foreign eyes'.

One such place is the city of Zeleenograd, forty miles north-west of Moscow. Surrounded by several rings of minefields, fences and closely guarded gates, Zeleenograd was erected in the early seventies to serve as a kind of Soviet Silicon Valley. For foreigners, the entire city is off-limits. Soviet citizens wishing to work or visit there need special permission from the secret police. Arkov was employed in Zeleenograd, and his eye-witness testimony, later expanded upon in an interview on British television, offers a rare glimpse of the internal workings of the Soviet armaments industry:

Arkov: 'We can see that this military electronic equipment cannot exist without Western technology. Among the most popular integrated circuits produced in the Soviet Union, orientated only for military usage, are their Series 130 and 150. They are direct one-to-one copies of Series 5400 and 7400 from Texas Instruments.'

Question: 'You're saying that these Soviet microchips are exact copies of Texas Instruments chips? Did you see those chips? Did you see that they were identical?'

Arkov: 'I not only saw them. I designed equipment using them.'

When the transcripts of the Senate hearings on technology transfer – including Arkov's testimony – were released in November 1982, economist Anatoli Godakov from the Soviet Embassy arrived on Capitol Hill to pick up several copies.

The Soviet Union is a closed society – isolated from abroad, tightly controlled internally, manipulated by a state press and centrally regulated at all levels. Its border, stretching some 75,000 kilometres across the coastline and countryside of two continents, is closely guarded. Whether approaching from a Warsaw Pact country such as Poland or from NATO territory in Turkey, from a neutral neighbour in Finland or a hostile one in China, one is confronted with the same depressing sight: watch-towers, ploughed earth, minefields and barbed wire.

Casual visitors from the West flying over these fortifications by plane may leave the USSR without ever realizing how little they were actually permitted to see of the country. The list of available tourist attractions may seem almost unlimited. In Moscow or Leningrad, visitors can move about freely. Hundreds of other cities are at their disposal. By train or car, they can travel 6,800 miles across the expansive countryside. On closer examination, however, it becomes clear how strict travel limitations in fact are.

Of the 272 Soviet cities with populations of over 100,000, some 200 are closed to foreigners. Travel by car is limited to specified streets. Guides accompany the few trains that carry tourists. Routes and rest stops are regulated, changes not permitted. In 1972, the entire area east of the Volga was closed to foreigners. On another occasion, it was the area around the Black Sea. Reasons are seldom given. Even Intourist cities such as Kiev, Tallin or Alma Ata may suddenly be declared off-limits, forcing unexpected changes in travel plans.

Even before arriving in the Soviet Union, visitors are subjected to the scrutiny of the secret police. Their visas must be approved weeks in advance, their hotel reservations booked by state agencies, their movements listed in binding itineraries. Wherever a traveller goes, his means of travel, his lodging, even the people he 'accidentally' meets during his stay, can be manipulated at will should Soviet authorities so desire.

The visits of Western trade delegations are subject to particularly meticulous Soviet preparation. Businessmen are often startled to discover that their hosts have extensive dossiers on their companies, with details on company history, liquidity, market position and investment strategy, and on the personal finances and political views of the management. In contrast, Westerners generally know little or nothing about their Soviet counterparts. Contractors working in the USSR often complain that they are unable to obtain necessary names and telephone numbers from the local officials they are dealing with on a project.

The popular view in Western business and banking circles that Soviet industry is in a desperate state, hopelessly dependent on outside aid, is carefully cultivated by the Kremlin leadership – if only to gain access to the billion-dollar loans generously distributed by capitalist financial institutions. Visiting delegations are often shown carefully selected technological goods that will impress upon them the obsolete and underdeveloped condition of the Eastern economy. Considering the general condition of the consumer industry, this is not difficult.

The Soviet obsession with secrecy, by no means limited to foreigners, goes far beyond purely military matters. Soviet law on the subject is unequivocal: 'Important economic information on the wealth of our country – on discoveries, inventions and improvements *of a non-military nature in all areas of science, technology and the economy* – is a government secret.' Thus, the impression Westerners receive of their technology may be seriously misleading.

Several multinational corporations buy top technology from the Soviets. The USSR exports patented pharmaceuticals to chemical giants such as Dupont, Bristol-Myers and 3-M and advanced production-processing to multinational metal corporations such as Kaiser Aluminium and Olin. Engineers at the Perkin Elmar Corporation subscribe to the *Soviet Journal of Spectroscopy* and the Varian Corporation got the idea of using lasers in the production of their microchips from a Soviet lecture in New York.

The oil men of Houston may hold a reputation as the world's best well-drillers, but it was Soviet engineers who sank their bits deeper into the earth's crust than anyone else: over sixteen kilometres into the depths of the Komi Peninsula. Harvard biologist Walter Gilbert was awarded the Nobel Prize for his genetic research on DNA, but his work, as the American scientist later acknowledged, was stimulated by Soviet colleague Andrei Mirzabekov.

The continuous steel casting plant in Novolipetsk and the electroslag melting line in Dneprospetstal are described by John Kiser as 'sophisticated industrial technology at work'. Kiser, a former US Ambassador to Stockholm, completed the first in-depth study of technology being transferred from East to West. Total sales of technology travelling out of the USSR – mostly marketed through the Moscow agency Lizenzintorg – are minimal: roughly 100 licences in the past fifteen years. 'But why should it surprise us,' asks Kiser, 'that the Soviets possess sophisticated technology?'

The Moscovich may be no Mercedes and a Soviet refrigerator hopelessly unable to compete with the products of General Electric or AEG, but Soviet high technology is by no means backward. There is no technology gap between East and West. It exists within Soviet society itself – between the consumer industry, supplying the needs of the general public, and the military-industrial complex, which has enjoyed priority in the Kremlin since the days of Stalin.

While ordinary citizens in the factories and fields of the USSR suffer the hardships of chronic shortages, deficient products and poor planning, top technology is reserved for the electronics laboratories of Zelenograd or the munitions factories of Gorky, the shipyards of the Red Fleet in Sudomekh or the test-flight facilities of the Red Air Force in Vladimirovka. This is where the contraband of the Western embargo-runners is delivered, installed, programmed and repaired: the VAX-780s and PDP-11s, the hardware from Bruchhausen and the software from DeGeyter, the IBM manuals from 'Gerkins' and the voice-scramblers from Batachev.

It is a world where the *crème de la crème* of the Soviet scientific élite is employed – and spoiled with luxurious limousines and dachas. Their offices and labs are furnished with Italian leather armchairs and French lamps, colour-coded desks and costly carpets – ordered in the West and smuggled to the East along with strategic electronic contraband. It is a world no Western visitor will ever see. It is a world never mentioned in *Pravda* or *Isvestia*. And the gatekeeper is an organization with the name Komitet Gosudarstvennoy Bezopasnosti (State Security Committee), better known by its initials, KGB.

The Soviet secret police was founded on 20 December 1917 by Felix Dzerzhinsky, confidant and personal friend of Lenin, who once described the organization as the 'spearhead of the revolution'. The building at No. 22 Lubyanka Street in Moscow, which Dzerzhinsky and his first agents confiscated from the All-Russian Insurance shortly after the revolution, has remained its headquarters. Only the name of the street has been changed. Today it's called Dzerzhinsky Place.

The seven-storey KGB building with its adjoining Lubyanka Prison is situated in the heart of Moscow only two blocks from the Kremlin. Around the corner at Kutovsky Prospekt or, translated Avenue is an apartment complex for high-level Party functionaries, where, among others, Leonid Brezhnev, Yuri Andropov and Konstantin Chernenko have lived.

Two departments of the KGB are best known in the West: the Fifth Directorate, which deals with internal dissidents, and the First Directorate, which runs foreign espionage. But the KGB has numerous other functions and operations. The Second Directorate keeps a watchful eye on the racial, religious – and often rebellious – minorities in the multifaceted Soviet society; the Third Directorate monitors the military. Other departments deal with secret codes, assassinations and *dezinformatsiya*, the fine art of manipulating Western media. A special force of some 300,000 border guards man the watch-towers and minefields on the outer perimeters of the Soviet state.

In short, the KGB is responsible for anything and everything that the Kremlin leadership regards as 'security'. Under the leadership of Lavrenti Beria, the KGB supervised the barbaric purges of Stalin, during which about one million people starved in Soviet concentration camps, another million were shot and countless others died in prison.

At the time of Beria's reign, a young man – son of a railroad worker – was earning his first favours with the secret police. After

Stalin's death in 1953, the young man joined the foreign service and soon became Soviet Ambassador in Budapest, where he played a key role in the bloody suppression of the Hungarian revolution. On 3 November 1956 he invited Defence Minister Pâl Maleter, a leader of the popular uprising, to negotiations in the Soviet Embassy. But instead of meeting a peace delegation, Maleter was confronted with Soviet soldiers who arrested him. The Hungarian hero was later executed. The Ambassador rose to become head of the KGB and later Chairman of the Communist Party and Premier of the USSR. His name was Yuri Andropov.

The KGB has grown steadily since 1917. Shortly after the Second World War political detainees and prisoners of war were forced to build an eight-storey addition to the main building at Dzerzhinsky Place. Soon after, the spacious offices were partitioned into smaller rooms to accomodate the ever-expanding staff. Andropov was the first KGB boss with extensive experience abroad and when he took over the organizaiton he erected a new crescent-shaped concrete and glass buildings on the outskirts of Moscow for the foreign espionage operations of the First Directorate.

This building is now the home of Directorate 'T', which is staffed by highly specialized scientists and engineers from a wide variety of disciplines whose sole task is the illegal procurement of Western high technology.

Almost immediately after taking office, Andropov began recruiting young students from the élite universities for work in Directorate 'T', and today the Moscow office alone employs a staff of over 1,500 analysts. In addition to the home offices, Directorate 'T' maintains its own KGB residences abroad (Line 'X') at embassies, consulates, trade missions and tourist agencies. Western sources estimate the total number of agents working for Directorate 'T' to be around 20,000.

When Andropov advanced from the KGB to the Kremlin leadership, Vitaly Fedorchuk took his place at the top of the KGB. But Fedorchuk's administration was short-lived: from May to December 1982. Today's chief is Viktor Chebrikov, a graduate of the metallurgical institute of Dnepropetrovsk and a man regarded as a top specialist in the illegal acquisition of Western know-how.

When the ' spearhead of the revolution' was founded back in 1917, military and political secrets of the capitalists were the main targets. Times have changed. Today, the spears of their spies are pointed at manufacturing technology. Precision production processes, the USSR has realized, are more likely to advance its military prowess than are stolen Western weapons prototypes. A nation that masters the manufacturing of laser mirrors, infra-red optics, microchips and light-weight metals is very close to the military application of these technologies. Many of the highest-priority Soviet espionage targets are thus production techniques which do not bear a top-secret classification.

Marc DeGeyter was after civilian software, 'Michael Gerkins' wanted commercial IBM machines, and the PDP-11s in the Elmont case are popular models used for a wide variety of civilian tasks by non-military companies. Civilian technology was also a prime target for Guennadi Batachev when he slipped out of his green KGB uniform and into a pinstriped business suit for his Cologne shopping spree.

'The Richard Müller case demonstrates the way Eastern bloc agents work,' says US Customs chief William von Raab. 'Acquisition of technologically valuable goods has absolute priority with the Soviets. According to our information, they judge it even more important than purely military data.'

Soviet espionage interest in non-secret information was further documented in February 1980 in Hamburg, Germany, when the KGB had no less than four intelligence officers among the group of official Soviet representatives at the Scientific Conference for Security and Co-operation in Europe. Two leading members of the delegation, Nikolai Berdennikov and Igor Milovidov, had been exposed as spies during previous diplomatic stays in London. Two other agents were spotted among the technical 'advisers'. Their presence at the Hamburg conference, where military secrets were certainly not available, throws a telling light on Moscow's view of East-West scientific forums.

The KGB has a reputation as an all-powerful, ever-present intelligence service and it is, without doubt, a feared instrument of the Soviet state both within the country and abroad. Its role in Moscow's strategic stealing, however, has often been overestimated in press reports. The KGB has its limits. Its influence ends where the might of the military-industrial complex begins.

The Soviet Military-Industrial Commission (often known by the initials VPK) is an organ of the Presidium of the USSR with powers comparable to those of the KGB. They may even reach further. The twelve cabinet members composing the Commission, heads of the most influential ministries of the USSR, supervise and co-ordinate the entire armaments industry of the Warsaw Pact. The VPK answers only to the very top of the Kremlin hierarchy – to the Central Committee, where annual priorities for the acquisition of Western technology are set.

The VPK serves as broker in the acquisition of Western technology. On the one hand, it receives all available overt and covert intelligence on newest developments in the West. On the other, it evaluates the needs of the various Soviet ministries, state committees and institutes of the military-industrial complex, dividing them into 'principal objectives' (which are military) and 'simple objectives' (which are civilian). The Commission is the switchboard, where the lines of supply and demand meet. Its members draw up master shopping lists that are binding for all Soviet ministries. Their decisive power stems from their control over generous acquisition funds, which they distribute – in Western currency.

The intelligence reaching the VPK, and the orders emanating from it, are by no means solely a matter for spies. Eastern bloc offices operating openly in the West have just as much of a place in the acquisition process as do the cloak-and-dagger methods of the secret services. Legal purchases – often subsidized by the West – are cheaper, and, since they often include long-term maintenance and spare-parts arrangements, more reliable. Legal acquisitions are delegated primarily to the State Committee on Science and Technology (GKNT), headed by Guriy Marchuk.

The GKNT is well known to Westerners trading with the Soviets. It serves as the official negotiating partner for all governments and private companies seeking Eastern business. GKNT representatives are always present at the negotiating table when trade delegations from East and West meet. The most prominent member is Dr Dzhermen Gvishiani, a son-in-law of Alexei Kosygin and Vice-Chairman of the GKNT. What many of the political leaders, scientists and businessmen who deal with him don't know is that Gvishiani personally used to lead an espionage ring in the West.

The intelligence operations of the Soviet acquisition programme begin with open-access information. The GKNT collects and analyses the flood of scientific and technological literature pouring into the Soviet Union each year from the West. Over 35,000 newspapers and magazines in 65 different languages are gathered annually by Soviet sources in 125 different countries. GKNT technical readers pore through a total of 1.5 million articles, hunting for significant technological developments and passing relevant articles on to interested offices. Some publications, such as *Aviation Week*, are judged to be so significant that latest issues are rushed to Moscow via Aeroflot, being translated into Russian en route.

Detailed background on specific equipment is gleaned from electronics fairs, where order numbers and even the photographs that the Soviets have been known to include on their shopping lists for embargo-runners are openly available. Anyone who has ever visited an important high-tech exhibition is familiar with the Eastern bloc visitors. They arrive early, head straight for the stands of Western companies and stuff all available data sheets, technical flyers and advertising brochures into their shopping bags. The literature often deals with equipment they cannot purchase legally. Many Western businessmen wonder what they do with it. The answer lies in the offices of the GKNT.

Soviet defectors have reported that one of their most reliable sources of technological intelligence is 'Comrade Regpatoff' – the Soviet nickname for the Registered Patent Office of the United States Government. They also rely heavily on the Library of Congress, in one case having blatantly ordered US army maintenance manuals for missiles and artillery. The librarians mailed them off – free of charge – in accordance with a treaty on scientific exchange dating back to the 1800s.

The US Department of Commerce created a 'Technical Information Service' to help American companies keep up to date on the newest technological developments. Its largest user, however, turned out to be the USSR – with orders one year topping 80,000 free government reports. Three-quarters of the publications the Soviets received came from the Department of Defense, the Department of Energy or NASA. The special irony of this case was that the Commerce Department is the government agency ostensibly responsible for stopping the high-tech drain.

On high-priority projects, the GKNT may ask for outside help. In 1979, for example, two members of the Washington Embassy appeared in the public library of Milan, Tennessee, and copied several pages from the environmental impact study prepared for a local industrial project. It was hardly their interest in the flora and fauna of Tennessee that prompted the trip. The proposed factory was an addition to the Milan arsenal, where the top-secret explosives RDX and HMX were to be produced. A Pentagon investigation of the incident later revealed that 'the technical details contained in it – when combined with other published materials – would permit the reconstruction of the entire production process'.

The scope of GKNT involvement in covert acquisition efforts was revealed in January 1985, when German intelligence officials obtained possession of a secret Soviet shopping manual prepared for spies working in the West. Written by the GKNT in co-operation with KGB experts from Directorate 'T', the handbook for high-tech thievery was officially entitled *Svodnoye Zadaniye Informatsionnoy Tekhnicheskoy* ('Co-ordinated Requirements for Technical Information Tasking'). Internally, Soviet officers were said to refer it as 'the book of rare and endangered species'.

Not surprisingly, much of the equipment sought by the Soviets concerns high-priority military know-how, such as the electronic guidance systems for in-flight navigation and targeting of intercontinental missiles. But the twenty-seven chapters also cover a broad spectrum of dual-purpose technology ranging from theoretical physics and astronomy to machine tools and mining techniques. Many items seem quite innocuous. Chapter 14, for example, is devoted to agricultural machinery and includes a section on the 'quadwrench' transmissions used by John Deere, International Harvester and Caterpillar in American tractors. Another section deals with maintenance-free batteries. Both, however, also have significant applications for tanks and other military vehicles.

A final chapter consists of a yellow-pages directory listing materials and manufacturers, suppliers and subcontractors, prices and order numbers. The Cyrillic text breaks into Latin terminology when identifying a targeted free-world firm or when quoting from a Western source, such as *Aviation Week*. Local export laws and means of evading them are also described.

The thick, soft-bound volume is kept under lock and key in the tightly guarded registries of Soviet consulates and trade missions, accessible only to agents of the KGB, the GRU and other military and diplomatic personnel who might gain access to embargoed Western technology. Its binding is sewn and its pages numbered to inhibit theft, and Soviet officials are not allowed to remove the book from the document room, where they read it in enclosed cubicles.

During détente student exchange programmes increased dramatically – a development greeted in many circles as a contribution to international understanding. While most Western students (average age 18-25 years) took advantage of their stay in the USSR to study Rachmaninov, Dostoyevsky and others their Soviet counterparts preferred practical areas of study; not Leonard Bernstein, James Faulkner or Ernest Hemingway, but rather laser optics, microelectronics, infra-red optics and nuclear physics were the primary curriculum choices of the Soviet 'students' – most of them middle-aged scientists with an average age of thirty-five and extensive professional experience.

It certainly would be an exaggeration to claim that all Soviet students in the West are spies. But it is a reasonable assumption that those receiving permission to study with the *glavniy protivnik* (main enemy) in the West have been thoroughly investigated before leaving home. During their stay in the West, Soviet students are required to report interesting technological developments to the local embassy. After returning home, their invaluable experience is likely to qualify them for high-priority scientific assignments. And high priority in the Soviet Union means military.

In special seminars at MIT or Stanford, Eastern exchange 'students' could start a course with an empty notebook and end it with a do-it-yourself microcomputer. During a single year, they would plot their microchip with computer-aided design and transfer it to silicon using computer-aided layout. They would construct, mount, pack and test it in one of the nation's most modern research institutions. In short, they were exposed to the entire palette of modern computer production, including extensive hands-on experience with a number of embargoed state-of-the-art devices.

'We delude ourselves,' concludes Los Alamos expert Dr Lara Baker, 'if we think the Soviets enter the black market in search of strategic components in a helter-skelter style, buying up dual-use commodities without rhyme or reason. The truth of the matter is that the Soviets and their surrogates buy nothing they don't have a specific, well-defined need for. They know exactly what they want – right down to the model number – and what they want is part of a carefully crafted design.'

East-West scientific and technological exchange programmes have unwittingly contributed to this design. In general, Soviet delegations consist of highly specialized experts, many of whom are working on classified military projects in the USSR. In 1976, for example, a Soviet scientist named S.A. Gubin managed to take part in an American development project for air-fuel explosives, a large blast weapons system. During his assignment he ordered a number of relevant documents from the National Technical Information Service. His professor was a consultant to the US Navy on secret explosive devices. After concluding his stay in the States, Gubin returned home to continue his research – this time for the Red Army.

As part of a French-Soviet exchange another scientist named Nikolai Sobolov was assigned to a research institute in Marseilles. But the methods of the budding Soviet researcher met with the disapproval of his French associates when he was caught stuffing a secret laser head into his trouser pocket. Sobolov was fired on the spot and expelled from the country.

But the man who had given him his instructions, Soviet Consul Guennadi Travkov, stayed on. Working under diplomatic cover, Travko offered an aerospace worker a speedboat as a 'gift' for information on underwater biology. From a pilot he then tried to buy blueprints of the highly sophisticated Mirage-2000 Doppler radar system. The pilot, however, reported the incident and French authorities were able to apprehend Travkov on 9 February 1980. At the time of his arrest, the diplomat was searching for the secret documents – in the town rubbish dump. He was later identified as an officer of the GRU.

Travkov's GRU colleague Yevgeniy Barmyantsev, who was posing as a military attaché, was caught in a similarly embarrassing situation in a suburb of Washington on 16 April 1983 – rooting in a hollow tree for a green rubbish bag. In the bag FBI agents found eight undeveloped 35mm films with pictures of secret army documents on laser weapons. The hollow tree stood exactly 24.5 miles from the city limits of Washington – US travel restrictions allow Soviet diplomats to travel not more than 25 miles from the country's capital.

The Glavnoe Razvedyvatelnoye Upravleniye, or GRU, has recently been scoring the biggest high-tech heists for the Soviets. It is the espionage arm of the Red Army. It was founded three years after the KGB and exists as an independent organization within the intelligence community – with its own administration, agent rings, training centres and even independent lines of communication back to the USSR. Its Department 'B' maintains a staff of qualified scientists specializing in technology acquisition at its residences abroad, similar to the KGB's line 'X'.

For a long time, Kremlin leaders took a dim view of the GRU. Western agents had succeeded in penetrating the upper echelons of its hierarchy in 1958, and again in 1962. When they were uncovered, Khrushchev reorganized the service, relegating the GRU to the outer reaches of power. For over a decade the GRU had to play second fiddle to the omnipotent KGB.

As a department of the Joint Command, however, the GRU continued to enjoy the special trust of Moscow's military leaders. The acquisition of strategic, tactical and technical intelligence remained its official domain. Over the years, as the expertise of military intelligence became increasingly important to the strategic plans of the Kremlin leadership, GRU influence began to grow. Today, its budget for foreign technology acquisition is believed to be larger than that of the KGB.

The methods of the KGB and the GRU have remained strikingly similar. Sometimes they are very direct. In 1973, GRU officer Viktor Delnov – an employee of the Soviet Embassy in Washington – had to be physically pulled from the cockpit of an A-7 fighter. While visiting an Air Force installation he had suddenly pulled out a camera and begun photographing the instrument panels. At the next stop on his tour, Delnov approached an F-4 fighter and brazenly began unscrewing the nose cone of a Maverick air-to-air missile under the wings. Before that, as was later revealed, he had tried unsuccessfully to recruit a US Air Force intelligence agent for the Soviets – while shopping at Sears.

Viktor Kedrov, who recruited West German high-tech trader Werner Bruchhausen, was an intelligence officer of the GRU. Before his promotion to Vice-President of Elorg in Moscow, where he directed many of Moscow's key smuggling operations, he had served as a military spy at the Soviet Embassy in London and at the Soviet Trade Mission in Copenhagen. The short, stocky Russian also recruited Danish spy Bent Weibel in the first major case of computer espionage in the West that led to a conviction. Weibel was sentenced to eight years in a high-security Danish prison. Kedrov, who carried a diplomatic passport, returned to Moscow unscathed and was rewarded with a string of promotions. Today he is serving as a member of the Soviet negotiating team at the MBFR disarmament talks in Vienna.

Technicians of the GRU also man the worldwide eavesdropping installations of the USSR. Since the electronic listening posts were originally established to collect military intelligence, their operations fall under the domain of the Red Army. They are now being used to collect high-technology data, and NATO experts are convinced that the Soviets are using modern Western electronics to do it. One of the most important GRU outposts is situated on a mountain peak called Der Brocken which is in the Harz area of East Germany.

The eighteenth-century poet Heinrich Heine once praised the view from the 3,426-foot Brocken, which offers a splendid panorama of the German countryside to the west. But today, the hilltop look-out is closed to romantic poets. It is reserved for the radar beacons of the Red Army, which scan deep into the strategically vital Elbe plains of West Germany. The high-frequency eavesdropping antennae perched there can also pick up thousands of telephone conversations between the Federal Republic of Germany and West Berlin. The West German post office beams the calls – bundled onto a microwave beacon – right by the Eastern espionage outpost.

Tapping into a microwave signal isn't difficult. Amateur equipment will do the job. With the help of radio scanners, listeners can pick out interesting telephone numbers for individual eavesdropping. Unlike conventional methods for tapping cables, which can be detected by measuring the voltage, eavesdropping on air waves leaves no telltale electronic trace.

Modern computers have long since been able to transform the spoken word into the bits and bytes, storing an infinite number of conversations on magnetic tape. State-of-the-art main-frame computers can easily handle the billions and trillions of bits of information involved in such an operation. Modern electronics make it possible – assuming one possesses modern electronics.

The Soviet station in Lourdes, Cuba – covering twenty-eight square miles and manned by roughly 1,500 Soviet technicians – is the largest electronic eavesdropping installation in the world, East or West. From there, according to reports in the *Boston Globe*, agents of the GRU are intercepting 'all international voice and data messages that reach the US by satellite'.

'The subject was virtually taboo for discussion even within the intelligence community before the intelligence board got a secret briefing on it in 1974,' recalls Secretary of Commerce Lionel Olmer. Olmer was a member of the President's Foreign Intelligence Advisory Board and he remembers the terror the discovery of Soviet interception from Lourdes struck in a number of hearts in Washington at the time. It meant that virtually all uncoded transatlantic messages – from data banks and diplomats, from loyal allies and illicit lovers – were vulnerable to Soviet tapping.

Listening devices, of course, were nothing new to Washington. Large-scale antennae had been mounted for years atop the Soviet Embassy, picking up signals from the State Department, the CIA and the Pentagon. A virtual forest extended from the roof of the Soviet Consulate in San Francisco, pointing south towards Silicon Valley. In fact, the top-secret blueprints of the atomic submarine Trident were known to have fallen into Soviet hands when a careless employee transmitted them to his office via telefax.

Security sources now fear that even internal data on the pricing and marketing policies of Western companies is being systematically scrutinized in the East. 'I firmly believe,' says Raymond Tate, 'the Soviet Union has for many years manipulated a lot of commercial markets in the world.' Tate should know. He is the former head of the American eavesdropping authority, the National Security Agency (NSA) at Fort Meade, Maryland. 'They have a significant cash-flow problem. How do you make money in a cash-flow problem? You turn your intelligence system around and use it to get all sorts of data you can use in commercial ventures.'

When GRU operatives head for cover, they often turn to Aeroflot. The Soviet airline, which maintains offices in nearly every major city of the Western world, is a logical choice for military intelligence agents. Although Aeroflot is widely regarded as a civilian airline, its organizational structure is rigidly militaristic. Most of its 450,000 personnel have either reserve or former military status. Management hold ranks with equivalents in the Red Army. Aeroflot aircraft (the IL-76, for example) are designed to military specifications and configured for aerial reconnaissance. The top man is Soviet Air Marshal Bugayev.

In times of crisis, the entire fleet is at the disposal of the Warsaw Pact. In times of peace it is often used by the intelligence services. Aeroflot has flown clandestine arms shipments to the PLO in Lebanon and to Zimbabwean guerrillas in Mozambique. It has flown Cuban insurgents to the underground war in Angola and KGB agents to secret preparations for the invasions of Czechoslovakia and Afghanistan. During the initial stages of the Afghanistan war Aeroflot cancelled roughly half of all its domestic flights because the planes were booked by the military.

Aeroflot planes bristling with antennae regularly stray from civilian aviation routes to fly over sensitive and restricted Western airspace. On 8 November 1981 two Soviet passenger planes diverted from their planned course. One wandered over a navy base in New London, Connecticut, the other over a General Dynamics shipyard in Groton, where a Trident submarine was under construction. Aeroflot often takes advantage of its landing rights in Luxembourg for low-flying excursions over the NATO military bases of West Germany in Bittburg, Hahn, Spandahlem and Buchel. Almost routinely, Aeroflot requests permission for charter flights across the American continent – at times and on routes that coincide with a military manoeuvre, an intercontinental missile launch or an Air Force scramble.

In April 1984, an Aeroflot TU-124 en route from Bucharest to

Marseille left its designated course to fly over the French harbour of Toulon. Air controllers radioed the plane, demanding it leave the zone immediately. The area over Toulon has been listed on aviation maps as restricted airspace for decades. But the Soviet pilot ignored them. In the shipyards of the French navy below, the atomic submarine *Rubis* was in for repairs. The aircraft-carrier *Foch* was being outfitted with a highly sophisticated NATO navigation system. Just a case of bad luck, Soviet officials later explained. After all, it was Friday the thirteenth.

Aeroflot also pursues high-flying objectives on the ground. Or, to be more exact, underground. Generally, it's the agents of the GRU who seek clandestine cover in the offices of the airline. But colleagues from the KGB have also been spotted there. Either way, it's espionage, and Aeroflot officials have been caught red-handed at it in and expelled from – Great Britain, Belgium, Spain, France, Cyprus, The Netherlands, Greece, Indonesia and Italy.

As early as the 1960s, Soviet intelligence officers posing as airline representatives were concentrating their efforts on the the illegal acquisition of Western high technology. Their target was the French-British supersonic passenger plane Concorde. There was no way for the Soviets to get the plans legally and company watchmen caught a good dozen intruders in the closely guarded grounds of the plant. Two top agents eventually did manage to obtain the sensitive blueprints, as was revealed at a later espionage trial. Disguised as Czechoslovakian priests, they had stuffed microfilm photographs of the documents into a toothpaste tube and smuggled them to the East on the Ostend-Warsaw Express.

The man behind the scheme was none other than the Paris chief of Aeroflot, Sergei Pavlov. Paris police found piles of secret documents on Concorde at his home when they arrested him. President Charles de Gaulle was so infuriated by the incident that he insisted on personally signing the extradition papers.

Shortly after, the Soviets had constructed their own supersonic jet liner. The TU-144, dubbed 'Concordski' by Western aircraft designers, made its maiden flight in 1968. But its introduction into commercial service was delayed for over ten years by serious design flaws. At the time, the local Paris press speculated that French counter-intelligence had got wind of the scheme and made small but vital changes in the blueprints before letting them pass to the Soviet spies. Whatever the reason, one TU-144 crashed in a spectacular incident at the Paris Air Show in 1973; another fatal crash was registered shortly after the inauguration of commercial service in 1977.

The only scheduled flights ever flown by the Soviet jetliner were on a remote route between Moscow and Alma Ata in Soviet Kazakhstan. In mid-August 1984, Tass confirmed that the carbon-copy Concorde had been withdrawn from service – for good.

When détente began to boom in the early 1970s, security restrictions within the Western aeronautics industry were relaxed. In 1973, for example, when Aeroflot expressed official interest in buying licences for passenger planes, American companies opened their doors. Aeroflot representatives, or intelligence officers posing as such, eagerly toured the facilities of Lockheed and Boeing, while sales personnel tried to attract the lucrative accounts. In the end, the Soviets bought nothing.

'Don't kid yourselves,' one Soviet confided to his American counterpart in a late-night conversation at the hotel bar, 'we aren't here to buy. We don't have the money. Besides, how could we sell our planes to our Eastern allies if we ourselves are buying your products? No! We're here to learn your secrets.'

On 14 November 1983, the telex machines of the Soviet news agency Tass were banging out their usual diet of Politburo propaganda when something strange happened. Between stories on the stationing of NATO missiles in Europe and the cost of cleaning snow from Moscow streets, Tass ran a Russian-language report on a revolutionary computer development in America. According to the text, a new photo-echo memory system had been developed that could transform electronic impulses into optical signals and process 'electrical images received with the help of air reconnaissance, almost in real time on board the aircraft'. The new US computer, Tass continued, also allowed 'the transmission of reconnaissance information to military units in the same form as in photographic air surveillance'. After roughly 400 words, the transmission was interrupted in mid-sentence.

Something was very wrong. Alerted Western embassy officials at first feared that the Tass report – apparently released through a switching error – could be based on top-secret information. A quick check revealed, however, that it was simply the Russian translation of an article from *Aviation Week* (23 May 1983). The embarrassing incident publicly demonstrated what Western intelligence experts had long known: Tass journalists concentrate a good deal of their time and energy on an élite circle of Soviet readers at the headquarters of the GRU, the KGB and the military-industrial complex.

According to estimates of the FBI, roughly one-third of all Tass employees are employed by Soviet intelligence. Besides their journalistic duties, it is their task to scout Western technological publications for new developments that might be of interest to the Soviet military. Oleg Chirokov, head of the Paris office of Tass, was expelled from France on 5 April 1983 on espionage charges. Neutral Switzerland also threw out a Soviet reporter – and with him his KGB officer. Novosti newsman Aleksei Dumov was accused by Berne authorities of turning his news bureau at Waldhainweg 19 into a 'centre for agitation and subversion'.

Even more disturbing than the traditional methods of the trade are the espionage prospects presented by new computer technology.

Electronic data banks have long since replaced conventional libraries as the keepers of the major research results of the world. The billions of bits of new information coming daily from the world's centres of scientific study can be managed only by computer. Minute details from the vast depths of their electronic memories can be located in seconds and flashed to faraway terminals. Without instant access to this information, the research facilities of leading universities and multinational corporations in many branches of business, engineering and science could lose their rank on the razor's edge of technology almost overnight. Electronic information is as important to the strength and growth of a modern industrial society as steel and coal once were. Those who possess it are out front. Those who don't are destined to lag behind.

For the time being, the Eastern bloc is lagging behind. Its experts are frantically setting up their own data banks, for example at the Robotron computer works in East Germany's Karl Marx City. But they have a long way to go. The United States, where over 100 million abstracts on economic, scientific and technical research projects are keyed annually into electronic files, is up front. At Chemical Abstracts alone some 400,000 new articles are read, reduced and recorded on magnetic tape each year. England, France and Germany also possess modern data banks on specialized topics. Thus, Soviet researchers needing such facilities turn their attention Westward.

For many years their access to this Western know-how was legal, even officially sanctioned. Moscow's Academy of Science participated in Lockheed's 'Dialog' with US government approval – at least until 1980, when CIA experts sounded the alarm. Since then, Soviet scientists have been forced to sidetrack their requests through Hungary, which continued to enjoy unrestricted access to the strategic information in Dialog.

If all else fails, intelligence service can easily tap into lines or illegally copy tapes. Eastern bloc electronic thieves have been caught red-handed in – and expelled from – France, Holland, Germany and the United States. Often the information they sought was not secret, yet still highly useful for an enemy intelligence service.

The USSR was also an official participant at the International Institute for Applied Systems Analysis in Laxenberg near Vienna. Along with Western scientists, Soviet experts hooked into satellite relays around the globe and were soon reaping huge research benefits. But not only that. The Reagan Administration believes they were also tapping into a strategic Cray-1 high-speed computer at Reading in England – and using it to simulate atomic bomb blasts.

Computer expert Dr Carl Hammer, who was called in to study the incident, is sceptical: 'The data-lines were too narrow to handle the complicated calculations the Soviets were accused of doing.' Since electronic bank burglars seldom leave telltale traces, it is hard to know exactly what the Soviets were up to in Reading.

Less confusing is the case of a data bank robbery in Holland. The Soviets had set up a local branch of their computer company Elorg in the small town of Hilversum – ostensibly to sell Soviet hardware to the West. Understandably, customer interest was minimal. 'In some months our sales volume was under $200,' reports former Elorg employee Gerard Lohuis. The Dutchman worked for the Soviets until it got too hot for him: 'Our company was being subsidized to the tune of two hundred million dollars a year from an account in the federal budget of the USSR.'

From a Soviet viewpoint, the Dutch office was anything but a losing business. Company representatives succeeded in copying magnetic tapes from police files and mobilization data from military archives. The copies, says Lohuis, were smuggled out by Soviet technicians travelling back and forth to Moscow. When the Dutchman started talking, Elorg director Vladimir Khylstov started packing. The Soviet 'businessman' was expelled by Dutch authorities – along with a certain G. Burmistrov from the Soviet Trade Mission in Amsterdam, who had also participated in the operation.

Burmistrov's cover as a trade representative was no accident. Official Soviet trade missions play a major role in the acquisiton of Western technology – by fair means or foul. The abuse of the German mission in Cologne as a front for KGB agent Guennadi

Batachev and at least ten other Soviet spies has been detailed in Chapter Nine. In February 1984, the Norwegians said goodbye to two KGB agents named Artamonov and Ovtkin when their involvement in the Treholt affair – a high-level espionage case that shook the government – came to light. Both were using their jobs at the Soviet Trade Mission in Oslo as a cover.

The USSR maintains forty-seven state-owned foreign-trade offices in the West, plus some 300 import and export companies with heavy Eastern financing. Since the demand for their technology is negligible, so is the economic justification for their existence. Except, that is, for the invaluable cover they offer for ostensibly legitimate inquiries and contacts in the business world. In the same fashion, Eastern trade fairs often serve a dual purpose – promoting legitimate East-West trade where possible, and as a front for clandestine operations when necessary. On several occasions representatives from Western firms exhibiting in the East have awakened in the morning to discover that prize equipment has vanished from their booth during the night. The loss has been described in the Soviet press aptly as 'thievery'. According to Josef Arkov, the Senate witness behind the glass screen, the thieves are often acting on government orders. Arkov reports the case of one Soviet acquaintance who worked as a watchman at international trade fairs in Moscow: 'In league with the KGB, the man used his position as security guard to steal several pieces of high-technology equipment. He was rewarded handsomely for his thievery. Not an especially intelligent man, he could never have earned on his own the PhD degree he was subsequently awarded.'

For a number of reasons Moscow prefers to run many of its clandestine operations through the intelligence agencies of its satellites. East Germany's geographical, cultural and linguistic ties with the West, for example, qualify it as a prime player in the twilight world of Soviet computer espionage. The East German intelligence service (Staatssicherheitdienst) set up its own specialized high-tech operation (Sektion Wissenschaft und Technik) in 1970. Its resounding successes in the acquisition of IBM 360/370 computers have been described. The largest KGB office outside Moscow is maintained in East Berlin, where some 1,200 Soviet analysts devote themselves exclusively to espionage operations against West Germany.

The annual German *Frühjahrsmesse* in Leipzig is reported to be very promising terrain for communist agents. Due to the heavy influx of Western businessmen it is an ideal recruiting ground for well-paying Soviet black-marketeers. Spies working in the West often travel there to meet their masters for lengthy, and inconspicuous, briefings. Former East German intelligence officer Werner Stiller (who fled to the West on the Berlin subway in 1979) reports that dozens of his former colleagues travel to Leipzig in specially equipped espionage buses. Directional microphones and mini-cameras, Xerox copiers and X-ray machines are among the equipment carried by the mobile field units, designed to deal with a number of situations at very short notice. Many of the internal East German documents that Werner Stiller managed to smuggle out on his train ride to freedom bear the initials 'SU'. According to Stiller, this means they are earmarked for the big brothers in Soviet intelligence.

The Hungarian company Mahart KFT was used by Richard Müller to funnel shipments through to Mashpriborintorg in Moscow. The Hungarian intelligence service played a key role in the acquisition of a strategically vital magnetic bubble memory system. Czechoslovakian contacts and forwarding addresses were prominent in Werner Bruchhausen's operation. Romanian and Bulgarian espionage agents have been active in a number of other cases. But two of Moscow's most stunning successes are credited to the Polish intelligence service Sluzba Bezvieczenstwa, or SB.

The tale of the SB's California capers reads like a John le Carré thriller. Among the players are two American high-tech engineers, seven FBI undercover agents, twenty KGB spies and a CIA mole in Poland. Among the locations are dead drops in Los Angeles, a hotel room in Geneva and the Soviet Embassy in Warsaw. Among the props are top-secret atomic-missile plans, extensive eavesdropping equipment and $100,000 in a plain brown envelope. The star of the story, at least from the Soviet perspective, is a young SB super-spy named Marion Zacharski.

Zacharski was president of the Polish-American Machinery Corporation (Polamco), a state-owned trading company established in 1976 to import Polish machine tools into the United States. As in the case of Elorg in Holland, the Eastern company wasn't making much money. In fact, in one year they suffered losses on sales amounting to $5.1 million. But somebody somewhere seemed to think they were doing just fine. After all, Zacharski had succeeded in selling Polish machine equipment to a top-secret nuclear testing site in Nevada. Two Polamco employees were even admitted to the site to install the machines, which was used to prepare American atomic weapons for testing. ('Nothing was compromised,' a

Department of Energy spokesman later claimed. 'We got a machine for $250,000 that would have cost us $1 million.')

The Hughes Aircraft Corporation couldn't make that claim. There is no doubt that Zacharski managed to steal its state-of-the-art look-down/shoot-down radar system. In 1979, the 29-year-old Polish agent recruited a major informant at Hughes and was soon funnelling scores of secrets back to Poland. Zacharski had approached his target, American computer consultant William Bell, as a neighbour and tennis partner. Both lived at the Cross Creek apartment complex in Playa Del Rey, California. At first, they were just friends. Then Zacharski loaned Bell large sums of money. For the American, the path soon led to financial dependence, microfilm photography, dead drops and rendezvous with his new masters in hotel rooms in Innsbruck, Linz, Vienna and Geneva. Bell turned over dozens of documents, among them plans for a 'quiet' radar system of the new B1-B strategic bomber, the look-down/shoot-down system used in US F-15 fighter planes, and details on the Hawk, Patriot and Phoenix missiles. In the end, Bell was arrested and sentenced to an eight-year prison term.

The goods went straight to Moscow, where a reverse-engineered Soviet version of the Hughes radar was soon sighted at Vladimirovka, a testing site of the Red Air Force located on the Caspian Sea. While flying at over 20,000 feet MiG pilots successfully intercepted target drones with a radar signature of less than one square metre, at altitudes below 200 feet. The tests simulated an attack by American cruise missiles.

Ironically enough, the fact that Zacharski was working for Polish intelligence was well known to American authorities. The FBI had been tipped off in 1979, long before the recruitment of Mr Bell. Undercover agents trailed the Polish agent for two years, monitoring his movements and tapping his telephone. But instead of arresting him – or at least warning the American engineer – they allowed the entrapment to continue. And vital secrets were passed to the Warsaw Pact.

The astute Zacharski was well aware of his clumsy followers. In fact, he often approached the FBI agents in their car, engaging them in a chat. On one occasion in November 1980 the Polish spy told his shadowers, 'You'll probably make it to my daughter's fifth birthday party at Burger King.'

'We'll get her a present,' the undercover agents replied. And they did. The cat-and-mouse game between the FBI and the Polish spy, with as many as seven pursuers tracking Mr Zacharski at any one time, produced a total of 2,500 pages of wire-tap and surveillance logs. But aside from an occasional traffic violation, there was no evidence of law-breaking. It was the CIA that had identified him as a foreign intelligence officer, and the testimony of William Bell that finally led to his conviction. Zacharski was sentenced to life imprisonment.

The CIA information on Zacharski came from a 'mole' in Warsaw – a double agent who had penetrated deep into the upper echelons of the Polish intelligence service. The informant was priceless, and the CIA wanted to keep him where he was for as long as possible. His testimony thus could not be used publicly to incriminate Zacharski. The American agent – later identified in official communiqués only as 'The Source' – had another important case to solve before he was allowed to relinquish his post and flee to the safety of the West.

'The Source' was asked to turn his attention to a Polish company named Unitra which maintained extensive business contacts with the West. Unitra manager Zdidzislaw Przychodzien, officially a member of the Polish Ministry of Machine Industry, was known to be a lieutenant-colonel in the SB. In his dealings with his agents, the ageing Polish master spy identified himself only as 'The Minister'. With the help of a Palo Alto entrepreneur (codename: 'Big Man'), Przychodzien had succeeded in recruiting yet another West Coast electronics expert for Eastern bloc espionage. The target this time was James Durward Harper.

Mr Harper fell victim to much the same ploy as William Bell: casual friendship, financial dependence and, finally, espionage. For several years Mr Harper received Polish shopping lists of desired Western technology, which he broke down into smaller lists and farmed out to various purchasing agents, smuggling the contraband to the East. Harper's preliminary high-tech deals read much like many other cases. The dramatic part of the tale involves his role in the sale of vital American plans to strengthen the concrete silos of Minuteman missiles against a pre-emptive Soviet attack. The Minuteman is considered the heart of the US nuclear defence force and the KGB had been combing the world for these plans for years. Harper found a way of getting them. Details of the deal were later revealed in an unusually detailed FBI affidavit on the Harper case.

According to the FBI, Harper and 'Big Man' flew to Switzerland in May 1979 for a meeting with Polish operatives in a Geneva hotel room. After agreeing on the price for the documents they were planning to steal, the two Americans then took separate flights on to Warsaw, where government cars whisked them off to meet 'The Minister' in his country villa outside town. 'The Big Man assured the Minister that I could be trusted,' Harper recounted under interrogation, 'and the Minister said he was very interested.'

On 5 June 1980 James Harper returned to Warsaw with the documents. But a team of eagerly waiting Polish experts was disappointed with their condition: the coveted papers had been stashed in an underground hideaway. They were wet, stuck together and out of sequence. A twenty-man KGB contingency was expected in from Moscow the next day to examine the contraband, and five SB technicians had to spend the entire night cleaning, separating and drying the missile plans with a hair-drier.

On 6 June the salvaged papers were turned over to the freshly arrived KGB team at the Soviet Embassy in Warsaw. After thoroughly examining them, the Soviets disappeared into an adjoining room. When they returned, they nodded and the American was given an envelope with $100,000 in hundred-dollar notes.

Harper's third meeting took place at the ticket office of the Museum of Anthropology in Mexico City. For the first time he was travelling on his own. Dressed casually in jeans and a polo-neck sweater and wearing a large medallion round his neck to make him easier to spot, the 49-year-old American waited uneasily for an unknown contact to approach. A Polish agent introducing himself as 'Jacques' greeted him with a warm handshake, presenting the torn half of a crumpled laundry receipt. Harper had the other half.

Harper continued to meet his Polish masters over a period of years in Vienna, Guadalajara, Brownsville and Tijuana, altering his appearance with sunglasses, varying hair lengths, a beard or a moustache, or occasionally clean shaven. He turned over documents on the MX missile and the Ballistic Defense Advanced Technology Center in Huntsville, Alabama.

Polish spy Zdidzislaw Przychodzien later received a personal commendation from then KGB Chief Yuri Andropov for his role in the sensational intelligence coup. The CIA mole, who revealed the operation, was allowed to return to the safety of the West. And James Durward Harper, arrested by federal agents on 17 October 1983, was convicted and sentenced to life imprisonment.

But the vital American missile secrets were gone for ever.

A Soviet scientist is caught red-handed slipping lasers into his pocket in a Marseilles research lab, a diplomat is arrested rooting in a French rubbish dump, a military attaché rooting in a Maryland tree trunk. Electronics experts in Holland have been caught at it. So have airline employees in Paris and trade mission officials in Cologne. Academics collect intelligence for the Academy of Science, students snoop for the GKNT: Tass covers for the KGB, Aeroflot for the GRU. Polish machine companies were involved in Los Angeles, German trade fairs were involved in Leipzig.

The list of players and passive participants could be expanded almost indefinitely. The plain fact is that no Eastern institution is untouched by the global Soviet drive for Western technology. From a Moscow perspective there is no distinction between legitimate business and clandestine espionage operations. Both salesmen and spies serve the same masters. Their ideals are identical and so are their ends: the ultimate victory of the socialist system.

Soviet spying, of course, is nothing new. But the Soviets' unremitting obsession with Western manufacturing know-how is. The inability of Eastern science to develop comparable technology of its own has forced the Kremlin into an all-out offensive to steal the West's. The Soviets build it into their armaments and point it back across their borders at the West, saving billions of dollars' worth of research and development costs in the process. And the West is compelled to spend billions more to keep up.

Western intelligence sources have no doubt that acquisition efforts now hold first priority within the Soviet espionage services. What are our governments doing about it? How effective are Western counter-measures? Do we take the problem seriously, and are we prepared to pay the price necessary to stop it?

Source Notes

Arkov: US Senate Subcommittee on Investigations (hereafter Senate Hearings), Washington DC 1982, p. 27; BBC *Panorama*, 21/2/1983; Jack Anderson, *Washington Post*, 10/12/1982.
Western purchases in the East: 'When West Taps into Communist Technology', US News and World Report, 17/1/1983; *Washington Post*, 14/8/1983; *Christian Science Monitor*, 22/2/1983.
Kiser quote: *Washington Post*, 14/8/1983.
Law on state secrets: William F. Scott, 'The Myth of Free Travel in the USSR', *Air Force Magazine*, March 1983.
KGB (background): John Barron, *KGB*, Scherz Verlag, Munich 1974; Barron, *KGB Today*, Readers Digest Press, New York 1983; *New York Times*, 13/11/1982; *Die Welt*, 30/11/1982; *Handelsblatt*, 19/5/1981; Inter-

view with CIA Chief Casey, *US News and World Report*, 8/3/1982; 'Das Schwert triff Unschuldige', *Der Spiegel*, 9/7/1984.

Quote from von Raab: Reuters, 15/11/1983.

Scientific conference in Hamburg: *Die Welt*, 28/2/1980.

MIK: Henri Regnard, *Défense Nationale*, December 1983, pp. 107-21; 'Red Star Wars', the *Economist*, 15/9/1984.

GKNT: Jack Vorona, Senate Hearings, p. 112-16; 'The KGB's Spies in America', *Newsweek*, 23/11/1981; *Die Welt*, 28/2/1982; Ralph Kinney Bennett, 'The Great Russian Raid', *Readers Digest*, March 1984.

Milan library: Senate Hearings, p. 116; *Human Events*, 12/6/1982; Caspar Weinberger, 'Technology Transfer Control Program', Report to Congress, 2/1983.

Soviet students: *Die Welt*, 27/4/1982; Tad Szulc, 'To Steal Our Secrets', *Parade*, 7/11/1982; Arnaud de Borchgrave and Michael Ledeen, 'Selling Russia the Rope', *New Republic*, 13/9/1980.

Quote from Baker: Senate Hearings, p. 57.

Gubin: *International Herald Tribune*, 10/11/1979; 'Controlling Scientific Information', CQ Weekly Report, *Congressional Quarterly*, 9/7/1982.

Solowjow: *Frankfurter Allgemeine Zeitung*, 23/4/1983.

GRU: 'How Russia Steals', *US News and World Report*, 25/5/1981; *Newsweek*, 23/11/1981; annual report of the German counter-intelligence (Verfassungsschutz), 1984.

Barmyantsev: Reuters, 22/4/1983; AP, 21/4/1983.

Soviet listening posts: *Boston Globe*, 5/4/1983; *Christian Science Monitor*, 25/4/1983; *Washington Post*, 22/4/1983.

Aeroflot: John Taylor, 'Gallery of Soviet Aerospace Weapons', *Air Force Magazine*, March 1983; *Der Spiegel*, 30/3/1972; Senate Hearings, pp. 11-17; *Die Welt*, 16/4/1984.

'Concordski': *Newsweek*, 20/8/1984; *Aviation Week*, 20/8/84.

Tass: *International Herald Tribune*, 18/11/1983; *Christian Science Monitor*, 7/4/1983; *Frankfurter Allgemeine Zeitung*, 23/4/1983.

Neues Deutschland on data banks: 28/9/1981, quoted in Klaus Krakat, 'Neue Tatbestände der Mikroelektronik', *FS-Analysen*, West Berlin, September 1981, p. 94.

Laxenburg incident and quote from Hammer: Szulc, *op.cit.*; *New York Times*, 25/9/1983.

Elorg: *Die Welt*, 6/4/1976.

Soviet Trade Missions: Reuters, 6/12/1983; see also sources for Chapter Nine.

Arkov quote: Senate Hearings, p. 30.

Leipzig Trade Fair: *Die Welt*, 13/3/1980.

Satellite states: *Aviation Week*, 28/11/1983; 'Blaupausenexport', *Capital*, March 1977; *Die Welt*, 30/11/1982; 'Idealer Tummelplatz für Industrie-Spione', *Der Spiegel*, 30/3/1972.

Zacharski and Przychodzien: *New York Times*, 5/10/1982; E.A. Burkhalter, 'Soviet Industrial Espionage', *Signal*, March 1983; David Wise, 'How our Spy Spied', *Los Angeles Times*, 23/10/1983; *Wall Street Journal*, 23/1/1984; Warren Richey, 'Polish Espionage in the US', *Christian*

Science Monitor, 4/1/1984, 6/1/1984 and 12/1/1984; *USA Today*, 20/10/1983; *San Jose Mercury*, 18/10/1983 and 19/10/1983; *Chicago Tribune*, 23/10/1983; 'Soviets deploying new fighters', *Aviation Week*, 28/11/1983.

THIRTEEN

CoCom – The Toothless Watchdog: What Are We Doing?

The snowplough dredging its way through the drifts of a winding mountain road in the foothills of the French Alps came to a grinding halt. A car parked carelessly on the shoulder of the road was blocking its path; its door hung half-open. Someone might be in distress, the plough driver thought as he yanked up his handbrake. He heard music blaring from the car radio as he approached. But at first glance he knew that it was too late for help. A snowy corpse sat drooped over the wheel, blood from a gaping gunshot wound clinging to the frozen skin. It was an apparent suicide.

Homicide experts arriving at the grisly mountain scene a few hours later found a handgun about six feet from the body. Three spent cartridges were in the chamber. The man had been killed, the police discovered, by a single bullet that had penetrated the head, exited, and was nowhere to be found. An autopsy would reveal that the fatal shot had been fired at a distance of several yards. The 'suicide' was a cheap set-up. It was clearly an assassination – and a professional one.

The dead man, found on 25 February 1983, was Lieutenant-Colonel Bernard Nut, an undercover agent of the French counter-espionage organization DST (Direction de la Surveillance du Territoire). Monsieur Nut was no ordinary spy. He had succeeded in penetrating the innermost circles of the KGB's Directorate 'S', a top-secret arm of Soviet intelligence which infiltrates Soviet-born agents into Western societies using assumed identities. Soviet 'S' agents had scored major successes in the piracy of French technology. For a long time, no one had suspected that the Frenchman in their midst was a double agent. Even diplomats at the Paris

Embassy had trusted Bernard Nut as a loyal Soviet agent, speaking openly in his presence about KGB operations.

The intelligence funnelled out by their 47-year-old officer proved priceless to the French, leading to the exposure and arrest of several high-ranking KGB operatives. Among them was Patrick Guerrier, a 25-year-old archivist at the state-owned coal company Charbonnages. Guerrier was apprehended at a clandestine meeting in the suburb of Meaux as he passed documents to a Soviet Embassy attaché. Nut also uncovered major espionage operations against the French naval base at Toulon, where the nuclear hunter-killer submarine *Rubis* was stationed. His biggest coup, however, was the unmasking of the Bulgarian/KGB connection behind the attempted assassination of Pope John Paul II. It was a tip from Bernard Nut that led to the arrest on 12 February of Viktor Pronin (an Aeroflot official in Rome) in connection with the Vatican shooting. Three days after the arrest, Bernard Nut lay dead in an Alpine snowbank.

Contrary to many popular notions, spooks seldom kill each other. It is an unwritten rule of their game. Given the stakes in this case, however, the KGB hierarchy apparently thought it would be worth risking an exception. It was, as it turned out, an epic miscalculation.

The murder of Bernard Nut – a French military officer gunned down on French soil – touched off a wave of high-level resentment, even fury, within the Paris Government. It sent shock waves right up to the very top of the Elysée Palace. Unfortunately for Moscow, the incident coincided with several other developments that day and the slaying was the straw that snapped French patience, prompting a historic decision that François Mitterrand had been contemplating for several months.

In November 1982, the French President had ordered a DST investigation into the damage done by Soviet technology theft. Originally, concern had been aroused by the remarkable increase in Soviet staff at the Paris Embassy. Since 1973, the number of Soviet diplomats in the French capital had risen from 200 to 700, the total number of Soviet citizens in France from 1,000 to 2,400. While three representatives of the USSR had been sufficient to staff the offices of the United Nations in 1973, they now numbered forty. In the same period, the number of personnel at consulates in Paris and Marseille had risen from six to thirty-six.

The DST report, which hit Mitterrand's desk shortly before the news of Bernard Nut's murder, confirmed his worst fears: the new arrivals in Paris were hardly dedicating themselves to diplomatic affairs. They were using their assignments as a cover for espionage. The sheer number of warm bodies, counter-intelligence officials warned, had turned their job into a nightmare. The French reckoned they needed a twenty-man team to observe a suspected spy for any extended period of time. There were already more suspected spies than they could handle, and the number was growing by the day. Line 'X' – the overseas arm of the KGB technology specialists at Directorate 'T' – had planted its agents at every available institution. They were posing as representatives of Aeroflot and Intourist, Tass and Soviet trade missions. Following the tightening of US embargo measures across the Atlantic, DST officials had noted a sharp increase in illicit activities. France had become a major hunting-ground for technology spies. 'We discovered their field workers were suddenly working overtime,' one expert reported, 'and those who normally did office paperwork were out on the streets looking for contacts.'

Moscow's interest in military projects came as no particular surprise. The French had a lot to offer. They were international leaders in the development of miniature neutron warheads; their computer-guided Exocet missile had demonstrated its lethal efficiency in the Falklands War; and the Mediterranean coastline was studded with several choice targets. There were intermediate-range nuclear missiles on the Albion Plateau and long-range strategic bombers in Orange. At a nearby airstrip, secret test flights for the Mirage-2000 fighter-interceptor were under way, and Marignane Arsenals were tinkering with an advanced French-German combat helicopter.

Most of all, however, the French were disturbed by blueprint bootlegging of civilian know-how. From computer electronics and glass-fibre cables to infra-red optics and navigational instruments, France was on the cutting edge of much advanced technology which would one day decide the long-term economic and military potency of Western Europe. All of these fields were targets of the experts from 'X'. Only half of all Eastern espionage operations, the DST report warned, were still aimed at traditional targets in the armed forces, in defence industries and in public politics. The Soviets wanted technology. And they were getting it. Nearly 30 per cent of all top-of-the-line French developments had already been plundered.

For President Mitterrand, who had his own ambitious plans for the French defence industry, this was not good news. He knew that the Rogers Plan for expanding conventional forces in Europe would mean billion-dollar contracts, and he wanted French companies to get their piece of that lucrative pie. Ever since assuming office, Mitterrand had carefully and quietly expanded ties with relevant West German and British industries. Widespread Soviet theft was now threatening his plan. With the Concorde copy TU-44 and the Airbus forgery IL-86 still fresh in French memory, the Paris government decided to act.

On 31 March 1983, thirty-three days after the slaying of Bernard Nut, preparations were complete. Prime Minister Pierre Mauroy summoned Soviet Ambassador Yuli Voronsov to the Foreign Ministry and announced the immediate expulsion of forty-seven Soviet citizens from France. The reason, Mauroy stated flatly, was espionage. Forty diplomats, five commercial officers and two journalists – among them KGB station chief Nikolai Chetverikov – were granted time only for a brief farewell party and some hurried shopping on the Champs-Elysées. On 5 April television cameras and newspaper photographers recorded the historic departure of the forty-seven at Charles DeGaulle International Airport. Laden with bulging shopping bags and clutching bouquets of flowers, the Soviets were driven in six grey mini-buses to a waiting Aeroflot IL-86 plane and jetted back to the USSR. It was the most sweeping house-cleaning of Kremlin spies since 1971, when London threw out 105.

Reaction from Moscow was surprisingly mild. Tass huffed and puffed about 'unfriendly acts' and 'hysteria', but no retaliation followed. The French had done their very best to discourage it. When Mauroy announced the purge at the Quai d'Orsay meeting, he presented Ambassador Voronsov with a second list of forty additional names – Soviets who would be asked to leave should their government 'overreact'. Mauroy added in no uncertain terms that any positions left vacant by *persona non grata* would not be open to future Soviet applicants.

'Retaliatory steps against French citizens living in the USSR,' Soviet leader Yuri Andropov explained in an interview with the German magazine *Der Spiegel* two weeks later, 'would have been a simple matter. In demonstrating restraint, we were guided by the overall interests of Franco-Soviet relations, which we appreciate and which have helped maintain détente in Europe for many years.'

When the expulsions were announced, Paris cited 'a systematic attempt by agents of several secret services of the USSR to acquire scientific, technical and technological intelligence'. The expulsions were directed primarily at the activities of Line 'X,' and this was new. For the first time, technological piracy figured in a major campaign of Western counter-intelligence. For years, the illicit deeds of this highly effective arm of the KGB had been registered with mounting concern in a number of Western capitals. The fact that it was François Mitterrand, a socialist leader, who took the first radical step to end Soviet snooping caught the world by surprise. *Le Monde*: 'The action washes Mitterrand, if that was necessary, of all suspicion that his freedom of action is limited by his coalition with the Communist Party.'

The real effect of the bold French stroke, however, was the global chain reaction it touched off. From Bonn and Brussels to Berne, Bangkok and Bangladesh, authorities were soon sending Soviet spooks packing. In the twelve months that followed, 135 Soviets were exposed as agents and forced to abandon their overseas assignments – more than ever before in the history of East-West relations.

On 22 April 1983, the US Department of State summoned Soviet Ambassador Anatoly Dobrynin and announced that three high-level diplomats were being declared *persona non grata*. Oleg Konstantinov, Third Secretary at the United Nations in New York, had been apprehended by FBI agents in Manhasset trying to obtain secret aerospace documents; his 44-year-old UN colleague, KGB spy Aleksandr Mikheyev, was snared seeking confidential foreign policy papers from a Congressional aide in Washington, while Yevgeny Barmyantsev, identified as a lieutenant-colonel of the GRU, was caught trying to gain access to military laser secrets in Maryland. That same day, on the other side of the world, authorities in Canberra, Australia, exposed and extradited Embassy secretary Valeri Ivanov for KGB activities.

On 26 April Stockholm recalled its Ambassador from Moscow. The Swedes, still fuming about a recent espionage affair at the Göteborg shipyards, were provoked by persistent Soviet submarine violations of their territorial waters.

Vice-Consul Vladislav Istomin was caught red-handed with NATO know-how in Geneva, while Danish counter-intelligence exposed Yevgeniy Motorov, chief of Line 'X' in Copenhagen. In Belgium, authorities halted the efforts of Soviet 'businessman' Yevgeniy Mikhailov to harvest computer hardware; in Tokyo an associate named Arkhadii Vinogradov was caught stalking Hitachi software.

Within six months London had expelled eight Soviets, Madrid four, Bonn three, Berne two, and Ottawa one. Even the Iranian regime of Ayatollah Khomeini took action, throwing out eighteen Soviet diplomats on 4 May. They were seen off at Tehran airport by

Soviets exposed as spies in the West between December 1982 and February 1984

17/12/82	Rome	1	Lt.-Col. Ivan Heliog (Military Attaché/GRU)
23/12/82	Stockholm	2	Yuri Averine (Soviet Consul-General/GRU); Lt-Gol. Piotr Skiroky (Military Attaché/GRU)
12/2/83	Rome	-	Viktor Pronin (Aeroflot/KGB): arrested
17/2/83	Cologne	1	Guennadi Batachev (STM/KGB): convicted, later extradited
24/2/83	Rome	-	Konayev (Soviet chemical company): arrested
3/83	London	8	Names not known
3/83	Toronto	1	Names not known
3/83	Madrid	4	Soviet shipping agency employees, names not known
3/83	Bonn	2	Names not known
3/83	Amsterdam	1	Names not known
5/4/83	Paris	47	Nikolai Chetverikov (First Secretary/KGB Station Chief); Vasily Golitsyn (Naval Attaché /GRU Chief); Oleg Shirokov (Tass); Vladimir Kulikovskykh (Tass)) Edward Sokolov (Marseille Consulate); J. Krivtzov (UNESCO); J. Matveyev (UNESCO); S. Yakubenko (UNESCO); and others
22/4/83	Washington	3	Yevgeny Barmyantsev (Military Attaché/ GRU); Oleg Konstantinov (UN/KGB); Aleksandr Mikheyev (UN/KGB)
22/4/83	Canberra	1	Valeri Ivanov (First Secretary/KGB)
26/4/83	Stockholm	-	Ambassador ordered home by Moscow
29/4/83	Berne	1	Aleksei Dumov (Novosti/KGB)
30/4/83	Copenhagen	1	Yevgeny Motorov (First Secretary/KGB)
4/5/83	Tehran	18	Diplomats, names not known
13/5/83	Brussels	1	Yevgeny Mikhailov(Elorg Manager/KGB)
19/5/83	Bangkok	1	Viktor Barychev (Soviet Trade Mission/GRU)
17/6/83	Tokyo	1	Arkhadii Vinogradov (First Secretary/KGB)
7/83	Geneva	1	Vladislav Istomin (Vice-Consul)
8/83	Washington	2	Anatoly Skripko (First Secretary); Yuri Leonov (First Secretary)
8/83	Brussels	1	Gruchine (First Secretary/KGB)
21/12/83	Bangladesh	9	Names not known
28/12/83	Bangladesh	6	Names not known
2/2/84	Oslo	5	Leonid A. Makarov (First Secretary/KGB); Stanislav Tsyibotok (First Secretary/KGB); Yuri A. Anisimov (First Secretary/GRU); Mikhail Ovtkin (Soviet Trade Mission/KGB); Anatoli A. Artamonov (Soviet Trade Mission/GRU)

an angry mob of Islamic revolutionaries hooting: 'Death to the traitors.'

A NATO report of the time estimated that 70 per cent of the staff at Eastern diplomatic missions were employed by intelligence services. The mass expulsions of 1983 were the first serious countermeasures taken by the West. It was not surprising that the initiative originated in Paris. Curious was the fact that it came from the Mitterrand Government. There was another organization based in the French capital which bore prime responsibility for such matters. It should have been in the forefront. But it wasn't.

The organization is called CoCom – the Co-ordinating Committee for East-West Trade. Housed in an inconspicuous backdoor building (Annexe D) of the United States Embassy, its international staff has the job of identifying militarily applicable technology, drawing up embargo lists and setting down policy guidelines for strategic trade. Its charter provides that member states develop and co-ordinate enforcement strategies. In short, the Co-ordinating Committee is designed to define, expose and combat technical and scientific espionage; it is the watchdog of the West.

CoCom was created on 22 November 1949, just a few months after the Atlantic Alliance was founded. The seven signatory nations were France, Great Britain, Italy, Belgium, Luxembourg, Holland and the United States. The Federal Republic of Germany, Denmark, Norway, Canada and Portugal soon joined, followed later by Japan, Greece and Turkey. Today, all NATO states, with the exception of Iceland and Spain, are members.

CoCom was conceived as a child of the Cold War. Shortly before its inception, the Soviets had imposed a Stalinist government on Czechoslovakia and blocked access routes to West Berlin. Continuing East-West tension promoted CoCom's early development. China invaded Korea and Moscow continued its brutal Sovietization of Eastern Europe, quashing popular uprisings in East Germany (1953) and Hungary (1956) with Red Army tanks. With the detonation of the first Soviet atomic bomb, nuclear energy became the first dual-purpose technology to be embargoed by the West.

Today, the internal workings of CoCom are carefully screened from public view. There is no sign on the entrance to Annexe D to indicate its existence, no entry in the local telephone directory. Information about its meetings is limited, if available at all. Camera crews or photographers trying to sneak an exposure of the grey façade in the Rue de La Boetie are rudely shoved aside by guards. Reporters' questions are traditionally greeted with a terse 'No comment'. On occasion, participants at CoCom meetings have been known to deny that a meeting had taken place at all.

The secrecy shrouding the Paris panel, however, is not so much motivated by fear of Eastern espionage. Rather, it is the squabbles among friends that are CoCom's best-kept secret. Ever since the onset of the 1980s, a heated controversy has been raging among member states about the wisdom of NATO embargo measures.

The conflict began with the invasion of Afghanistan. In response to it, President Carter imposed a grain embargo on the USSR, also announcing a sweeping review of all American East-West trade policies. Over 400 US export licences were cancelled overnight, among them those for computer components for the Kama River project. But when the American President turned to his allies hoping to find support for his sanctions, he discovered that CoCom had deteriorated from a hard-hitting regulatory arm of NATO to an indifferent provincial outpost dozing in a dull bureaucratic sleep. CoCom, watchdog of the West, had long since lost its bite.

Staff members – all fourteen of them – were ill-equipped for the job at hand. They could judge neither the significance of the new equipment they were supposed to be protecting nor the global scope of scientific smuggling they were supposed to be preventing. Most of them were trade diplomats. Technical and military expertise, absolutely essential to serious regulatory supervision, was available only during rare high-level meetings. There were no simultaneous translators, no stenographers, not even a functioning Mimeograph machine. The total annual budget was a laughable $500,000.

The embargo lists of CoCom were thus hopelessly obsolete long before they went into effect. Innovations in Silicon Valley and elsewhere moved far faster than the bureaucratic machinery designed to protect them. 'If CoCom had existed in the year 3000 BC,' lamented one member, 'the wheel would still be in the export lists.'

Efforts on the enforcement front were hardly more spectacular. The Paris organization had no computers to record and correlate data on the scores of phoney companies, front organizations and middlemen being used; no data-processing equipment to trace the tangled shipping routes and unravel the twisted corporate networks. What little intelligence CoCom did have had simply been jotted onto hand-written file-cards. Employees spent their working days transcribing, translating and distributing minutes of the countless, but generally unproductive, CoCom meetings.

All this, of course, was fine with most Europeans. Interest in trade restrictions had waned in the fat years of détente between 1972 and 1980. The number of strategic products on the embargo list declined from 300 in 1951 to less than half that number by 1980. Remaining restrictions were shot full of holes by constant exemptions. In 1979 alone, member states submitted over 1,500 applications for exemptions to CoCom rules. Many countries on the Continent, in particular the Federal Republic of Germany, had become embarrassingly dependent on Eastern trade. All were earning billions of dollars in their dealings with Warsaw Pact countries. A weak embargo policy, they thought, was in their very best interest.

In the wake of the Afghanistan shock, President Carter began planning new priorities for CoCom. He wanted its facilities modernized, its personnel bolstered, its general mandate expanded. He suggested CoCom move from the Embassy annexe building to its own headquarters. He wanted a secretary-general and a staff of full-time military advisers installed. He now regarded Soviet theft of military know-how as a matter of grave concern and he appealed to Western nations to support his initiative.

German Chancellor Helmut Schmidt, whose low opinion of Jimmy Carter is now a matter of public record, regarded the US embargo initiatives as ill-conceived, untimely, even stupid. His criticism was shared in London and Paris. European governments were familiar with the appeals of the Carter Administration. And they distrusted them. All too often they had grudgingly consented to co-operate with an unpopular Washington policy – only to see the Americans themselves abandon it without notice.

Carter was in a weak bargaining position. His own Administration had contributed substantially to the relaxation of strategic trade policies. American companies had joined the Eastern business boom with verve, quickly overtaking the Europeans in both the quantity and the quality of their high-tech sales. They had led the way in computers, peddling more electronic wares to Moscow than all other CoCom countries combined. Over half of the 1,500 applications for exemptions in 1979 had been submitted by Washington. US companies had supplied over $200 million worth of top technology to the USSR. And now, suddenly, Washington was arguing that such transactions posed a fundamental threat to Western security.

European leaders wouldn't support Carter. If Washington wanted to restrict its own exports, they argued, let it. But they were quite unwilling to follow the lead taken by a wavering White House. Detached, disinterested, on occasion even bemused, they sat back to watch the first insecure steps of Jimmy Carter on the slippery stage of embargo politics.

US Computer Exports to the USSR (in computer units)

1972	USA	20
	other Cocom nations	18
	total	38
1973	USA	41
	other Cocom nations	36
	total	77
1974	USA	57
	Other Cocom nations	37
	total	94
1975	USA	162
	other Cocom nations	97
	total	259
1976	USA	122
	other Cocom nations	36
	total	158
1977	USA	67
	other Cocom nations	73
	total	140
1972-7	USA	469
	other Cocom nations	297
	total	766

(*Source:* Kenneth Tasky, 'Soviet Technology Gap', *Soviet Economy in a Time of Change*, US Joint Committee of Congress, Washington DC, 10 October 1979.)

The American President announced his decision in a televised speech on 4 January 1980. He wanted to hit the Soviets where it would hurt most: in the bread-basket. The main thrust of his action was an embargo on the sale of American grain, on which the USSR depended heavily. At the time, its own agricultural industry was in serious trouble. Although 1978 had produced a record grain crop (235 million tons), 1979 was a typical Soviet disaster (only 179 million tons).

Traditionally, the USSR writes off one quarter of its harvest to transportation losses, rodents, mildew and thievery. One million tons were already allocated to Vietnam and North Korea, another million to Afghanistan. The poor 1979 harvest meant that the Soviet Union would need to import 34 million tons. The lion's share – 25 million tons – was on order from the United States.

Bread is a mainstay of the Soviet diet. It is one of the few commodities in the USSR which is seldom scarce. Despite the squeeze, officials felt assured they could continue to meet demand for it. 'Rations for supplying the Soviet population with bread and grain products,' Leonid Brezhnev announced on 12 January 1980, 'will not be reduced by a single kilogram.' The problem, however, was not so much bread for the people as feed for livestock. The embargo would be felt first and foremost by the Kolkhozniks on Soviet agricultural collectives. Their herds were fattening on grain from the American Midwest. If the impending deficit forced a wholesale slaughter of cattle and swine, the situation could become explosive. Meat shortages in Eastern-bloc countries have been known to cause social upheavals and rioting.

Moscow apparently got wind of Jimmy Carter's intentions. The day before the presidential announcement, the Soviets placed a last-minute order for an additional 3 million tons of American grain. Soon Soviet purchasers swarmed out to scour world markets for alternative sources. Their biggest finds were made in Latin America. They closed long-term contracts with fifteen countries, importing coffee and sugar from Colombia, fruit conserves and spices from Mexico, rice from Costa Rica and bananas from Ecuador. In Argentina they purchased 83 per cent of the country's total grain exports. Canadian wheat sales rocketed. Europeans were soon buying huge quantities of American soya beans for reprocessing and resale to the Soviets. In the north German port of Hamburg, hordes of freighters brimming with Eastbound grain were sighted steaming out of the harbour. By October, *Pravda* was boasting that Jimmy Carter's grain embargo was a flop.

Many European heads nodded knowingly.

Circumvention of the American ban did, however, extract a high price from Kremlin treasuries. The Soviet Union spent a total of over 2 billion dollars on contracts with its new agricultural partners. Attempts to substitute barter arrangements for cash payments failed. The wares the Soviets had promised in exchange for grain – primarily farm machines – couldn't be delivered. They were badly needed at the agricultural collectives at home. Another problem was cash. Most of the grain-sellers demanded hard currency, and brokers at international commodity markets noticed a sudden surge of activity, as Moscow traders put millions of dollars' worth of oil, diamonds and precious metals up for sale. A year later, when commodity prices plummeted, they were forced to finance their continuing grain imports with short-term loans – at outrageous interest rates of up to 17 per cent.

Still, the Soviets seemed able to cope with the American embargo with relative ease – a fact that was interpreted in many circles as evidence of the futility of trade sanctions in general. One reason for the ineffectiveness of the embargo was revealed by Fred Asselin, a US Senate staff investigator at the Subcommittee on Investigations, when he testified at technology transfer hearings on 5 May 1982:

Mr Asselin: A former Compliance Division investigator told the subcommittee minority staff that he was given the assignment of investigating embargo violations. He said no other agents in the Compliance Division were assigned to assist him. . .

Senator Nunn: You mean to testify that based on your investigation, the grain embargo that resulted after the Soviets invaded Afghanistan had one person in the Commerce Department checking on violations?

Mr Asselin: Yes, sir. . .

Senator Nunn: So you have a major policy decision by the President of the United States on a major foreign-policy issue involving the United States and the Soviet Union, involving all our allies, involving the credibility of our foreign policy and economic policy around the world, and you have the Commerce Department assigning one individual for enforcement purposes?

Mr Asselin: That's right.

Most American farmers co-operated voluntarily with the regulations of their government. The problem was not compliance. The problem was that the grain embargo was ill-conceived.

It was designed to punish a nation for its foreign-policy behaviour. 'The Soviet Union,' Jimmy Carter said, 'must pay a concrete price for its aggression.' But no trade embargo will work unless it has widespread support from many countries, a factor which Jimmy Carter simply ignored. His action also failed to capture the public imagination. It was hard for people to understand what guns for the battlefields of Afghanistan had to do with bread for the tables of Soviet citizens. The brunt of the embargo was felt, as Soviet dissident Roy Medvedev pointed out, by 'the small man who had nothing to do with the invasion and little influence on those who did'.

Most seriously, the grain embargo failed to provide an adequate response to Moscow's mounting military aggression. Whatever the President's intention – whether to teach the Soviets a moral lesson or to whip them into submission – it was a delusion. Carter lacked a cohesive political strategy. Worse, his action helped unify the states of the Warsaw Pact while it brought divisiveness to the Atlantic Alliance.

From the Kremlin's perspective, the cost of the grain embargo had been an acceptable one. The problem could be reduced to a matter of mere money. High-tech trade restrictions, however, were more serious. The equipment needed for Warsaw Pact armaments programmes could not be purchased in Costa Rica, Argentina or even Canada. Carter's cancellation of computer exports thus caused grave concern in Moscow. While Soviet leaders hurriedly developed contingency plans, they continued their worried watch on the Western Alliance.

By mid-1980, with US elections approaching, Carter began to feel the hot breath of his Republican presidential rival. Ronald Reagan was a hardliner on Soviet affairs and political pressures on the White House started mounting. Carter pursued his CoCom initiatives with new vigour. He pressurized the member nations to abandon their policy of promoting Eastern trade with government subsidies. He presented a 'Military Critical Technologies List' of know-how that American defence officials considered vital to Western security. The Pentagon denial list, about the size of a large telephone directory, included all the bread-and-butter exports of Western Europe's burgeoning Eastern trade: advanced machine tools, modern steel plants, sophisticated oil-drilling and petro-chemical equipment, and technology for automobile production plants.

In Europe, resentment was growing. Leaders in London, Rome, Paris and Bonn sought to limit the damage done to East-West relations by Afghanistan. They wanted to salvage détente and they were enraged by the new American proposal, which went to the core of their vital economic interests. West Germany, for example, was selling 64 per cent of its total export of automated lathes to the USSR. France and Britain, too, were far more dependent on Eastern trade than the United States. They expressed willingness to accept modest changes in CoCom procedures. An across-the-board freeze on Eastern exports, however, was out of the question. The Europeans announced publicly that they would fight such a move tooth and nail.

The full extent of Alliance irritation surfaced on one occasion during the Washington visit of Count Otto Lambsdorff, West Germany's trade minister. His hosts were complaining about subsidies for Eastern trade in general and German government credits called Hermes Guarantees in particular, when Lambsdorff suddenly exploded. As one eye-witness reported, he screamed at startled

Commerce Department officials, ranting that Washington was trying to ruin the German economy, slamming his walking-cane on the conference table for emphasis. Upon his return home, the minister carried his criticism to the media – a reliable sign that allied relations have reached a new low – claiming the American initiatives were aimed at bringing German-Soviet trade to a standstill.

The US had its own reasons for anger. Several American companies had been forced to abandon lucrative contracts with the East, only to see European competitors snap them up – often with the explicit approval of their governments. The Armco Corporation, for example, had been negotiating over the construction of an electric steel plant in Novolipetsk for four years. Most of the contracts had already been signed when President Carter suddenly cancelled the export licences. Helplessly, the American company was forced to look on while the state-owned heavy-equipment manufacturer Creusot-Loire of France made a grab for the million-dollar deal. Armco's losses were $6.5 million on negotiating costs, $16.7 million on profits and an expected $20 to $30 million on service and spare parts orders. It was not an isolated incident.

Despite its influence as a superpower, the United States was unable to coerce its partners into co-operation. CoCom is not a treaty organization. Its charter is not anchored in international law. All decisions are based on an informal 'gentlemen's agreement'.

And CoCom's members were not behaving like gentlemen.

Ronald Reagan fought and won his election campaign on the technology issue, and the team he took with him to Washington was well suited to the issue: Caspar Weinberger, Fred Iklé and Richard Perle, a trio of hardliners whose first stop was the Defense Department's technology office. They found it in a state of total chaos. Staffing was inadequate; files were either non-existent or unusable. The defence budget was boosted by $25 million, personnel increased by twenty-five, and a modern data-processing system called Fordtis installed. Secretary Weinberger optimistically earmarked $2 million for CoCom modernization and generously transferred an additional $30 million from his budget to the Treasury Department to bolster enforcement efforts.

William von Raab, the new Chief of Customs, invested the new money in a special task force. At the time, only four agents were ferreting out high-tech leaks at the nation's hundreds of airports and harbours. He trained over 400 new recruits and stationed them quickly at US embassies and consulates around the world. 'Operation Exodus' was officially established in October 1981. Within the first twelve months of its existence, 2,330 illegal shipments were seized, valued at a total of $148.8 million.

Before Reagan's arrival, the US Department of Commerce bore primary responsibility for strategic trade violations. The new Administration transferred major authority to Customs and the Department of Defense. At Commerce, Reagan reinstated Lawrence Brady, who had departed during his dispute with Carter over the Kama River project, promoting him from a deputy department head to assistant secretary. As chief of his enforcement branch Brady chose the young California Federal Prosecutor Dr Theodore Wu, who had won national recognition for his handling of the Spawr and Bruchhausen cases.

One of Reagan's first presidential actions was to direct a Central Intelligence Agency investigation into the consequences of the technology haemorrhage. As a result of the devastating CIA report, discussed earlier in this book, a specialized team of intelligence experts was formed at the Langely headquarters under the name 'Technology Transfer Assessment Center'. Its members soon joined Customs and Commerce officials in an inter-agency task force, travelling to the capitals of the Western world to co-ordinate US enforcement activities with those of other governments.

Ronald Reagan hardly intended to limit his technology initiatives to a reshuffling of the Washington bureaucracy. He believed that Carter's problems with the Europeans resulted from a lack of resolve. After a mere six months in office, the new President broached the delicate subject of embargoes at his first summit meeting in Ottawa. He addressed a personal appeal to the leaders of the ten nations gathered there and one tangible result was the high-level meeting of CoCom which followed on 19 January 1982.

For the first time in over twenty-five years, cabinet-level representatives of the CoCom member states assembled in the Rue de La Boetie to discuss new strategic trade initiatives. They were greeted with a barrage of facts and figures from US security experts. With slides and charts, diagrams and satellite photographs Pentagon specialists briefed the assembled ministers on the awesome advances of the Warsaw Pact: SS-18 atomic missiles built with ball-bearing grinders from Vermont; SS-20 launch vehicles designed with IBM computers; nuclear warheads constructed with Western CAD/CAM systems. The subjects ranged from 'A' for aeronautics to 'Z' for ZIL trucks, and included over 160 Eastern weapons systems built with Western technology.

Customs officials elaborated on the complex corporate constructions and covert smuggling routes used by embargo-runners – nearly all passing through Europe – and named names of notorious high-tech pirates who, although exposed and indicted in the United States, were continuing their devious dealings from European soil. Intelligence experts detailed the inner workings of the KGB's Directorate 'T' – with over 20,000 agents rustling electronics manufacturing equipment at outposts all over the world.

'It was,' as one European participant concluded, 'an extremely impressive presentation. We were all simply floored.' The CoCom meeting could have ended as a resounding success. But things didn't turn out that way.

The technology issue, demonstrated so vividly in Paris, was blurred by other American initiatives which coincided with the CoCom meeting. At the same time, the Reagan Administration was pushing vigorously for a reduction in lending to the Soviet bloc which, in the Americans' view, was paving the way for KGB crooks to steal NATO know-how. US financial institutions, like the New York Chase Manhattan Bank, had long since reduced their Eastern holdings. But European banks continued to extend loans to the East. Poland's debts alone had risen from $1.2 billion in 1971 to the dizzying height of $26.5 billion by 1981. Chances were, they would never be able to pay even the interest.

White House efforts on the financial front focused on a mammoth natural-gas project then under negotiation between Moscow and several European countries. The West was to provide capital and technology to build a pipeline connecting the natural gas fields at Urengoy in Siberia with Western Europe. The Soviets were dependent on foreign know-how to tap their vast deep-earth Arctic reserves. But they were not the ones footing the bill. Contracts called for the Soviets to receive hard-currency earnings of between $35 billion and $70 billion. In return, Moscow promised to deliver cut-rate gas to the West Europeans – when construction of the pipeline was completed.

Not only were the profits way out of proportion; the transaction gave Moscow long-term leverage over the West. Once the pipeline was completed, there was no guarantee the Soviets would deliver their part of the bargain. The Europeans, Washington believed, were setting themselves up for blackmail. If the worst came to the worst, Moscow could threaten to cut energy supplies and the political pressure to consent to its demands would be enormous: from housekeepers who feared for their home heating, from bankers who feared for their loans and from industrialists who feared for their profits. The Soviets had been known to violate contracts on other occasions for reasons of political expediency. There were plenty of precedents: Yugoslavia in 1948, Israel in 1956, Finland in 1958, China in 1964 and Poland in 1981.

Export licences for the US companies participating in the pipeline deal, Caterpillar Tractor and General Electric, were cancelled by the Department of Commerce in December 1981. It would be advisable for the Europeans to follow suit with their companies, Washington warned. Otherwise, the US government might resort to steps of its own to punish Continental companies. It was an ominous economic threat. But President Reagan was firmly convinced that he would be spared the fate of his predecessor. Alliance politics, he believed, was merely a question of resolve.

The Europeans viewed the American announcement as an intolerable infringement of their national sovereignty. Once again, Washington was attacking a trade practice that went to the core of European economic interests. Besides, under European law valid private contracts could not be cancelled at will by the government merely because foreign policy had changed. European leaders would not contemplate violating agreements already signed and sealed with the Soviets. So they balked. Paris: 'In France, the French rule alone.' London: 'I do not believe it was right to do this.' Bonn: 'We will abide by all existing contracts.' Criticism of Washington came from the highest levels of government and was announced publicly.

For Ronald Reagan, things were getting slippery on the diplomatic stage. Six months had passed since the high-level CoCom meeting and no progress was being reported from Paris in high-tech negotiations. Delivery deadlines for the pipeline deal were approaching fast. Right to the finish, the White House hoped the Europeans would give in. To add weight to US demands, a special task force was formed under the leadership of Secretary of State George Shultz. It worked late into the night developing strategies to deal with companies which refused to co-operate with the American initiative. Options were discussed with President Reagan at his West Coast ranch, and approved by him.

On the morning of 27 August 1982, the French freighter *Borodine* heaved anchor and steamed out of the port of Le Havre. On board the ship, bound for Riga in the USSR, were three compressors for the Siberian pipeline in Urengoy. The *Borodine* sailed with the explicit approval of the Paris Government. Within thirty minutes of its departure, US sanctions took effect. Secretary of Commerce

Malcolm Baldrige immediately cancelled the American trading privileges with America enjoyed by two participating companies: Creusot-Loire, the state-owned French equipment manufacturer, and Dresser France, a Paris-based subsidiary of Dresser Industries of Dallas. The US company was ordered to end all technical communications with its French office. In Pittsburg, technicians flipped a switch at Dresser's computer base, cutting data lines between corporate headquarters in Texas and Paris. Terminals at Dresser France suddenly went blank.

For Commerce Secretary Baldrige the step was a 'moderate action'; for Dresser it meant near disaster. The computer connections to Texas main frames were a corporate lifeline. Electronic brains at the company's data base transmitted a torrent of up-to-the-minute information on latest technological innovations, international financial developments, designs and drilling results. Offices and construction sites in over 100 countries of the world were hooked into the Dresser network. Cut off from the rapid flow of vital data, the Paris subsidiary was virtually paralysed. Within days, an Australian account worth $3 million was cancelled.

Bonn was hoping its good relations with Washington would spare it from a similar fate. When West German Foreign Minister Hans-Dietrich Genscher breakfasted with George Shultz in New York on 4 October his optimism was growing. The German freighter *Horst Bischoff* had unloaded pipeline parts from AEG-Kanis in the Soviet port of Klaipeda the day before. The Secretary of State made no mention of it. But after the meeting, when Genscher looked through the *New York Times*, his spirits collapsed. Four German companies were on the US black list. Genscher's response: the Federal Republic of Germany would continue to abide by its contractual obligations.

Italian Prime Minister Spadolini suffered a similar fate when he travelled to Washington for talks two weeks later. Shortly before his arrival, US customs had seized thirty crates containing rotary blades in New York harbour. The shipment, addressed to the Italian company Nuovo Pignone, was also destined for the Siberian pipeline in Urengoy. But Spadolini, too, remained steadfast.

Ultimately, Ronald Reagan was forced to see the futility of American strong-arm tactics. His own efforts to enforce a pipeline embargo had proved just as ineffective as Jimmy Carter's sorry attempt at a grain ban. On 11 November 1982, a year after he launched his anti-pipeline programme, the President surrendered. When West Germany's newly elected (and staunchly pro-American) Chancellor Helmut Kohl arrived in Washington a few days later, the agony was over. The two Western leaders could address other issues in a more relaxed climate. There were pressing political reasons for Reagan's retreat. The stationing of nuclear missiles was about to begin in Europe and anti-Americanism on the Continent was running high. The months ahead would be turbulent enough, and Reagan figured this was no time to be straining relations with loyal allies.

If West Germany's Christian Democratic Chancellor was treated to carrots in Washington, his Social Democratic counterpart in Austria got the stick.

Bruno Kreisky's visit to Washington was preceded by a barrage of interviews in Austrian newspapers. In the Vienna *Presse*, US Assistant of Defense Fred Iklé denounced the complacency of the neutral Alpine republic on the issue of illicit technology transfer. For years, Austria had served as a staging area and sanctuary for Moscow's most notorious high-tech traffickers. Scores of local companies, including a number of renowned corporations, were cooperating in the shady strategic scam. In fact, Iklé declared, over 100 of them had landed on American export denial lists.

While government circles in Vienna were pondering Iklé's statements, wondering which companies he meant, Richard Perle from the Pentagon appeared in the *Presse* with the answer: one of the companies involved was the Gesellschaft für Fertigungstechnik und Maschinenbau (GFM) in Styre. Rotary forges sold to the Soviets by the state-owned Austrian metals-manufacturer were being used to construct armour-piercing smooth-bore cannons for the Red Army. Perle: 'The cannon for the T-72 tank is produced on the Austrian equipment, and the same goes for a number of cannons of the Soviet navy.'

The press campaign came as an embarrassment, to say the very least. Kreisky was planning a good-will tour to the American capital. On his agenda were licences for a joint venture between the Vöst-Alpine steelworks and American Microsystems Inc. The crisis-ridden Austrian corporation planned a $46-million chip-making factory which, Kreisky hoped, could become the cornerstone of a European Silicon Valley in Austria. Export licensing applications, however, had got lost in the Washington bureaucracy. At least, that's what Kreisky thought. He wanted to expedite them.

In Washington, the Austrian leader learned differently. At a tête-à-tête in the White House, Kreisky was told no licences for the Vöst venture would be issued unless Vienna agreed to co-operate with

Western enforcement agencies. A detailed contract proposal had been drawn up. And Kreisky signed. 'We didn't get everything we wanted,' an American official later commented, 'but we got a lot.'

The tactics, described by *Business Week* as 'a little economic blackmail', proved effective. In October 1984 Austria announced it would tighten its export regulations and introduce stiff penalties for violators. They dubbed the law 'an autonomous Austrian solution' to the problem. *Izvestia* accused the US of gross interference in Austrian affairs.

The same squeeze was soon applied to the government of Sweden. Stockholm was reminded that crucial components for Swedish Air Force fighter-interceptors were made in the USA. If deliveries were to continue, co-operation was expected. In April 1984, after years of futile negotiations on the Datasaab case (described in Chapter Ten) the Swedish Foreign Office finally declared it was prepared to pay a civil penalty of $1 million. Datasaab was entered in the export denial lists.

Gentle persuasion of a similar nature was also used in Switzerland, Finland, India, even Hong Kong. In bilateral talks with the United States, a number of CoCom member states also demonstrated good will. European Customs authorities adopted the Pentagon's 'mushroom book' – a layman's guide to the complicated high-tech wares sought by KGB smugglers. Belgium tightened its export regulations, Japan introduced new travel restrictions for Soviet diplomats, and the British special task force 'Project Arrow' was scoring major successes. But the progress achieved in bilateral negotiations paled in comparison to the meagre results coming out of CoCom. New bite for the old dog was still nowhere in sight.

Neighbours near the Rue de La Boetie in Paris had noticed the lights at the CoCom headquarters burning until the small hours. National delegations had been meeting there regularly since October 1982. Washington presented proposals to update 160 items in ageing CoCom embargo lists, adding new technology and deleting those no longer regarded as strategically significant. The Europeans, however, consented only to the deletions. The introduction of new embargo restrictions in the fields of microelectronics and metallurgy, glass fibres and gas turbines continued to meet stiff resistance. An export ban on lasers, which obviously possessed great military potential and had already bolstered Warsaw Pact arsenals, was rejected. The American request for a technical advisory staff for CoCom was denied, as was the request for a new headquarters and for modern computer equipment. In fact, even the request for US dollars, earmarked for the Paris organization by Defense Secretary Weinberger in 1981, was turned down. 'Many CoCom members,' a Commerce Department spokesman remarked in disgust, 'are hesitant partners, to put it mildly.'

While European negotiators stymied progress in Paris, European companies were making a killing on Eastern markets, snatching up the lucrative accounts their American competitors had been forced to abandon.

Caterpillar Tractor of Pretoria was forced to drop an $85 million contract for 200 pipe-layers. The profits were mopped up by the Japanese company Komatsu, which took an order for 1,500 similar machines.

At the 1983 spring trade fair in Leipzig, US exhibitors watched enviously from their nearly empty stands as the West Europeans closed contracts with eager Eastern buyers: Siemens of Germany sold microprocessing equipment; CIT-Alcatel of France sold digital lines; the Italians were peddling a new needle-matrix printer; the British offered a new word-processor.

In April 1983, Count Otto Lambsdorff was proclaiming that the Bonn government saw no need for any changes at CoCom. Six months later, the German minister travelled to Moscow with the German-Soviet trade commission, where Leonid Konstandov promised German contracts for large-scale Soviet industrial projects. Both announced their intention to expand bilateral trade. The USSR, Konstandov emphasized, was especially keen on the new technological innovations.

On 3 November 1983 Luxembourg representatives of fifteen Western banks, spearheaded by the Deutsche Bank of Germany, approved new multimillion-dollar loans for the destitute Nadlovy state bank of Poland.

Thus, it was the intelligence service which achieved the first major breakthrough. With the aid of a 36-year-old KGB defector named Vladimir Kuzishkin (who walked into the British Embassy in Tehran in June 1982), deciphering experts managed to crack several KGB secret codes. The incident provided Western eavesdroppers with their first reliable intelligence on the internal workings of Line 'X'. The British were extremely alarmed by what they heard, as were officials in other Western capitals who were told of the results. The French DST report and the murder of Bernard Nut did the rest.

By early 1983, things were moving. In addition to the Soviet spies

– now leaving Western capitals in droves – the discreet travels of US inter-agency teams, combined with mounting publicity on the technology issue, were prompting European enforcement officials to take action. The odyssey of the *Elgarin*, and the high-level attention given to the case in Washington, accelerated efforts. A number of important arrests followed. Werner Bruchhausen, who had been living free in and working with impunity from his German base of operations for years, was finally arrested and charged in Düsseldorf. Volker Nast and three other cohorts of the Richard Müller organization were imprisoned in the Baltic port of Lübeck on 13 December 1983. Megabuck himself, now on the run, found there were several countries where it was better not to show his face. In Britain, the new high-tech task force apprehended Bryan Williamson, who was to face trial for the first time.

But just as counter-intelligence and enforcement agencies began to make genuine progress, security experts were alarmed by another event that was soon causing deep concern and a high-level reassessment of the strategic significance of high-tech thievery. It happened on 3 June 1983 in the Memorial Sloan Kettering Hospital in New York City.

Systems manager Chen Chui spotted the problem immediately. Upon arrival at the hospital's data centre that Friday morning, his machines had informed him of a breakdown the night before. Apparently someone had been tampering with the computers. Five new files had been opened in the electronic brain, permitting access to its secret program. Portions of the memory had been erased. Mr Chui informed Sloan Kettering management. There was reason for alarm. The VAX-11/780 main-frame computer ran five X-ray machines at the New York cancer clinic, as well as answering inquiries from eight other hospitals across the country. An error in the computer program could lead to lethal overdoses of radiation in patient therapy.

After a crisis meeting, Mr Chui returned to the computer room, erased the new files and reprogrammed all access codes. With that, he thought, the problem was solved. But the following morning he discovered to his horror that the uninvited visitors had returned, this time planting a 'spy program' in the computer memory. It requested all users to reveal their secret passwords – a trick, Chen knew, that would enable the intruders to return to the computer's data base at will. They were dangerous. Kettering officials called the police. And the FBI.

By mid-August, the trail had been traced to West Allis, Wisconsin. From the attic of his home, 21-year-old Gerald R. Wondra had tapped into the Manhattan main frame and easily sliced through its layered electronic protection systems. His tool was a simple Apple-II home computer. Wondra belonged to a local group of young electronics enthusiasts who called themselves 'The 414s'. Cracking computer codes was their passion.

Investigators soon discovered that the youngsters had violated computers not only at the New York cancer clinic, but also at a consulting firm in Dallas, a bank in California and a cement company in Canada. Allegedly, they had even succeeded in penetrating non-confidential portions of a program at the Los Alamos National Laboratory – where atomic bombs were designed. They called their hobby 'hacking'. The phenomenon portrayed in the Hollywood thriller *War Games* (in which a teenage youngster cracks a Pentagon code and nearly provokes a Third World War) had been demonstrated in reality, at least on a modest scale.

Hacking immediately captured the public imagination. Dramatic cases of computer crime at financial institutions were already raising considerable doubts about the reliability of expensive data-protection systems. Now neighbourhood hot-shots were penetrating the fringes of national security computers. 'If this is what kids can do on a lark,' Adam Osborne of the Osborne Computer Corporation was soon asking, 'can you imagine what people are doing who are serious about this?'

Dr Willis H. Ware, data security expert at the Rand Corporation, welcomed the media commotion: 'The incident has been very useful in forcing the attention of the Federal Government to the issue.' For years Dr Ware and others had warned of the dangers of computer penetration. They were less worried, however, by the mildly malicious mischief of teenage tinkerers. Their concern was the KGB.

Early in the 1970s, Willis headed a government committee charged with investigating the vulnerability of high-security data systems. Its conclusion: advanced equipment was making computer-tapping easier by the day. Bugs could be attached to terminals or data lines; microwave transmissions intercepted in the air. Magnetic disks and tapes were easy to conceal and easy to steal. Protection programs, it was feared, could malfunction during a power failure, allowing open access to anyone. Computer switches and terminals – even electric typewriters – emitted weak radio-frequency radiation (known in the intelligence world as 'Tempest'), which could be intercepted and deciphered by finely tuned wireless receivers hidden in a nearby building, or parked in a nearby van.

Today, modern main-frame computers have become absolutely essential, monitoring nearly everything in the military that moves – from the supersonic speeds of bullets and ballistic missiles to the tedious tempo of slow ships and spare parts. Computers serve as guardians of the secret reconnaissance of Western spy-satellites, the unseen positions of NATO nuclear submarines or the identities of Western spies who have penetrated deep into Eastern establishments. They contain emergency plans for a nuclear alert, connect strategic bombers with one another and evaluate top-of-the-line weapons systems long before they are ever deployed. In short: computers know all the secrets that a superpower possesses.

The electronic share of total military intelligence is exploding. The Pentagon alone operates over 8,000 main-frame computers. Countless others are plugged into its international communications networks. Increasingly, top-secret information must be rapidly relayed from listening posts, reconnaissance satellites or military installations to evaluation centres at home, thus multiplying the opportunities for clandestine tapping. Sensitive magnetic tapes and disks, formerly locked away at night in high-security vaults, are now in constant use, never leaving their computers. There, of course, they are more vulnerable than ever. A computer is easier to crack than a safe.

In order to pinpoint potential soft spots in this network, 'Tiger Teams' were formed at the Pentagon and elsewhere – élite groups of specialists assigned to crack their country's computer codes. To the horror of their masters, they succeeded every time. Again and again, computers were reprogrammed or even completely redesigned, only to be penetrated once more. The Tigers tunnelled with relative impunity through layered software safeguards into the secret heart of strategic computer programs.

The tricks they played were simply fantastic. If an initial entry proved difficult, a 'trap door' was planted in the program which would flop open for the thief when he approached a second time. Tiger Teams revealed the darker side of the electronic revolution. 'They kept finding holes in what was already a Swiss cheese,' one official concluded. Particular concern was raised by their demonstrated ability to burgle a computer without leaving any telltale electronic traces. The National Security Agency had spent over $100 million to safeguard the top-of-the-line computer fleet at its cellar installation in Fort Meade, Maryland. Now, no one could guarantee that it had not already been compromised.

Computers, so vital to the defence of the West, had become one of its biggest security problems. Yet the most chilling conclusion was still to come.

In the world of electronic espionage and counter-espionage the Tiger Teams not only demonstrated that a trained expert was capable of cracking the most sophisticated of protection schemes – and living a superspy's dream inside the central nervous system of the NATO defence network; they were soon also exploring the menacing potential of software sabotage. Special programs, inserted clandestinely in the innermost data base of a strategic computer, could drive the entire system haywire.

A software saboteur could plant a program that would not be visible to even the most schooled eye. It could be designed to go unnoticed in routine situations. Triggered by a pre-set radio command or geographic parameter, the 'logic bomb' would be activated only in a real war, garbling communications, fogging radar or confusing navigational systems. Remote controls operated via satellite or internal timers accurate to a microsecond could also be used to switch them on. It was a military man's nightmare. Pentagon experts envisioned early-warning radar that refused to warn; helicopters and jet bombers that fell from the skies without apparent rhyme or reason; or ship-to-ship missiles that returned to sink the ship that had launched them.

Unlike hobby-hacking, serious military sabotage is no business for loners. A perpetrator would require a comprehensive knowledge of the system and its peripherals not available to single individuals, even those with high-security clearance. Equipped with the prepared program of an enemy intelligence service, however, a single agent – perhaps a trusted employee with an ID card dangling from his neck and a friendly wave for the security guard – could wreak absolute havoc.

The ugliest scenario is painted by Colonel Roger Shell of the National Security Agency: the re-targeting of nuclear missiles. A skilfully designed sabotage program, carefully concealed in the tangled bits and bytes of sophisticated software, could be programmed to ignore routine testing or electronic war-gaming, and thus go undetected for years in its quiet little corner of a missile guidance system. Not until the radio signals of a real alert reached it would the logic bomb go into action, commanding an atomic warhead to detonate in its home-town silo or reverse a trajectory, guiding a renegade rocket unerringly into Western targets in Washington, Paris, Hamburg or London. It is the ultimate threat of Moscow's computer spies: a lethal atomic boomerang soaring back to annihilate Western cities.

The Soviet military has neither the hardware nor the software capability to produce such systems. But there can be little doubt they are doing their very best to steal them.

Source Notes

Bernard Nut: 'Real Goal', *US News and World Report*, 18/4/1983; *Chicago Tribune*, 10/4/1983; *New York Times*, 6/4/1983; 'Diplomatic Expulsions', *Guardian*, 17/4/1983.

Mass expulsions: *US News and World Report*, 9/5/1983; *Long Island Newsday*, 20/4/1983; *New York Times*, 7/4/1983, 24/4/1983 and 24/7/1983; *Christian Science Monitor*, 25/4/1983; UPI, 8/4/1983 and 24/4/1983; AP, 7/1/1983, 18/5/1983 and 23/12/1982; Reuters, 5/4/1983; *Frankfurter Allgemeine Zeitung*, 23/4/1983; *Financial Times*, 31/8/1983; *ARD Tagesthemen*, German television, 2/2/1984; Erwin Brunner, 'Dossier', *Die Zeit*, 3/2/1984.

CoCom (background): Rolf Hasse, *Theorie und Politik des Embargos*, Institut für Wirtschaftspolitik, University of Cologne, 1973, pp. 195-202; Ellen Frost and Angela Stent, 'NATO's Troubles with East-West Trade', *International Security*, summer 1983; *Frankfurter Allgemeine Zeitung*, 28/5/1983; *Frankfurter Allgemeine Zeitung*, 20/11/1982; *The Times*, 14/12/1983.

Grain embargo: *Der Spiegel*, 18/2/1980; *Baltimore Sun*, 6/3/1983; *Frankfurter Allgemeine Zeitung*, 9/2/1983; *Neue Züricher Zeitung*, 5/3/1982.

Quote from Assilin: US Senate Subcommittee on Investigations, Washington DC 1982, p. 92.

Quote from Jimmy Carter: *New York Times*, 5/1/1980.

Quote from Medvedev: 'Ein Frost so Kühl', *Der Spiegel*, March 1980.

Andropov's *Spiegel* Interview: *Der Spiegel*, 25/4/1983, p. 130.

Lambsdorff's explosion: Eyewitness interview with the author.

Armco: *Baltimore Sun*, 5/3/1982.

Pipeline embargo: *Frankfurter Allgemeine Zeitung*, 12/1/1982, 16/7/1982, 25/8/1982, 15/11/1982, 13/3/1983, 28/5/1983, and 28/8/1983; *New York Times*, 13/3/1983; *Der Spiegel*, 11/10/1982.

Dresser Industries: *Baltimore Sun*, 6/3/1983; *New York Times*, 13/3/1983.

Kreisky and the cannons: *Der Spiegel*, 3/1/1983; *Business Week*, 4/4/1983.

Sweden: *Die Welt*, 10/4/1984.

Operation Exodus: *Newsday*, 21/2/1983.

London: *Guardian*, 9/9/1983.

Hacker, Tiger Teams and software sabotage: Background to this section came from NATO high officials and other sources who offered information only on the condition they remain anonymous. The problem, however, has been discussed in public. See: *Newsweek*, 29/8/1983; *New York Times*, 25/9/1983; J. Goldstein, 'Technology Transfer from the Defence Perspective', *Signal*, August 1983; Tad Szulc, *Current News*, 5/11/1982; Tad Szulc, 'To Steal Our Secrets', *Parade*, 7/11/1982; Lawrence Meyer, 'Hey Ivan, say "Cheese"', *Washington Post Magazine*, 4/12/1983.

Colonel Shell quote: 'Pentagon Computers: How vulnerable?' *US News and Report*, 31/10/1983; *USA Today*, 25/8/1983.

Index